Contesting the Corporation

In an age when large corporations dominate the economic and political landscape, it is tempting to think that their power goes largely unchecked. *Contesting the Corporation* counters this view by showing that today's corporations are fundamentally contested spheres driven by political struggle, power plays and attempts to resist control. Building on a wide range of theoretical sources, Fleming and Spicer present an analysis of the different ways in which power operates within the modern workplace. They begin by building a theoretical perspective that synthesizes previous investigations of power and resistance, identifying struggle as a key concept. Each subsequent chapter illustrates a different dimension of workplace struggle through an array of original empirical studies relating to sexuality, cynicism, new social movements and new-wave trade unionism. The book concludes by demonstrating that social justice claims underlie even the most innocuous forms of resistance, helping to transform some of the largest modern corporations.

PETER FLEMING is University Lecturer in Organisation Studies at the Judge Business School, University of Cambridge.

ANDRÉ SPICER is Associate Professor of Organisation Studies at Warwick Business School, University of Warwick.

Contesting the Corporation

Struggle, Power and Resistance in Organizations

PETER FLEMING
Judge Business School,
University of Cambridge

ANDRÉ SPICER
Warwick Business School,
University of Warwick

CAMBRIDGE
UNIVERSITY PRESS

CAMBRIDGE UNIVERSITY PRESS
Cambridge, New York, Melbourne, Madrid, Cape Town, Singapore, São Paulo

Cambridge University Press
The Edinburgh Building, Cambridge CB2 8RU, UK

Published in the United States of America by Cambridge University Press, New York

www.cambridge.org
Information on this title: www.cambridge.org/9780521860864

First published 2007

Printed in the United Kingdom at the University Press, Cambridge

A catalogue record for this publication is available from the British Library

Library of Congress Cataloguing in Publication data

Contesting the corporation: struggle, power and resistance in organizations/by Peter
Fleming and André Spicer.
    p.   cm.
    Includes bibliographic references and index.
    ISBN-13: 978-0-521-86086-4 (hardback)
    ISBN-10: 0-521-86086-5 (hardback)
    1. Corporate power. 2. Corporations – Sociological aspects. 3. Organizational
behavior. I. Spicer, André. II. Title.

HD 2741.F56   2007
302.3'5–dc22   2007002290

ISBN 978-0-521-86086-4 hardback

Contents

Acknowledgements

This book is the product of seven years of scholarly collaboration. The ideas developed in this book found their germ in the unusual and invigorating intellectual ferment in the Department of Management at the University of Otago in New Zealand; we would like to give our profound thanks to Shayne Grice, Malcolm Lewis, Marc Jones, Campbell Jones and Ralph Stablein for helping to foster this. The ideas were further refined at the University of Melbourne in Australia, and we would like to register our appreciation of Cynthia Hardy, Graham Sewell, Bill Harley and John Selsky for their extremely useful input at this stage. The concepts were finalised and committed to paper in our respective universities in England; André would like to thank his colleagues at the Warwick Business School for their support, and Peter would like to thank his colleagues at the Judge Business School, University of Cambridge, for theirs.

Many other people have been instrumental in providing space and inspiration for and constructive criticism of the arguments we have made in this book. They include Mats Alvesson, Johan Alvehus, Steffen Böhm, Martin Bringham, Christian de Cock, Chris Grey, Alessia Contu, Yiannis Gabriel, Dan Kärreman, Chris Land, Markus Perkmann, John Roberts, Stephanie Schreven, Melissa Strauss, Andrew Sturdy and Hugh Willmott.

Some of the ideas contained in this book have been presented to audiences before publication. In particular, we would like to thank the following groups for their insightful comments: the standing group on Philosophy of Organization in the European Group for Organizational Studies; the Biannual Critical Management Studies conference; the Department of Business Administration at Lund University in Sweden; the Department of Organization, Work and Technology at the University of Lancaster; the Department of Organization Behaviour, University of Nottingham; the Department of Accounting, Finance and Management, University of Essex; and the School of Business and Economics, Exeter University.

Some chapters in this book gain their inspiration from previously published material. Chapter 4 draws on 'Working at a cynical distance: implications for power, subjectivity and resistance', *Organization*, 10 (1): 157–79. Chapter 5 develops further the arguments in 'Sexuality, power and resistance in the workplace', *Organization Studies*. Chapter 6 is inspired by 'You can check out any time you like, but you can never leave: spatial boundaries in a high commitment organization', *Human Relations*, 57 (1): 75–94. And Chapter 7 gains impetus from 'Intervening in the inevitable: contesting globalization in a public broadcaster', *Organization*.

Introduction: Prisons, playgrounds and parliaments

THE sun never sets on the golden arches. These gleaming symbols of the iconic fast food giant, McDonald's, can be found scattered across the surface of the earth. They seem to have spread even further than the standards of ancient Rome, the cross of Christianity or the flag of imperial Britain. McDonald's is so ubiquitous that the film-maker Morgan Spurlock found that most children had difficulty recognizing the United States president and Jesus Christ, but they could instantly recognize Ronald McDonald. In the course of becoming the corporate power that it is today, McDonald's has transformed people's lives around the world in a way that emperors and governments have only dreamed of (Schlosser, 2002). It might be argued that it has swept away thousands of small businesses throughout the world and replaced them with chain stores; that it has applied the standardized techniques of mass manufacture to the job of cooking food and serving people; that it has systematically rolled back the rights of workers; that it has hastened the introduction of monoculture factory farming; that it has made fatty fast food a staple diet for millions of people; that it has aided the rapid decline in people's ability to prepare even the most basic food for themselves; and that it has even changed the shape of our bodies by encouraging obesity throughout Western nations. Whether or not we go that far, it is evident that the huge changes that McDonald's and other fast food restaurants have heralded reveal the kind of power that lies in the hands of the largest corporations. They have the power to change the landscape of business, the way we work, the way we eat and the way we live. Staring into the face of such an all-encompassing power might produce a sense of concern, disgust or even bitter outrage.

Such obvious bitterness would sit uneasily in the stomach of the listless customer as he waits for his drive-thru Mac attack. He might

1

stare forlornly across the car park into the suburban wasteland. Safely ensconced in his automobile he might imagine Ronald being crucified on his own sickly yellow cross. He might laugh to himself as he fantasizes about the pimply teenagers who work the grills, mocking the once happy clown as he writhes in agony atop the arches. But our cynical consumer knows that these are just flights of fancy. He shakes these follies from his poor head and focuses on the one thing that he knows is real – the delicious burger in his chubby hand. Inside the 'restaurant', the same kind of resigned cynicism plays on the mind of the migrant teenager as she flips what seems like the millionth burger patty of the day. This bored employee can't help thinking of the thousands of calories she is pumping into the greedy gullets of angry children. That cheesy manager with his 'motivational' slogans and plastic team talk certainly make our McWorker even more irate! She realizes that she simply has to accept this monotony and degradation if she wants to keep her job. But a small smile comes to her face when she thinks about the 'McShit' T-shirt that she is secretly wearing under her uniform.

Engaging in cynical flights of fancy and guerrilla T-shirt wearing is not the only way in which people have dealt with the bitterness they feel towards the golden arches. Many have turned their personal disquiet into action. In some cases this has involved individual consumer choices. Many consumers have pledged to avoid the golden arches at all costs. Some have begun personal crusades against fast food. The obese Californian, Steve Vaught, undertook an epic walk across the United States in an effort to shake off his fast food lifestyle. Countless others across the globe have engaged in more collective forms of protest. This includes residents in towns such as Torquay, Australia, who have fought a prolonged battle to keep McDonald's out of their community; protest groups such as 'Super Size My Pay' in Auckland, New Zealand, who have sought to improve the working conditions in McDonald's; activists such as Helen Steele and Dave Morris in London, who fought a gruelling legal battle to prove infringements on the part of McDonald's; and health campaigners, who have tirelessly pointed out the devastating consequences of fast food overconsumption.

As long as these protests remained small and relatively disconnected, McDonald's was largely able to ignore them. However, the mass pressure that has built up over the course of the last few years has brought the issues of health, the environment, urban planning and worker rights to the forefront in debates about McDonald's and other large multinationals. Indeed, even mainstream discussions about McDonald's long-term future now routinely refer to the increasing consumer disquiet dogging the organization. There has even been some indication that McDonald's may be the target of a wave of lawsuits similar to those faced by the tobacco industry. In some parts of the world McDonald's is in major decline. Naturally, senior executives are worried. The grandees of the corporation have begun to take these threats seriously. They have withdrawn their super-size options, changed their ingredients (introducing free-range eggs, for instance), transformed their menu and introduced a range of more 'healthy' options, put a stop to some of the more brazen attempts to 'educate' children about the benefits of McDonald's, redesigned their restaurants to look more like postmodern inner city cafés and in some cases improved worker conditions. They have even begun to shift their investment into 'healthier' food businesses, such as the British sandwich shop chain Pret à Manger. Taken together, these changes represent a significant shift in corporate strategy, which can largely be attributed to the millions of acts of protest across the globe.

Struggle for the corporation

The saga of McDonald's reminds us that the largest organizations have astounding power over our working lives, our consumption patterns, our bodies, the economy and our very way of life. The story also reminds us that the power of large corporations is far from unchecked. Any organization like McDonald's faces a thousand swarming refusals, ranging from the disgruntled employee who mocks his/her officious boss to the social movement that unveils corporate misdemeanours in the international media. At the very heart of organizational life is the ongoing struggle between those in the corporation who seek to assert power and those who seek to resist and perhaps destroy this power. It is this struggle that gives organizations a sense of vitality and a life-giving political pulse. It is this struggle that is the topic of this book.

Those studying modern workplaces have long realized just how important struggle is in organizational life. There is a large and prodigious body of research on workplace politics examining how people gain, lose and disrupt power in organizations.[1] Underlying this broad and complex discussion are three images of what power looks like in work organizations. Perhaps the most widespread image is that of the *prison*. If we take even the most cursory glance at the research on workplace power and politics, we find ourselves in a world of 'iron cages', 'cells', 'guards', 'wardens', 'panopticons' and 'imprisonment' (e.g. Weber, 1924/1947; Foucault, 1977; DiMaggio and Powell, 1983). The message is clear: when we enter an organization we intern ourselves and give away the freedoms enjoyed in the rest of our lives. We allow cretinoid managers to tell us what to say and when we can move our bowels. We adhere to a strict set of rules (both written and unwritten) that govern what we do and how we think. We accept the micromonitoring of everything from our keystrokes to our attitude. And, what is even more surprising, millions of us accept these mind-numbing and spirit-crushing regimes every day, and are often *grateful for it*. This image of the corporation as a prison has inspired countless studies of the ways people are controlled in and around organizations. Some typical forms of control include threats of violence, direct commands, the provision of incentives, technical systems, rules and regulations, group norms and various forms of ideology associated with corporate culture. Even the most 'free' workplaces, such as youthful 'creative' companies, have been shown to be replete with mechanisms of control (Ross, 2004). If we follow this line of argument, it is hard not to reach the conclusion that we live in a universal prison of organizational domination, from which escape is very difficult.

The view that we live in a prison of corporate control is certainly an important wake-up call to those who dream that the modern organization is the royal road to freedom. However, it does paint a rather pessimistic picture, a world of total corporate domination that would not be out of place in *1984* or *The Matrix*. Confronted with such a bleak dystopia, it is easy to resign ourselves nihilistically to keeping our heads below the trenches, enjoying what the system has to offer and accepting that we are doomed to be prisoners of work for the rest of our days. But such a wholehearted acceptance of corporate power takes the system far too seriously. It misses the many opportunities for misbehaviour and outright rebellion that are right under our noses. The recognition that organizations are, in fact, awash with various 'escape attempts' has led to the promotion of a second image: the corporation as *playground*. As a countermeasure to the pessimistic image outlined above, much research now focuses on worker resistance that pokes fun at the corporation. This type of subversion includes practical jokes, ironic repartee, mating rituals on company time, wilful rule breaking, farting in front of a team leader, game-playing, theft, sabotage and now even corporate 'culture jamming' (Kane, 2004). These everyday acts of rebellion remind us that, like any large institution, the corporation creates a huge vacuum in which to challenge its existence from within. Indeed, those studying resistance have shown how organizations are consistently under attack from nearly every possible angle imaginable. Shareholders, senior managers, middle managers, shop-floor employees, customers and stakeholders all undermine and challenge the corporation in their own transgressive ways. If we cast a playful glance at what actually happens in the daily behaviour in and around organizations, we are struck by the fact that it might actually be better described as organizational *misbehaviour* (Ackroyd and Thompson, 1999). Some have gone so far as to suggest that, if everyone soberly followed the rules legislated by managers, the machine would rapidly grind to a halt, and that it is only through this systematic misbehaviour, playfulness and rule-breaking that the corporation is able to continue functioning in a workable fashion (Bensman and Gerver, 1963).

The idea that the corporation is a playground gives us hope. It reminds us of the potential spaces of freedom possible in even the most oppressive corporate environments. However, overemphasizing the potential playfulness of corporate life runs the danger of ignoring the fact that, despite our everyday challenges, systems of control and domination continue to whirr on. By focusing only on play we begin to lose sight of the more profound political processes that fundamentally shape our organizational lives. Indeed, we miss how the space in which we play is made possible and even encouraged by the very forms of domination we seek to escape. Ultimately, by concentrating on jocular acts of subversion we ignore the structural political processes that make up organizations. In order to account for these processes, we would like to suggest a third guiding image for the study of politics and power in the workplace: the organization as a *parliament*. A parliament is an arena in which actors 'struggle' to have their voices heard as the latent conflicts of the social well-up. We hope that this image draws the reader's attention to how the 'prison' of corporate power is inextricably interlocked with the 'play' of resistance. Power functions only to the extent that it is engaged in a struggle with some form of resistance and transgression. Indeed, as expounded in a profound insight of Michel Foucault (1980), power works only insofar as people do not completely follow its demands. Conversely, resistance has an impact only insofar as it wields a degree of power (no matter how minuscule).

When we approach politics as an ongoing interplay of struggle, we are not led into either surrendering to the power of the corporate prison or whiling away our days in self-indulgent play (or heterotopia, as the case may be today (Hjorth, 2005)). Rather, we recognize that we are always implicated in an ongoing struggle to establish a particular kind of organization. Precisely because this is a struggle, the results are always precarious and open to challenge, compromise and reversal. There is always the possibility of asserting another form of organizing in face of the status quo. There is always the possibility that the organization elites currently enjoy will be torn asunder and replaced. When we approach organizational politics as struggle, we can begin to decon-struct the dualism of power and resistance, and focus on their interplay and mutual constitution. At this level, power and resistance begin to blur. Moreover, we suggest that the issue of struggle is at the heart of some of the keenest concerns we experience in the workplace: what are we struggling for, how do we engage in struggle and where are our struggles best placed? It is these questions we aim to address in this book.

The structure of the book

This book was written with four intentions. First, we hope to provide the reader new to the field with an introduction to the political dynamics of organizational life. Second, the book aims to provide an exploration of some of the most important forms of struggle that characterise contemporary organizations today. We now live in the age of the cynical knowledge worker, the gay office activist, the MBA (Master of Business Administration) who cannot face re-entering the ranks of the corporate dead zone, and the high-tech union organizer. Theories of social justice are only now catching up with the new social movements challenging corporate power. Third, we aim to contribute to current theories of workplace power and resistance by introducing the concept of struggle. We do this by adapting recent theoretical advances developed in the work of Slavoj Žižek, Peter Sloterdijk, Ernesto Laclau,

Nancy Fraser, and Michael Hardt and Antonio Negri, among others. And, finally, we hope that this work is a step towards building a genuinely critical social theory that takes us well beyond the cul-de-sac of postmodernism, a project that certainly began with a genuinely radical spark, but has subsequently matured into a veiled apologetic for the status quo.

In order to achieve these rather ambitious and admittedly daunting goals, we have organized the following nine chapters into three parts. The first part of the book outlines our theoretical framework. Chapter 1 provides an overview of the literature on power in organizations. We argue that power has been conceptualized in four ways: as coercion, manipulation, domination and subjectification. Instead of privileging one 'face' of power over another, we suggest that each represents a dimension that is of equal importance in organizational life. In chapter 2, we consider the different theories of resistance that have been discussed in organization theory. Paralleling the four faces of power, we identify four ways of thinking about resistance in the workplace: as refusal, voice, escape and creation. Chapter 3 proposes that power and resistance are underpinned by a deeper dynamic that we call 'struggle'. This chapter works through the political philosophy of struggle, and applies it to the politics of organizational life.

The second part of the book examines various forms of resentful struggle that currently characterize contemporary workplaces, especially in this age of high risk, cynical disappointment and low trust. In chapter 4, we focus on struggles around identity. We investigate how employees frequently engage in 'cynical distancing' as part of their struggles against empowerment, cultural controls and other forms of identity management that are currently *en vogue*. Chapter 5 considers struggles around sexuality in the workplace. Drawing on a case study of a call centre, we argue that sexuality is not necessarily a space of liberation but an object of ongoing contestation. Chapter 6 examines struggles around space and place in the same call centre. We unpack what we consider to be a fascinating contest over how the space of work is defined, controlled and resisted in organizations. We suggest that the division between work and private life is especially pertinent in this struggle.

The third part of the book moves away from resentment and identity politics to those forms of struggle that are overt, organized and collective. Chapter 7 discusses struggles around corporate language and the discourse of globalization. In particular, we examine the collective action undertaken by social movements protesting the commercialization of a public broadcaster in the name of globalization. In chapter 8 we propose that the question of justice underpins many forms of organizational struggle. In order to make this argument, we demonstrate how the campaigns of three prominent social movements (port workers, gays and shareholder rights campaigners) were all driven by strong and well-articulated social justice claims. In chapter 9 we discuss struggles for commonality. Drawing on recent political philosophy and the empirical studies outlined in the book, we consider how organizational struggle appears to create social connections and common causes whereby specific concerns are linked to broader, society-wide narratives regarding justice, equality and fairness.

Because this book is aimed at a number of different readers, we think that it should be read in different ways. For those of you who are relatively new to the field, we suggest beginning with the first and second chapters. They provide an introduction and overview of the current literature on power and resistance. These chapters should equip you to deal with the key debates and problems that are subsequently addressed in the remainder of the book. For more advanced readers who are interested in our theory of struggle, we suggest you begin with chapter 3. It provides an in-depth outline of our particular theoretical approach. For those who are more interested in our empirical work on this topic, we suggest you look at chapters 4 to 8. Each of these chapters is built around empirical case studies that examine how struggle unfolds in contemporary organizations. Finally, for readers interested in practical strategies of collective struggle, chapters 7 to 9 are recommended for both reformist and radical struggles in today's work organizations.

PART I

Theoretical framework

1 | *Faces of power in organizations*

> Power springs up whenever people get
> together and act in concert.
>
> (Arendt, 1970: 44)

Whenever we gather to undertake a task in common, power appears. This is because we all have different ideas about how even the most mundane and simple task should be accomplished. Just think how difficult it is to get a handful of people to agree upon a common time and place to meet. Our experience of coordinating a meeting of friends would lead us to expect no-shows, dissent, frustration, absolute uproar and even revolt. If such a simple task is troublesome, imagine coordinating hundreds or thousands of people in contemporary organizations. Interestingly enough, however, much mainstream organization theory views organizations as places where thousands of diligent souls work contentedly towards a universally accepted goal. If political squabbles appear, then this is the fault of a power-hungry manager, a few deviant subordinates or an organization that is in terminal decline. In this otherwise perfect world, good people in good organizations do not engage in politics. They just work towards the common good. But is organizational life really like this?

The widespread assumption that organizations are groups of people working together to achieve a common goal is naive. All the evidence suggests that, though we work together at times, we also frequently work against each other (e.g. Pfeffer, 1981, 1992). Indeed, there is rarely lasting agreement or understanding even about what the 'common goal' we desire actually is. Instead, there is contention around how people should labour, how the benefits should be distributed and how the products of our efforts should be consumed. To be blunt, power and politics are endemic in organizations.

In this chapter we argue that organizations have, in fact, become one of the most important sites of power and politics in contemporary societies. This is because many of the decisions about the allocation of the vital resources we all depend upon are increasingly decided within the walls of large organizations, whether private, public or non-profit (Wolin, 2004). Who has access to life-saving drugs, for example, is often determined during meetings between faceless government bureaucrats and representatives of large multinational pharmaceutical companies. The fate of a river is decided during a boardroom squabble in a large energy company. The jobs of thousands of workers hang in the balance of negotiations between a few business people. These common occurrences remind us that decisions shaping our worlds and livelihoods are often not publicly debated during a sitting of the local council, the national parliament or the United Nations. Rather, these decisions are made in the plush meeting rooms of a few major corporations. Some commentators even suggest that the multinational corporation in particular has overtaken the state as the most important site of politics today (Crouch, 2004).

What do we mean by the word 'power'? The concept has a long and complex intellectual history, and understanding how it works has been an ongoing concern in the field of political philosophy for many years. Within this field we can identify two broad traditions. On the one hand, we have the great normative tradition that attempts to establish the most rational way of organizing power in a society. Some famous contributors to normative political philosophy include Plato's *Republic*, Saint Augustine's *City of God*, Jean Jacques Rousseau's *Social Contract* and, more recently, John Rawls' *A Theory of Justice*.[1] A second tradition of research eschews normative judgements. Inspired by Niccolò Machiavelli, this approach considers the question of how power ought to be organized – a hopelessly utopian one that will always fall short of proposed ideals. Instead, the question is: how does power actually operate? How do people gain and maintain power within the realpolitik of social relations? Machiavelli's book *The Prince* sets out to answer these questions by developing what some consider the first realistic analysis of power.

It appears to me more appropriate to follow up the real truth of a matter than the imagination of it; for many have pictured republics and principalities which in fact have never been known or seen, because how one lives is so far distant from how one ought to live, that he who neglects what is done for what ought to be done, sooner effects his ruin than his preservation. (Machiavelli, 1515/1997: chap. 15)

What remains so interesting and perhaps shocking about Machiavelli's work is that he rejects normative niceties to stare into the bloody abyss of power in operation. Machiavelli inspired a host of twentieth-century social scientists who wanted to move beyond idealistic celebrations of participative democracy and identify who exactly held power in their communities. C. Wright Mills (1956), for example, argued that American cities were controlled by a small 'power elite' made up of a handful of individuals and families with close networks. According to Mills, this power elite controlled most of the important institutions, including businesses, the judiciary, local government and public administration. This argument prompted the lively 'community power debate'. The result was what some have identified as four distinct 'faces' of power.[2] The first face of power is *coercion* and involves one individual getting another to follow his/her orders. The second face involves the *manipulation* of agendas through 'behind the scenes' politicking. The third face of power is *domination* over the preferences and opinions of participants. The fourth face entails *subjectification*, whereby actors are constituted as subjects with certain understandings of themselves and the world around them.

We suggest that each face of power reveals different aspects of domination and politics in organizations. Each face has distinct answers to what power is, how it operates and how it is maintained in organizations. Moreover, exploring each face of power will provide us with a more precise and thorough way of thinking about the struggles that arise when we 'act in concert', a topic explored in the following two chapters.

Power as coercion

When you walk into your manager's office some familiar sights are evident: the large desk made of dark wood; a sizeable space with views over the city; an Italian leather office chair. You squelch into one of the smaller seats opposite the boss. As you try to relax your boss begins running through your current tasks. When he comes to the end of this monologue he says, 'Oh yes, there is another small project I would like you to do.' Your heart sinks. You know this project will be particularly tedious and that it is not within your official remit. You also know that your boss will be angry if you say no. In fact, if you did say no it could jeopardise your future progress within the organization. After accepting the project, you leave resenting him and the additional work you will inevitably have to do.

This vignette illustrates the most obvious face of power: direct coercion. This kind of power involves someone getting another person to do something that he or she otherwise would not have done. They are simply told what to do 'or else'. This example illustrates Robert Dahl's (1957: 203) understanding of power as 'A has power over B to the extent that he [sic] can get B to do something B would otherwise not do'.[3] This definition identifies some central aspects of power as coercion. First, we notice that power is *causal*: A is causing B to do something, such as write a report. Second, Dahl views power as *episodic*, as something involving actual and observable behavioural episodes. That is, there is a definitive behaviour of A asking B to do something, which can be observed if we are in the right place at the right time. Finally, according to Dahl, power is *situational*. That is, an actor may have power in some situations and spheres, but not in others. In the vignette above, we may accept our boss's request on a matter relating to a work task, but not when it comes to re-decorating our bedroom or the content of our diet.

What is it that allows A to make B do something that he/she otherwise would not do? In other words, what is the 'basis of power' (French and Raven, 1968)? Most obviously, perhaps A is simply a 'powerful' person. A might have the physical strength to threaten others, manifest through displays of brute force and stand-over tactics (Cannetti, 1962).[4] This draws our attention to the signifiers of physical threat that continue to haunt the contemporary organization. For instance, the business suit is designed to broaden the appearance of the shoulders and make the wearer look more muscular. As well as physical power, it is possible to claim that an individual's power is a product of his/her psychological make-up. We all know individuals who revel in politics and seem to actively seek out opportunities and situations that allow them to shape the behaviours of others. According to some psychologists, these individuals have specific personality types. For instance, a study of US presidents shows that they tend to be charismatic figures and have a high need for recognition and affiliation (House, Spangler and Woycke, 1991).

Physical strength or psychological constitution do not by themselves make an individual powerful. If an individual with unusual physical strength attempts to threaten individuals in a company, he/she would probably be dismissed for bullying. If that same individual found himself or herself in a management position in a sweatshop, such tactics might be accepted as inevitable (Ong, 1987). It is something about an individual's social *position* that makes him/her powerful. Max Weber (1924/1947) argues that actors in the official bureaucracy gain their power from the office they hold.[5] Their office has power by virtue of rational and written rules that give the office holders the right to coerce others below them. Most importantly, these powers are limited to certain tasks and rules, just as an on-duty police officer may ask for my name and address, but cannot when off duty.

However, many studies of power in organizations have noted that the power of some actors exceeds the 'legitimate authority' guaranteed by their position. The possession of crucial skills is often an important reason for this. In a classic study of two United States Air Force (USAF) wings, James Thompson (1956) found that the director of operations had a great deal more power than the squadron commander, despite the fact that the commander was officially superior. This was because the skills possessed by the operations director and his unit were vital to the functioning of the organization (keeping the planes safely in the air). Indeed, the operations director was far more important to the workflow of the organization and had more contact with senior management than the commander. These findings were developed by David Mechanic's (1962) analysis of power and the possession of scarce and critical expertise. He argues that critical expertise allowed even lowly organizational members (such as prisoners) to wield significant power.

Another important source of coercive power is the ability to cope with uncertainty. Michel Crozier's (1964) study of power dynamics in a French tobacco manufacturer illustrates this point. Because the company enjoyed a monopoly over the sale of tobacco in France, it had a relatively stable market and environment. It did not, for instance, face the prospect of a lithe new competitor entering the market with a better offer. The only source of real uncertainty came from the machinery, which malfunctioned periodically. Because they alone could deal with this uncertainty, maintenance engineers gained significant power within the organization. This power allowed them to shape decisions at the top of the hierarchy, including removing senior staff. Actors are also able to coerce others when they possess critical resources that the organization depends upon. This insight largely emerged from Jeff

Pfeffer and his colleagues' study of resource allocation in universities (Pfeffer and Salancik, 1974; Salancik and Pfeffer, 1974; Pfeffer and Moore, 1980). They set out to ask which departments were powerful at the University of Illinois. They found that those departments with access to the most critical resources (in this case, national research grants) were considered by colleagues in other departments to be the most powerful. Resource-rich departments also had access to the most powerful positions in the organization, such as membership on important university boards. They were also able to garner additional resources within the organization, such as grants for summer internships and internal research grants. The lesson is that those already rich in power and resources tend to get richer (Pfeffer, 1992).

Approaching power as coercion reveals three interesting dimensions of organizational politics. Power involves direct political acts and observable behaviours. The key political manoeuvre at this level entails gauging how much power an actor can wield and what form it might take. The second dimension concerns resistance and how power overcomes it through punishment and sanctions. The final dimension this perspective reveals is that power increases via certain mechanisms. Power is augmented through acquiring scarce resources, developing critical skills and/or collecting critical information (Pfeffer, 1992). But thinking about power as coercion is not without its problems. Does power operate only through overt and observable acts? This behavioural view may blind us to the more subtle exercises of power that take place 'behind the scenes' (Bachrach and Baratz, 1962). Moreover, the coercion approach tends to view power as something held by a bureaucratic office or authority (e.g. Crozier, 1972). Very few questions are asked about aspects of power implicit in the broader system associated with managerial and shareholder capitalism. Finally, a coercive approach to power generally focuses on the intended consequences of control. Many of the unintended consequences of power are not recognized (Bachrach and Baratz, 1962; Wrong, 1968). For instance, a managerial decision may aim to force employees to work harder, but also impact on their family and private lives.

Power as manipulation

You have been working in an engineering lab on a new engine for quite some time. After some reading, you come across a new technology that is used in Brazil. Following more investigation and some minor tests you discover this new improvement will reduce carbon emissions significantly. You are excited – this is precisely the kind of discovery that motivated you to become an engineer. But on the way home you begin to seriously consider whether this will actually appeal to senior management. Will they give you the resources you require? Consulting a few colleagues, you come to the conclusion that reducing emissions is really a non-starter in this company. Fuel-hungry North American engines are the order of the day. It would be very difficult to get the necessary funding to take your innovation forward and you would feel uncomfortable even broaching the new design. With some sadness you decide to shelve the idea for another day.

In this short scenario we find an example of a kind of politics that the study of coercive power cannot capture. There is no direct exercise of coercion here. Instead, there is an implicit shaping of issues considered important or irrelevant. This manipulation of issues and non-issues is 'the second face of power'. In a series of seminal articles, Peter Bachrach and Morton Baratz (1962, 1963) argue that power is manifested not only through direct decisions but through *non-decisions*. This is 'the practice of limiting the scope of actual decision making to "safe" issues by manipulating the dominant community values, myths, and political institutions and procedures' (Bachrach and Baratz, 1963: 632). While coercive politics involves the direct exercise of power and attempts to increase one's power bases, manipulative politics is the attempt either to fit one's activities within the boundaries of what is deemed to be normal or acceptable by elite groups or to challenge and contest these boundaries. For instance, those who are hoping to have an innovation accepted within an organization or market are advised to cloak propositions in acceptable garb so that it does not threaten the interests of the dominant coalition (Kelley, 1976). Studies of health care professionals show that, in order to cope with new auditing procedures, which threaten their professional autonomy, they develop surface compliance to these new rules while continuing their normal routine of activities (McGivern, 2005). Similarly, in a study of a building site, Stewart Clegg (1975) identifies how building contractors would use ambiguities in blueprints to transform 'objective' criteria to support their 'subjective' interests. In each of these cases, effort is targeted at changing the background rules of the game, rather than exercising power through direct behaviour.

In organizations, this type of power can involve three processes. The first is the *anticipation of results*. This is where actors foresee future expressions of power and thus comply with what they assume are the wishes of the powerful. It has been shown, for example, that the continued exercise of domination over individuals will result in feelings of powerlessness and personal worthlessness (Gouldner, 1970). Others may feel resigned in the face of domination and raise issues that question the directives of authority. It was noted in a study of strategic change efforts in three Australian organizations that employees were resigned to the vicious downsizing exercises (Connel and Waring, 2002). In a more pronounced case we find that repeated exposure of working-class people to brute exercises of power results in a sense of powerlessness and, in some cases, a lack of self-worth (Sennett and Cobb, 1977).

A second process associated with manipulation is the *mobilization of bias*. Here, some topics are organized into decision-making activities while others are organized out. In an investigation of the escalation of the American military involvement in Vietnam, it was found that scenarios not fitting the 'domino theory' (if Vietnam was taken by the communist forces, then the rest of Asia would fall) were systematically organized out of the decision-making system (Alexander, 1979). Likewise, during the decision about the site for a new airport near London, those options that were not located to the north or north-east were discounted. Similar results have been found in the acceptance of innovations within firms. In particular, innovations will be accepted only if they are perceived to be relatively conservative and to fit into the organizational elite's existing value system (Hage and Dewar, 1973; Kelley, 1976). The manipulation of bias allows options that do not accord with the wishes of dominant groups to be dismissed from the deliberation process.

The final organizational process whereby some issues are rendered non-decisions is institutionalized *rule- and norm-making*. Often issues are simply prevented from arising because they contradict entrenched and taken-for-granted rules and specifications (Selznick, 1949). For instance, women's access to managerial roles is frequently blocked by 'value-free' rules around issues such as working hours, transfer policies and lack of childcare. Because these rules were designed to favour men as managers, women find it difficult, if not impossible, to fit in with them (Kanter, 1977; Ashford, Rothbard, Piderit and Dutton, 1998). Without the need for a direct and conspicuous exercise of power, women were still disqualified from holding certain positions within the workplace. This form of power results in perfectly viable propositions and possibilities (e.g. women managers) being excluded when they do not comply with entrenched rules and norms.

While the manipulation approach to power extends our understandings far beyond coercion, some critics suggest that studies of manipulation are problematic since assumptions about power are difficult to falsify and not logically or empirically supported (Merelman, 1968). Since studies of manipulation move away from directly observable behaviours, it becomes a topic that is difficult to research empirically (Wolfinger, 1971). In contrast, Steven Lukes (1974/2005) argues that Bachrach and Baratz (1962, 1963) do not go far enough. He has three problems with the manipulation thesis. Not only does it continue an undue focus on individual behaviour (ignoring broader structural processes related to capitalism), it assumes that the absence of grievance is synonymous with the absence of conflict. This blinds us to the processes that structure our very desires so that we may not even want to articulate a grievance. Lukes' critique calls for a far broader conception of power that considers the domination of our preferences.

Power as domination

As you walk out onto the street, you realize just how late it is. You can't believe that you have been at work for so long. You should be used to this by now. Most days you spend twelve hours in the office, with only a fading tourist photograph of an Indian village to remind you of what it was like to be carefree. But this is what the job requires and you freely choose to work in this firm. There isn't anyone holding a gun to your head, is there? But long hours have their drawbacks. You very rarely get to socialize with friends. You need a few stiff whiskeys to get to sleep, and there really is no time to meet someone you could spend the rest of your life with. Even though you might want a family, you know that it is impossible. Anyway, you have made the decision. You're out to achieve big things, and this requires a few small sacrifices.

This vignette is all too familiar for thousands of workers (Sennett, 1998, 2006). It is a story in which there seems to be power at work, but it is not the kind of overt coercion identified by Dahl or the manipulation identified by Bachrach and Baratz. Rather, this dimension of power shapes our very preferences, attitudes and political outlook. This 'third dimension of power' discussed by Lukes (1974/2005) is domination. In his short but highly influential book he defines 'domination' as 'the ability to bring about significant outcomes' which 'will be present whenever it furthers, or does not harm, the interests of the powerful and bears negatively on the interests of those subject to it' (Lukes, 1974/2005: 86). This provides a far broader conception of what organizational power relations might involve. First, it demonstrates how some issues are legitimized while others are not even imagined. Second, it draws attention not only to existing or manifest conflict but also to potential or latent conflict. This reminds us that perhaps one of the most insidious ways that politics operates is by ensuring that conflict does not arise in the first place. Finally, Lukes argued that power involves situations in which, even though individuals may freely make a decision, their interests are being betrayed. We come to prefer acting in a manner that is anathema to our objective interests.

Is it not the supreme and most insidious exercise of power to prevent people, to whatever degree, from having grievances by shaping their perceptions, cognitions and preferences in such a way that they accept their role in the existing order of things, either because they can see or imagine no alternative to it, or because they see it as natural and unchangeable, or because they value it as divinely ordained and beneficial? (Lukes, 1974/2005: 24)

This approach to organizational power relations assumes that decision-making (and non-decision-making) 'is not the most important exercise of organizational power. Instead, this power is most strategically deployed in the design and imposition of paradigmatic frameworks within the very meaning of such actions as "making decisions" is defined' (Brown, 1978: 376). But how does this occur? Stewart Clegg's study of a building site focuses on the domination of *forms of life*. Although the bulk of the study analyses the interpretation and negotiation of rules, he notes that all these negotiations are determined by the single criterion of profit. On the building site there is 'the iconic domination of a form of life in which the ideal of profitability is King Harvest – it must be reaped' (Clegg, 1975: 155–6). In later work, Clegg (1979, 1981; Clegg and Dunkerley, 1980) significantly expands his conception of domination by identifying the basic and unquestioned ground rules that actors refer back to as their bedrock reality. Indeed, Clegg provides an impressive body of research that expands our understanding of how domination operates through shaping ways of life via the broader social structures of capitalism.

Others have focused more specifically on the role of *ideology* in producing preferences and wants antithetical to our interests (Ranson, Hinings and Greenwood, 1980). Ideology often works through patterns of corporate communication such as widely told narratives and stories. For example, Dennis Mumby (1987) demonstrates how a famous story of a security guard (who would not let the chairman of IBM through a security door because he did not have the correct pass) is an important instance of ideology. Perhaps one of the major manifestations of ideology in contemporary corporations is the dominance of *technical rationality*. Drawing on a radical Weberian tradition, technical rationality is defined as a reductive and single-minded focus on the efficient achievement of a given end (Habermas, 1971). Technical rationality is perhaps one of the most dominant criteria that infuse contemporary organizations (Alvesson, 1987). It works largely by reducing even the most challenging political matters to considerations of efficiency. Moreover, the dominance of technical rationality often favours the interests of those who are in positions of control while working to the detriment of subordinates. Perhaps the best illustration of the dangers of technical rationality is Zygmund Bauman's (1991) study of the organization of the Holocaust. The dominance of modern technical rationality, among a number of other factors, played a central role in allowing millions of Jews to be systematically slaughtered. Robert Jackall's (1988) study of the highly instrumental approach to the ethics of middle managers also demonstrates this point. The ideology of technical rationality structures personal ethics in such a manner that managers acted in ways that they would never have done outside their corporations.

The 'third face' of power may also operate through cognitive schemas that legitimate certain views while delegitimating others to the extent that they may never be considered. As neo-institutional theory argues, this happens chiefly when a particular 'collective rationality' spreads throughout an organizational field. As it spreads, patterns of legitimation make certain models, actions, ways of behaving and power relationships become normal and obvious. This locks actors into thinking about their behaviour in a certain way that rapidly becomes an 'iron cage' (DiMaggio and Powell, 1983). Patterns of legitimation diffuse through a process called 'cognitive isomorphism', whereby organizational actors copy recipes and scripts from other actors in their field (Meyer and Rowan, 1977). An organization will adopt these recipes and scripts not because they are technically efficient or particularly effective (sometimes they might be the very opposite) but because they are considered to be the most appropriate. For example, a classic analysis of chief executive officers (CEOs) in America's largest corporations found that, as models of corporate strategy spread, organizations increasingly favoured the recruitment of CEOs with a certain background (Fligstein, 1987). For instance, from 1959 to 1979 many CEOs of American companies had a finance background. Such a background was considered legitimate when expansion through unrelated mergers and acquisitions was the most acceptable way of doing business in an industry.

Studying power as ideational domination invites us to consider how a regime is established as taken for granted, normal and natural. Here, conflict does not arise because we are so immersed in a certain world view that we see nothing wrong or illegitimate with it. While this approach makes a significant contribution to the study of organizational power, it has not been immune to a range of criticisms. Are there objective interests that can be hidden from us through ideological mystification? Clegg (1989) argues that we should be wary of the notion of objective interests because it ignores how interests are divergent within groups and are politically contingent. It also assumes that academic investigators can identify what these real interests are and distinguish them from the fake or distorted ones. Moreover, this version of power views it as something that constrains, represses and prohibits. This approach downplays the 'productive' aspects of power. Thus we miss the active and dynamic ways in which the 'powerless' are engaged in the reproduction of their own subjugation (Barbalet, 1985; Knights and Willmott, 1989). And, finally, this approach focuses only on how power is exercised over agents by a single sovereign centre (Clegg, 1989). It thus misses aspects of power that are diffused through a number of fragmented relationships. To address these blind spots, a 'fourth face of power' might be considered (Digeser, 1992; Hardy and Leiba-O'Sullivan, 1998).

Power as subjectification

You know that in order to get the job you want you are going to have to work hard while you are at university. Of course, this involves applying yourself to coursework and projects. However, the really important thing seems to be crafting yourself into the kind of dynamic young professional that big businesses are after. To do this you think you might join a few clubs, take a few summer positions at reputable companies and hone your image. The motivation books you have been reading remind you that really believing in yourself will help you to achieve your goals. And they are right! You know that when the time comes you will have to show the recruiters that you are the dynamic professional that they are looking for.

The kind of power in the world of this aspiring university student is strange. He/she does not seem to be oppressed in the way described by those studying power as domination. Instead, we find an actor who exuberantly grasps hold of his/her own destiny. Such determined self-direction is typical of many modern exercises of power in which subordinates (workers, students, patients) are merely asked to be themselves (Fleming and Sturdy, 2006). This is the 'fourth face of power', and it involves a process of *subjectification*. Here, the focus is not on decision-making and non-decision-making, or the ideological suppression of conflict, but the constitution of the very person who makes decisions. The wide-ranging work of Michel Foucault has been influential here. According to Foucault, power is achieved through defining conditions of possibility underlying how we experience ourselves as people. Power, therefore, produces the kinds of people we feel we naturally are. As he famously argues, 'Power produces; it produces reality; it produces domains of objects and rituals of truth. The individual and knowledge that may be gained of him belong to this production' (Foucault, 1977: 194). That is to say, systems of power actively produce the kinds of statements that can appear, the interests of political actors and the desires they might hold. These productive relations of power are embodied in a whole set of micro-political techniques that are distributed throughout society via forms of knowledge. These are generally made up of bodies of arcane expertise (such as medicine), associated institutional forms (such as the clinic) and a whole range of practical techniques (such as procedures for operating). The result is that power 'reaches into the very grain of individuals, touches their bodies and inserts itself into their actions and attitudes, their discourses, learning processes and everyday lives' (Foucault, 1980: 39). These micro-modalities of power do not flow from a sovereign society-wide centre of domination. Rather, they involve a fragmented network of small-scale relations of force.

Initial studies of organizations inspired by Foucault's work focused on the various technologies of power/knowledge through which voluntary compliance is obtained. These systems of control are based on codified knowledge that creates disciplinary effects. Discipline may be defined as 'a configuration of power inserted as a way of thinking, acting and instituting. The disciplined member of the organization wants on his or her own what the corporation wants' (Deetz, 1992a: 42). Human resource management (HRM), for example, has been approached from this perspective (Townley, 1993a). The discipline of HRM establishes divisions within groups of employees through enclosure, the portioning of individual identifiable units and the ranking of employees. HRM also instigates the micro-monitoring of employee behaviour. The broad result is that employees come to internalize the discourse of HRM and enforce it upon themselves (Townley, 1993b). Studies of accountancy have yielded similar results by demonstrating how accountancy emerged as an important disciplinary control system (Hoskin and Macve, 1986). It was propagated through elite education institutions, such as the West Point military academy, and implemented during large-scale industrial projects, such as the American railroads (Hoskin and Macve, 1988). As a social technology, accounting systems, backed by managerial force, construct calculable subjects and render them more amenable to the business of capital accumulation.

Many studies of subjectification have focused on how organizations produce certain types of subjectivity and personhood (Knights and Willmott, 1989). Power is examined as 'a medium of relations in which subjectivity, as a complex, contradictory, shifting experience, is produced, transformed or reproduced through the social practices within which such power is exercised' (Knights and Willmott, 1989: 541). Subjectification has been most notably identified in discourses of corporate strategy. Strategy has been shown to involve a set of power/knowledge relations that appeared at a particular historical juncture, providing employees with a secure sense of self as strategizing agents (Knights and Morgan, 1991). When they take on this mantel of the 'strategising self', employees begin to think of themselves as calculative and future-oriented agents. Studies of total quality management (TQM) show a similar process, whereby the various discourses and practices associated with TQM are subjectively absorbed by workers on a production line, shaping how they think about themselves and their colleagues (Sewell and Wilkinson, 1992). Important here is the internalization of surveillance, so that employees monitor themselves and peers. As a result, 'the constant scrutiny of a panopticon gaze which penetrates right to the very core of each member's subjectivity creates a climate where self-management is assured' (Sewell and Wilkinson, 1992: 284). Wendy Hollway's (1991) study of personnel management reflects similar findings, showing how the individualized employee is created. The study identifies notable shifts in the construction of the worker during industrialism. During the dominance of scientific management, personnel management constructed employees as 'economically motivated' agents, whereas, with the rise of the human relations movement, the employee was understood as the 'sentimental worker'. Each of these new modes of subjectification fundamentally transformed personnel management practices as well as the very identity of employees (also see Jacques, 1996).

More recent studies have demonstrated a relationship between dominant discourses and subjectification. Here, discourse is defined as 'the structured collection of texts embodied in the practices of talking and writing (as well as a wide variety of visual representation and cultural artefacts) that bring organizationally related objects into being as these texts are produced, disseminated and consumed' (Grant, Hardy, Oswick and Putnam, 2004: 3, also see Hardy and Phillips, 1998). Some studies have shown how discourses of workplace equity policies shape what is possible and impossible for employees to reveal regarding gender issues within the workplace (Garnsey and Rees, 1996; Dick and Cassell, 2001). Similarly, service work deploys a discourse of consumer care that slowly infiltrates employee identity (Sturdy, 1998). The culture of the customer (du Gay and Salaman, 1992) has been linked to broader trends concerned with managing culture; as a discourse that encourages committed, loyal and dedicated employees, it targets the very identities of the workforce and aims to have them emotionally and psychologically attached to the firm (Casey, 1995, 1996; Barker, 1993). In his study of self-managing teams, James R. Barker (1993) reveals how subjectification constructed employees into agents who were hardworking, resourceful and reliable. This type of power infused workers' entire sense of self, and was thus difficult if not impossible to escape through conventional forms of resistance.

The final mechanism of subjectification we are concerned with is governmentality. Governmentality involves 'the conduct of conduct: a form of activity aiming to shape, guide or affect the conduct of some person or persons' (Gordon, 1991: 2). This ultimately entails a process of self-government, whereby external exercises of power are not required because individuals control themselves through auto-monitoring behaviour

(Burchell, Gordon and Miller, 1991; Dean, 1999). An excellent illustration of governmentality in organizations can be found in research on cultures of enterprise and the enterprising self (du Gay, 1996). This research shows how the culture of enterprise, which came to prominence during the 1980s in the United Kingdom, saw even basic employment being scripted in the rhetoric of enterprise. Many individuals began to engage in calculating behaviour, whereby they would reflect on how they could expand their portfolio of skills and 'become more entrepreneurial'. Similar processes were identified in Nikolas Rose's (1990) study of the human relations school, which brought to the fore techniques emphasizing self-actualization subjects. Each of these studies reveals a so-called 'liberal regime of control' by which the aim is to generate a sense of freedom and self-determination, ensuring that the subject freely chooses goals that advantage the powerful.

The study of subjectification has certainly extended our understanding of power to include the most microscopic aspects of organizational life. Instead of focusing only on large-scale structures and ideologies or contentious processes of decision- and non-decision-making, our attention is drawn to the fine-grained networks in which active participation in power relations is achieved. However, this kind of analysis has a number of evident shortcomings. Some have argued that studies of subjectification place far too much emphasis on the all-encompassing nature of 'micro-physical' operations of power and thus downplay agency and freedom. This effectively ignores how agents of subjectification often actively use, play with and undermine dominant discourses and disciplines (Newton, 1998, 1999; Ackroyd and Thompson, 1999). While this claim is certainly not applicable to all accounts of subjectification (also see Wray-Bliss, 2002), it does highlight the missing account of resistance in some studies of subjectification. Another criticism of the 'fourth face of power' concerns the obsession with micro-practices of control. This view of the organization underestimates the continuing influence of wider structural relations of force linked to capitalism, the nation state, kinship and so on (Reed, 1998, 2004). Perhaps more seriously, the Foucauldian tradition has little truck with normative claims associated with emancipation – or, at least, how power might be used otherwise. Ultimately, by making power absolutely immanent and technical, all aspects of social life are reduced to micro-exercises of social engineering. There is little room for reflections about a future emancipatory freedom in this cold vision of organization.

Conclusion

In an oft-quoted passage, Charles Perrow (1972: 14) reminds us that 'organizations must be seen as tools... A tool is something you can get something done with. It is a resource *if* you control it. It gives power others do not have. Organizations are multipurpose tools for shaping the world as one wishes it to be shaped. They provide the means for imposing one's definition of the proper affairs of men [sic] upon other men.' Organizations are indeed powerful entities. We scarcely need to be reminded how they help to multiply the power of its individual actors manyfold. They build cathedrals and fly across continents; tasks that we would have attributed to giants or gods in the past. These superhuman powers arise from the fact that organizations are systems that allow us to act in concert. Indeed, Hannah Arendt (1958, 1970) argues that, if power is anything, it is the product of human collective endeavour, and it follows that we should only expect power and politics to spring forth from our organizational endeavours.

In this chapter we have traced through the various forms of power that are involved in the process of organizing. We have seen that there are at least four major dimensions, or faces, of power in work organizations. The first and most obvious face is coercive power. This involves making decisions and directly enforcing them upon others. The second face of power is the manipulation of issues through sorting important topics from non-important ones. This involves the anticipation of results, the mobilization of bias, and institutionalized procedures that systematically exclude some topics from political discourse. The third face of power consists of domination, so that actors' very political preferences get shaped in a way that is counter to their own interests. The fourth and final dimension of power is subjectification, which produces voluntary compliance in subjects of power by moulding them into certain types of people. In the next chapter we develop these faces of power by concentrating on the question of resistance. Then we synthesize our understandings of power and resistance by outlining the concept of struggle in chapter 3. The notion of struggle, we hope, will integrate the most useful features of the frameworks discussed above and provide a more plausible understanding of how power and resistance intersect in contemporary workplaces.

2 | *Faces of resistance at work*

If my manager insults me again, I will be
assaulting him.
After I fuck the manager up, then I'll shorten
the register up.

(Kanye West, *Spaceship*)

Any analysis of power in the context of modern organizations must
also be sensitive to the many ways in which it is resisted. Resistance can
take various forms in complex workplaces, some of which may not be
obvious. For example, imagine a female IT employee who is asked to
work overtime in the evening for a month, a demand that conflicts
directly with her family life. This is a classic articulation of power, in
which the company extends the working day and in doing so encroaches
more and more on the lives of its employees. The employee may gleefully
agree to the request, and put her family life aside in order to impress her
superiors. On the other hand, she may simply refuse, with recourse to
the authority of the local union. This resistance may evoke a more
forceful use of power by the superiors. The employee may then comply
grudgingly, expressing her resistance in less blatant ways, such as
sabotage, working to rule and cynical distancing. On the other hand,
she may simply quit and find employment elsewhere.

This scenario hits upon some rather complex issues concerning the
question of workplace resistance. If the employee continues to work,
but is secretly cynical, is this cynicism to be considered a form of
resistance? Does resistance have to be behavioural in order to be
effective? In this example, family life is the motivator for resistance.
Does resistance always have to have a clear-cut rationale in order to be
expressed? Why do workers resist in the first place? If workers are not
resisting then does that mean they are consenting to relations of power?
Can workers both resist and comply at the same time?

This chapter explores the current views regarding these questions and builds upon the analysis of power developed in the previous chapter. It will be recalled that four 'faces' of organizational power were identified: coercion, manipulation, domination and subjectification. In this chapter we suggest that each face of power points to a corresponding dimension of resistance: resistance as refusal, voice, escape and creation. Each instance of resistance can be identified in the above example. Refusal is the blocking of power by simply saying no. Voice is the attempt to gain legitimate representation within the realm of legitimate power relations, such as the use of a union authority. Escape is the distancing of oneself from the realities of power via cynicism, irony and humour. And creation is the confounding of subjugation by crafting an alternative identity. Our IT worker subverted the company-sponsored identity of the all-hours worker by constructing herself as a family-committed mother, wife, etc. These four categories may be present in the same sequence of resistant activities, or may be articulated individually. We feel that each category of resistance is useful for elucidating the political economy of working life in which so many find themselves embroiled today. The exploration of them in this chapter will serve as a platform from which we will develop the concept of 'struggle' for analysing the power/resistance nexus in the next chapter.

Conceptualizing resistance

'Resistance' is one of those tricky concepts that is difficult to define in any unequivocal manner, and therefore we must proceed with a number of precautions. First, worker resistance does not really exist 'out there' in a position of positive factuality but is necessarily an abstraction that *we* have invented in order to make sense of certain organizational practices and behaviours. In many cases those doing the resisting may not be cogently articulating to themselves: 'We are now resisting.' As Paul Edwards, David Collinson and Giuseppe Della Rocca (1995) point out, there will be situations in which employees do not consciously define themselves as resistant but a closer examination may reveal aspects of organizational subversion. Conversely, employees might volubly define their activities as oppositional but, in reality, be motivated by other intentions. Second, as a construct, the term 'resistance' obviously draws inspiration from the Newtonian theorem in classical physics regarding the interactions of large moving bodies:

every motive force can be neutralized by an equal and opposite force. This metaphor involves assumptions about the ways in which power, domination and opposition intersect. And, third, we must keep in mind the shifting and evolving nature of the concept in organization studies. It is not the case that it has just a single meaning, but is a contingent signifier that is evoked now and then to represent certain behaviours. The meaning of 'resistance' has undergone a series of re-evaluations, making one single definition not only unfeasible but undesirable, given the importance of theoretical fluidity in contemporary organizational analysis. Moreover, because of the multiple and specific nature of the phenomenon, broad, catch-all generalizations of 'resistance' may be clumsy and sometimes misleading.

Having said that, the following are some typical definitions of 'resistance' that we find in the critical organization studies literature: '[A] reactive process where agents embedded in power relations actively oppose initiatives by other agents' (Jermier, Knights and Nord, 1994: 9); '[A] wide range of behaviour – from failure to work very hard or conscientiously, through not working at all, deliberate output restriction, practical joking, pilferage, sabotage and sexual misconduct' (Ackroyd and Thompson, 1999: 1–2); '[A]ny individual or small group act intended to mitigate claims by management on workers or to advance workers claims against management' (Hodson, 1995: 80, quoted in Edwards, Collinson and Della Rocca, 1995). David Collinson makes an extended statement:

Workplace resistance may seek to challenge, disrupt or invert prevailing assumptions, discourses and power relations. It can take multiple material and symbolic forms, and its strength, influence and intensity are likely to be variable and to shift over time...resistance constitutes a form of power exercised by subordinates in the workplace. (Collinson, 1994: 49)

Or, in a Japanese context, Dorinne Kondo comments:

Resistance can take the form of various overt or covert acts, from outright strikes and rebellion to less obvious strategies such as socialising new workers to the intricacies of the piece-rate system, to practices creating sense of solidarity among women, such as their efforts to 'humanise the workplace' by holding baby showers... (Kondo, 1990: 223)

While some of these definitions are so broad that they include even the most banal and mundane act as a form of resistance, we can tease out a few points of commonality that may be helpful. Common to these definitions and descriptions is the idea that resistance represents a particular *relationship with power*, one which does not simply repeat or reiterate its discursive logic but blocks it, challenges it, reconfigures it or subverts it in a way not intended by that power and which has 'favourable' effects for subordinates. How 'favourable' is defined will depend upon the political context in which those who resist are embedded (i.e. it may not look favourable to other insiders or an outside observer). If power in the workplace involves a set of rules and influences that attempt to determine the coordinates of work behaviour and subjectivity, then resistance is an act that disrupts this process in favour of those who are being dominated. In the lexicon of resistance we see adjectives such as 'challenge', 'question' and 'criticize' dovetail with nouns such as 'discontent', 'oppression', 'disadvantage' and 'injustice'. Given the emancipatory values informing the scholarly tradition of critical research, the power that is resisted is usually assumed to be somehow 'dominant' and the subjects who resist either symbolically, economically or structurally subordinate, such as women, workers, indigenous peoples, ethnic minorities, etc. This is not a simple matter of delineating the 'goodies' from the 'baddies' but a result of inspecting closely the often intersecting and contradictory relations of domination that make up particular systems of power and resistance.

If resistance involves a relationship with power that does not simply repeat its demands apropos behavioural and subjective directives, then the forms it takes will be diverse. A survey of the present literature, much of which we discuss below, reveals that the concept of resistance has typically been classified by way of certain sociological dualisms: organized and unorganized, formal and informal, and individual and collective.[1] Unfortunately, these dualisms miss important elements of commonality that blur some of these distinctions. For example, identity-based forms of opposition may be present at both the individual and collective levels. Unorganized forms of resentment and dissent may shore up organized forms of resistance, and so on. Stephen Ackroyd and Paul Thompson (1999) offer a more sophisticated framework, which defines resistance or 'organizational misbehaviour' as acts that *appropriate* specific elements of the organization. Subordinates may appropriate time, work, products and identity when they misbehave. Our reading of the literature focuses less on what the employee 'takes' from the organization and more on what the dissatisfied do. We suggest that each face of power discussed in chapter 1 corresponds to an expression of resistance associated with refusal, voice, escape and creation.

Resistance as refusal

As mentioned earlier, the first face of power involves A coercing the actions of B, thereby making B do something (or *be* someone, as the case may be in the context of today's identity-based controls) that he/she would not otherwise have done. This involves a singular economy between individuals or groups in which A is in a position to direct the actions of B. As John French and Bertram Raven's (1968) adaptation of this analytic argues, the source of this power may derive from legitimate authority, expertise, economic monopoly and so forth. B's refusal to do what A tells him/her to do represents the classic image of resistance: the aim is to block the effects of power by undermining the flow of domination rather than change it. By its very nature, therefore, refusal is generally a visible strategy of resistance, because B is put under the spotlight when he/she does not follow the commands of a superior, the edicts of a bureaucratic apparatus or the normative rules of a corporate culture programme. In this sense, refusal is a risky aspect with which all forms of resistance toy because it activates the eye of authority, and may result in either compromise or further punitive sanctions.

In the beginning, every act of refusal is a form of passive resistance, because it responds to a demand or directive of power by simple non-compliance. There are, of course, degrees of action within this general rubric of passivity. For example, a common response to a programme of change in organizations is to support the process rhetorically during the obligatory worker–management meetings and then continue as one has always worked. B refuses the directives of A by not directing his/her behaviour in the way that A desires. The power of A does not necessarily involve orders demanding a change in behaviour. It may simply involve structures that support an already established status quo, such as a bureaucratic procedure or a wage–labour relationship between temp workers and management. Refusal to comply with the status quo may involve not going along with it by choosing a different course of action, such as strike action. While this action still involves a moment of passivity in which one does not comply with 'the way things are done', it then evolves into a more active articulation of refusal. The initial refusal, if visible and openly communicated to those most likely to object, will trigger a response from superordinates. How B replies to this response from A will determine whether we can call the refusal active or passive. Passive refusal means continuing to behave as one does when he/she refused in the first place. Active refusal may involve an escalation of opposition in which it is A's response that is then targeted by the resistance.

Many accounts of refusal in the workplace derive from a classic Marxist approach and highlight overt attempts to subvert capitalism. The broader perspective from which these accounts of refusal are developed is anything but homogeneous and uniform, and it is therefore difficult to summarize in any cursory fashion. However, some general themes are identifiable. Karl Marx argued in his early writings that class struggle and revolution were fundamental features of all human history hitherto. The division of society into those who control economic resources and those who depend on them for survival was an inherently antagonistic one and often the fulcrum of historical change. With the overturning of feudalism and the emergence of capitalism, a new class system developed around commodities, wage labour and the private ownership of the means of production (technology, capital, materials, etc.). In *The Communist Manifesto* (1848), Marx and Friedrich Engels argued that capitalist society was becoming increasingly divided into two camps: the bourgeoisie, who legally own the means of production, and the impoverished proletariat, who have only their labour power to sell at an exploitative rate. Resistance manifests itself in the proletariat's refusal to accept or perpetuate its own subordination in the capitalist system. As research has demonstrated, this refusal may take the form of strikes (Hyman, 1972), go-slows, theft (Mars, 1982) and sabotage (Dubois, 1979). While early writers in the Marxian tradition viewed revolutionary change (towards a socialist society) as the final goal of all acts of resistance, second-generation theorists such as the Italian Marxist Antonio Gramsci (1929–35/1971) revealed the ways in which resistant groups such as unions, workers associations and so forth may incorporate workers more profoundly in the capitalist social order. Unions, for example, fight for higher wages and improved working conditions, which reproduce rather than undermine the fundamental assumptions of capitalism. This is still a refusal of capitalism, but only of the harsher elements of this particular way of organizing work. As Andrew L. Friedman (1977: 54–5) puts it, 'The most powerful forms of resistance are double-edged swords. In challenging only aspects or symptoms of capitalist social relations, they allow the possibility for capitalism to accommodate such challenges by offering concessions and by co-opting institutions which were intended to marshal worker solidarity...'

Pivotal in the Marxist perspective is an appreciation of the dynamic that is created between management and labour when workers refuse to obey. In his classic study, Richard Edwards (1979) traces the historical dialectic of control and resistance as it unfolded in US industry. Under capitalism, the 'workplace becomes a battleground, as employers attempt to extract the maximum effort from workers and workers *necessarily* resist their bosses' impositions' (Edwards, 1979: 13; emphasis added). He argues that capitalist control of the labour process is automatically met with refusal, which then forces managers to develop better modes of control. That is to say, worker resistance engendered by a dominant mode of control sets off a new search for methods of controlling the labour process. Throughout the history of American industry Edwards has identified a number of these 'structures of control'. First came *simple* control, whereby workers were governed personally by a supervisor through direct orders, violence and similar techniques. This mode of control failed because personal supervisors proved no match for the newly unionised labour force. This led to the development of *technical* control, when machines regulated the nature and speed of work. Insurrections and increasing worker knowledge of work tasks led to the development of *bureaucratic* modes of control, which relied upon a programme of formal rules and career paths to direct the activities of large numbers of workers in the burgeoning corporate enterprises of the 1960s and 1970s.

Refusal, then, is the dimension of resistance concerned with blocking power. Although it is perhaps most commonly understood from a Marxist perspective in the literature, resistance as refusal is not necessarily exhausted under this theoretical rubric. For example, what Ackroyd and Thompson (1999) call 'sex games' is motivated not by classic class politics but by the refusal to treat the work environment as a hyper-rationalized zone. With the desexualization of organizations following the Industrial Revolution and bureaucratic rationalization of the work sphere (Burrell, 1984), sexual acts assume a form of transgression that undermines the libidinal economy of capitalism (see chapter 5). In the context of high-commitment organizations, refusal might also take place in the misty realms of subjectivity and psychic identifications. As Peter Fleming and Graham Sewell (2002) argue in relation to dis-identification in commitment-based human resource models, subjective refusal to buy into the corporate culture has practical effects insofar as it thwarts a key aspect of the employment contract – the managerial demand to assume the subject position of the happily managed.

Resistance as voice

It may be that resistance aims not just to block power but also to gain access to power, in order to express voice via the legitimate organs of domination. Recall that the second face of power operates through non-participation, whereby subordinates are excluded from the means of decision-making authority. An important dimension of resistance appears to correspond with this particular face of power, in that it seeks to gain access to the flows of domination in order to participate in the decisions that affect them. Voice may mean a number of things in this context. As studies of the October Revolution in Russia demonstrate, the most radical way of expressing voice is to supplant and replace those in authority with an alternative set of organizational principles (Žižek, 2004). All forms of revolution aim to undermine the hegemony of a class or elite by establishing an alternative voice in its place. This will usually involve a significant revision of the power hierarchy – not simply a changing of the guard. A less radical, but perhaps more common way in which voice is expressed as resistance is to let one be heard by those in control in order to change particular aspects of power relations in favour of those being affected by them. Organizing a woman's group in order to voice grievances about sexual harassment or discrimination might be an example of this type of voice. Trade unionism also involves an important element of resistance through voice within the institutional parameters of the organization. The rise of social movements outside the workplace – the 'right to be lazy' or anti-globalization movements – is also an example of voice being mobilized to impact upon the decision-makers in offices of authority. Less obviously, some forms of resistance through voice may not be overt, identifiable and organized. Sporadic sabotage, for example, sends a clear signal to authorities that all are not happy with the organization (Brown, 1977). But this type of voice is unlikely to gain legitimacy in the organization or seriously affect the imbalance of power that derives from non-participation (unless, of course, it becomes an organized campaign).

As we shall argue in chapter 9, in order to speak to power and achieve participation in an organizational structure that has eschewed wider involvement, a space must either be utilized or created wherein one's voice can be heard. There are many ways in which this space can be formed. In Western societies, for example, the public sphere still offers a relatively legitimate space to engage in criticism of company policy or managerial initiatives. A public sphere is a realm that is structurally removed from the means-end logic of the economy on the one hand and the modern state on the other hand (Arendt, 1958). The public sphere can, of course, take different forms, including the European coffee houses of the Enlightenment, the public square, the newspaper, the broadcast media and now the digital media (Habermas, 1991). In order for such a space to be meaningful, people must also be empowered to appear legitimately, part of which involves having enough dignity to do so. Indeed, for Amartya Sen (1985), one of the central preconditions for a political actor is 'being unashamed to appear in public' (Sen, 1985: 15). In practical terms this means imparting sufficient recognition to actors for them to be able to participate in the public sphere confidently and without fear of persecution (Honneth, 1995). The speaker must be recognized as a free fellow actor who has something important and relevant to say. A contemporary example of this space is the growth of independent regulatory watchdog institutions that provide support for whistle-blowing activities. This gives organizational members access to the media in order to raise public attention about wrongdoing within a company. Another type of 'public appearance' that is not likely to be sanctioned by managers is protesting in public spaces or within the media. Picketing outside an animal experimentation laboratory or creating a subversive website regarding one's organization are good examples. Organizational members may also challenge significant authorities to appear in public. Public relations officers are now well versed in this activity.

Space for resistant voices may also be created through alternative organizational structures. Labour organizations such as trade unions and, at the broader level, the International Labor Organization (Aronowitz and Gautley, 2003) use the power of numbers to voice grievances about working conditions, pay, etc. The ability of unions to give a voice to workers is demonstrated in David Collinson's (1994) study of a woman's resistance to gender discrimination in an office environment. In this case, an employee due for promotion announced to her superiors that she was pregnant. Later she was passed over for the promotion, with a less qualified candidate being offered the position instead. While the company had a well-articulated equal opportunities policy, it was clear to the employee that she did not get the promotion because she was about to take maternity leave. As Collinson (1994: 42) suggests, 'Jane might have decided to resist by her full entitlement of statutory maternity leave and then resigning from the company.' Jane could have also remained with the company and grudgingly accepted the decision. Instead, she went to her union representative, who then discussed the issue with management. Jane's supervisors applied pressure in order to stop the action, even arranging a very early morning meeting, knowing full well that Jane's morning sickness would impair her participation. An important part of the union's strategy was gathering knowledge from management about their selection criteria. Eventually, the union recommended a submission to the Equal Opportunities Commission, which was pre-empted by Jane's supervisors instantly promoting her. In this case, the union provided a persistent, rational and informed voice for Jane.

While unions have traditionally been the prime organizational form for providing workers with a voice, new forms of collectivity are now emerging outside the classical union framework. For example, new social movements such as the anti-globalization collectives now provide some voice for the disgruntled employee, consumer and citizen. These groups have been important for widening the politics of organization to include the environment, immigration, consumerism and Third World relief. Gaining inspiration from books such as Naomi Klein's (2000) *No Logo* and Michael Hardt and Antonio Negri's (2000) *Empire*, protests in Melbourne, Genoa, Seattle, Prague and Davos, to name but a few, were swiftly organized in an informal manner, creating a convincing counter-narrative regarding the inimical effects of international business. Underground associations such as Ya Basta and *tute bianche* (white overalls) protested at international business meetings organized by, for example, the World Trade

Organization, the G8 and the World Economic Forum in order to gain maximum media exposure. In some countries, these informal networks have developed into de facto political parties. Examples include the Fuerzas Armadas Revolucionarias de Colombia (FARC) and the Ejército de Liberación Nacional (ELN) guerrilla forces in Colombia, which are opposed to transnational oil and mining companies. Other groups are more fluid and network-based, such as the Zapatista Front of National Liberation (EZLN) in Chiapas, Mexico, and Ken Wiwa's Mossop movement in Nigeria. The Zapatistas are a diffuse network of disenfranchized indigenous groups in the Chiapas district (including the Tzeltal, Mam, Chol, Zoque and Tojolobal peoples). Their expressed aim is to create what they call 'democratic room' in order to facilitate struggles against land privatization, transnational agribusiness and the machinations of the North American Free Trade Agreement.[2]

Resistance as escape

The third face of power is what Lukes (1974/2005) associates with the domination of preferences, with the result that we pursue goals antithetical to our objective interests. To paraphrase one of Lukes' most famous statements, is not the most profound form of power that which obscures actors' best interests from themselves? Preferences may be layered upon the subject in a manner that simply reproduces their position of subordination. The mechanics of this reproduction operates in a variety of ways; employees may, for instance, be exhorted to think of the company first rather than themselves. The hierarchy that consolidates the split between those who manage and those who are managed may be 'naturalized' so that it comes to be seen as inevitable and immutable. Regimes of paternalism and commitment may have employees identify with the company so that they come to enjoy their powerlessness. An important stream of research has demonstrated how it is not only positive sentiments (e.g. commitment, loyalty, dedication, consent, etc.) that can blind actors to the true nature of their subordinate position. Certain negative sentiments associated with dissent and resistance may also do this. What Stanley Cohen and Laurie Taylor (1992) call 'escape attempts' are those strategies used to disengage mentally from the world of work. In the context of working-class counter-cultures, for example, commentators have pointed to cynicism, scepticism and dis-identification as common avenues of escape. Such escape attempts may unwittingly function as a 'safety valve' (Brown, 1987; Rodrigues and Collinson, 1995) or 'ideology' (Fleming and Spicer, 2003) that preserves rather than subverts the status quo, in that they allow workers to let off steam in a manner that does not necessarily harm the existing regimes of power.

This interpretation of resistance (especially escape attempts via cynicism, scepticism and irony) has its origins in a stream of research that identifies the functional elements of conflict (Piccone, 1978; Burawoy, 1979). Employee cynicism in the context of culture management and high-commitment discourse has been highlighted as a key example of reproductive resistance. Gideon Kunda's *Engineering Culture* (1992) gives an ethnographic account of employees escaping managerial discourse of commitment through cynicism. Cynicism was a way of keeping the insidious culture from impinging upon the ego, a manoeuvre Kunda calls 'cognitive distancing'. He explains: 'Cognitive distancing – disputing popular ideological formulations – is manifested when one suggests that one is "wise" to what is "really" going on. Being "wise" implies that despite behaviours and expressions indicating identification, one is fully cognizant of their underlying meaning, and thus free of control: autonomous enough to know what is going on and dignified enough to express that knowledge' (Kunda, 1992: 178).

Building on Kunda's work, Hugh Willmott (1993) argues that, although the corporate culture may capture the subjectivities of many employees, some are inevitably cynical. Willmott evokes Peter Berger and Thomas Luckmann's (1966) concept of 'cool alternation' to explain this response, whereby individuals subjectively distance themselves from the roles they play. He then extends Kunda's (1992) findings to describe how such a mode of cynical dis-identification can actually incorporate workers into the relations of power they seek to escape (and thereby operate in an ideological fashion). Cynicism at 'Tech' allowed employees to resist seduction by the corporate culture but,

a less obvious and perverse effect of playing the game of cool alternation was an undermining or numbing of a capacity directly to criticize or resist the cultural logic. Why so? Because the very possibility of engaging in the playful ironicizing of the Culture was interpreted as evidence of Tech's commitment to openness, freedom of expression, etc. (Willmott, 1993: 537)

According to Willmott, therefore, that there exists a possibility to be cynical about the culture is something that is perceived by employees as a sign of the company's dedication to freedom. It is this dedication that consequently forestalls any initiative to organize more effective forms of opposition on the part of employees. Employees subsequently become trapped in a 'vicious circle of cynicism and dependence' (Willmott, 1993: 518) that disarms them of any ability to challenge the existing power structure. Collinson (1992, 1994) develops Paul Willis' (1977) study of 'the lads' by focusing on male manual workers in a British lorry manufacturing firm called Slavs. The shopfloor workers were very cynical towards the new emphasis on 'communication' and 'teamwork' because the contradiction between the saccharine rhetoric and their actual second-class status within the firm was too great. Like Willis' 'lads', the workers developed a counter-culture that overtly celebrated manual labour and masculinity (getting their hands dirty) and cynically derided managerial work as effeminate and beneath them. The outcome of this type of resistance, however, also had a sinister and self-defeating aspect. Indeed, Collinson uses the phrase 'resistance through distance' to describe cynicism, because it resulted in workers voluntarily disengaging from the management process (perhaps the real seat of power) and thus perpetuating the very conditions that they were resisting. The counter-identity of masculinity appeared to rely upon a fundamental denial of the more concrete and practical aspects of managerial power at Slavs.

Cynicism here was not seen as real opposition because it could not practically challenge the distribution of resources, management's right to manage or asymmetrical decision-making processes. Cynicism and other kinds of subjective opposition consequently are 'unlikely to be effective forms of resistance given the disciplinary processes that characterise contemporary organizations' (Collinson, 1994: 51). For sure, opposing management in this manner appeared to represent a corrosive resistant attitude that 'significantly limited worker's otherwise radical oppositional practices...' (Collinson, 1994: 33). A similar reading of worker cynicism can be found in Paul du Gay and Graham Salaman's (1992) analysis of enterprise. In pointing out the supposed lack of meaningful resistance to strategies of enterprise culture in the organizations studied, they argue:

Certainly the discourse of enterprise appears to have no serious rivals today... [E]ven if people do not take enterprise seriously, even if they keep a certain cynical distance from its claims, they are still reproducing it through their involvement in everyday practices within which enterprise is inscribed. (du Gay and Salaman, 1992: 630)

This argument is developed from Slavoj Žižek's fascinating description of what he calls the 'ideology of cynicism': 'Cynical distance is just one way to blind ourselves to the structuring power of ideological fantasy: even if we do not take things seriously, even if we keep an ironical distance, *we are still doing them*' (Žižek, 1989: 32; emphasis original). Du Gay and Salaman (1992) similarly insist that, even though we may negatively distance ourselves from the dictates of enterprise culture, the real measure of organizational resistance lies in *how we act*. If we merely criticize organizational power relationships and then proceed to go through the motions, then nothing has really changed. If anything, in fact, we are duping ourselves by our cynical expressions, because we gain an erroneous and illusory sense of self that suppresses rather than facilitates insurrectional activity.

This analysis of resistance as escape is convincing in a number of regards. We mentally dis-identify with our prescribed social role yet still perform it and are thus blind to the material nature of power. But it has become a target of criticism itself in recent years (see Fleming and Sewell, 2002; Fleming and Spicer, 2003). It tends to privilege traditional conflict as the only standard by which to judge the efficacy or legitimacy of resistance. Indeed, as the term 'escape' implies, when we ironically dis-identify with the organization we are not really changing anything – but what does change mean in this context? More recent research on identity, subjectivity and subjugation has broadened the parameters of resistant activity and analysed its political status in the context of contemporary work forms. This problem in relation to cynical resistance is very germane to today's organizations, which entice workers with culture management and empowerment, and will be explored in more depth in chapter 4.

Resistance as creation

The fourth face of power explored in chapter 1 relates to the Foucauldian motif of subjectification, in which actors become attached to an identity that is the very product of relations of domination (Foucault, 1979, 1980). Power operates by constituting identities and individualities in a manner that is productive to the maintenance of certain organizational imperatives (consent, commitment, innovation, creativity, subordination, etc.). As David Knights and Hugh Willmott (1989) point out, this understanding of power is markedly different from the Marxian approach, in that it does not use economic structures to read off underlying interests. Indeed, interests are the very product of power, although this point continues to be an issue of debate (see Clegg, 1989, and Eagleton, 1991). For many commentators, the Foucauldian concern with identity, ethics and care of the self marked a major departure from more traditional approaches, which treated resistance as a synonym for 'industrial struggle'. Resistance no longer had to conform to the industrial image of overt, organized and confrontational action (Kondo, 1990; Bennett, 1998). For some, Foucault allows us to think about resistance in new and broader ways that do not rest solely upon the nomenclature of dialectics, true interests and overt antagonism (Knights and McCabe, 2000; Thomas and Davies, 2005; Mumby, 2005). Because power is increasingly mobilized at the often imperceptible level of subjectivity, self and the ethical body in non-absolutist states, it is also here that an ambiguous site of various practices of subversion appears. Indeed, Foucault argues that resistance 'against the submission of subjectivity...is becoming more and more important, even though the struggle against forms of domination and exploitation have not disappeared. Quite the contrary' (Foucault, 1982: 213). This point about new forms of power requiring updated notions of resistance is made succinctly by Sally Engle Merry (1995) in the context of cultural studies.

The transition from understanding resistance as conscious collective actions such as peasant uprisings to more subtle, unrecognised practices such as foot-dragging, sabotage, subversive songs and challenges to the law's definition of personal problems...parallels the development of new conceptions of power as produced in social relationships, discourses and institutions... The turn to micro-resistance parallels Foucault's emphasis on the micro-techniques of power. As power surrounds and infuses every action, the significance of small acts of resistance to these minute forms of power becomes more important. (Merry, 1995: 15)

This Foucauldian sensibility seems to have shifted our attention away from class struggle to those subtle micro-practices that do not necessarily aim for 'revolution' but nevertheless allow subordinates to construct counter-spheres within forms of domination, change the trajectory of controls and quietly challenge power relations without necessarily leaving them (de Certeau, 1984). This approach to employee resistance has become increasingly popular in critical organization studies, with identity, alternative discourses and quotidian subversions coming to the fore in many accounts of recalcitrance (Knights and McCabe, 2000; Ezzamel, Willmott and Worthington, 2001; Fleming, 2005a, 2005b; Thomas and Davies, 2005). Following the Foucauldian approach, an important aspect of resistance is the creation of alternative identities and discursive systems of representation within the context of broader flows of domination. An important influence on this way of analysing resistance is the application of Foucault's work by Michel de Certeau in *The Practice of Everyday Life* (1984). He understands resistance as an everyday tactical process of 'making do' with the materials at hand. Resistance from this perspective 'insinuates itself into the other's place, fragmentarily, without taking it over in its entirety, without being able to keep it at a distance' (de Certeau 1984: xix).

From this perspective, resistance involves using power to create something that was not intended by those in authority. Many examples of this 'making do' have been identified in organizations. In the context of commitment and loyalty programmes, workers often rescript the official culture in order to render it absurd or hypocritical (Kondo, 1990; McKinlay and Taylor, 1996). Martin Parker (2002a) has demonstrated how sponsored terms such as 'autonomy', 'self-management' and 'trust' are often turned back on the organization as an instrument of critique, along the lines of: 'We are not *really* allowed to manage ourselves. We are not *really* trusted.' Another example is humorous parody, in which employees absorb the dominant discourse in order to implode its legitimacy through 'sending it up'. Here, the geography of resistance is one of intimacy rather than distance, as Judith Butler (1998: 34) explains in reference to cynical parody: 'Parody requires a certain ability to identify, approximate, and draw near; it engages an intimacy with the position it appropriates that troubles the voice, the bearing, the performativity of the subject...' A similar idea has been explored in relation to the seditious practice of *over-identification*, a tactic in which workers resist the discourse of culture management by taking it too seriously and over-identifying with certain norms and beliefs (Fleming and Sewell, 2002). A favourite lampooning strategy among unions, for example, is to follow a cultural script to the letter, swiftly short-circuiting its administrative legitimacy. A kind of cultural working to rule (fixing hundreds of company stickers to your car, or swamping the suggestion box with not entirely useless offerings) may have similar subversive effects.

Other research in this tradition has studied the ways in which employees resist subjugation by creating alternative self-narratives and identities. Quickly attaining classic status in this respect is Dorinne Kondo's *Crafting Selves* (1990). In this study of part-time female workers (or *patō*) in a Japanese confectionary factory, she observed employees resisting the oppressive corporate culture by forging alternative discourses about the company. The dominant discourse espoused by management revolved around the concept of *uchi no kaisha* – 'our company'. This discourse was designed to instil a sense of pride and loyalty among workers and foster an emotional attachment to the firm. However, front-line managers tended to be authoritarian, and the wages the women received were low, even by industry standards. Because of the patriarchal nature of the local culture, *patō* found it difficult to resist in any overt way. They therefore engaged in subjective resistance by expropriating the language and identity of *uchi no kaisha* and turning it back on itself, in order to highlight the injustices of organizational life. Kondo writes that,

by paying careful attention, then, to the ways the boundaries of *uchi no kaisha* are drawn, we can see how workers can give a particular spin to the meanings of such an idiom, wresting it from *shachō* [company president] and turning it to their advantage, yet creating ironies and contradictions for themselves in doing so. (Kondo, 1990: 202)

Kondo's study attempts to demonstrate that, when the identities of employees' are a predominant control mechanism, this also becomes an important site of resistance. An important aspect of Kondo's study is the rejection of the notion that authentic real selves underlie acts of resistance. Authentic selves are not projected through resistance but created (see also Fleming, 2005a; Thomas and Davies, 2005). The assumption of a 'pristine space of authentic resistance' (Kondo, 1990: 224) erroneously positions subjectivity outside power. She particularly takes issue with James Scott's *Weapons of the Weak* (1985), an influential study of peasant resistance in Malaysia. Scott found that the peasants complied with relations of power on the surface but refused to accept and internalize the ideological justifications asserted from above. He calls the resulting internal autonomy a 'hidden transcript' that was shared among labouring peasants and protected them from the tyrannical class relations. But Kondo rejects Scott's theory of mental autonomy, because it posits a social sphere that is separate from power in which more authentic discourses reside. We are given the impression that resistance is propelled by a pre-existing ego that is the author of its own subjectivity and actions. She compares Scott's findings to her own:

Scott's individual who hides the transcript still retains the character of a whole, consciously intentional subject who holds well-informed, uncontradictory opinions apart from the imposed values of the dominant ideology. The 'less authentic' side which comes into play in situations of unequal power is simply a kind of mask, donned for expediency's sake. Nowhere do we find people like my co-workers in contradictions, that they simultaneously resist and reproduce, challenging and reappropriating meanings as they also undermine those challenges. (Kondo, 1990: 221)

Following Kondo, the presumption of an autonomous mental space that has informed a whole tradition of radical perspectives on resistance assumes that dissent both emanates from an authentic self (as the agent of resistance) and makes self-liberation its primary *raison d'être*. This tautological notion of authenticity also implies a sense of genuineness and purity, an eternal 'origin' that is untouched by outside forces, the most recent articulation being Michael Hardt and Antonio Negri's (2000: 157) rather romantic claim that the 'poor are god on earth'.

Conclusion

Each of the dimensions explored above represents a particular aspect of dissent that might be found in any act of opposition. We have suggested that they map onto the faces of power discussed in the previous chapter, but we do acknowledge the fuzzy nature of such a mapping. This is more a heuristic exercise than a concise relational model. One problem with many of the analyses of resistance described above can be found in the very term 'resistance'; as a metaphor relating to the action and reaction of moving bodies, it assumes that power comes first and then resistance attempts to neutralize that power through refusal, voice, escape and creation. Others have argued that perhaps resistance comes first and then invites further acts of power (Ackroyd and Thompson, 1999), but such a reversal still maintains a linear causal relationship between power and resistance. The metaphor separates power and resistance into two antagonistic camps that periodically collide when the conditions are ripe. The 'face' of power lies between A and B, whereby one is detached from the other. Many have theorized about the gravity that locks them in a turbulent embrace, with notions such as dialectics. While the research on this topic has been very valuable in elucidating the politics of organization, we argue that the concept of 'resistance' needs to be transcended if we are to describe more accurately the kinds of conflicts in today's workplaces. It is suggested in the next chapter that it is at the inter*face* between power and resistance that the notion of 'struggle' comes into play.

3 | *Struggle in organizations*

> If there is no struggle there is no progress.
> Those who profess to favour freedom and yet
> depreciate agitation...want crops without
> ploughing up the ground, they want rain
> without thunder and lightning. They want
> the ocean without the awful roar of its many
> waters... Power concedes nothing without a
> demand. It never did and it never will.
>
> (Douglass, 1857/1985: 204)

Our intuitive understanding of power and resistance is rather strange. We often draw a strict contrast between the diabolic world of power and the liberating world of resistance. This division has almost religious dimensions. On one side of the pearly gates is a devilish realm of power where employees are directed by dark-suited overlords. This is Dante's inferno, where sinners are meted out excruciating punishment by a complex hierarchy of devils. On the other side of the pearly gates we have a world of sweetness and light, where emancipated employees frolic in a corporate playground overflowing with opportunities for naughtiness.

Like most intuitive understandings, this stark contrast between power and resistance is naive. It is a bedtime story of baddies (presumably the powerful manager) and goodies (presumably the oppressed worker). In such stories the baddies are always unfailingly bad and will not cease to exercise their diabolic power to achieve their dastardly plans. The freedom-fighting goodies will, of course, be resolutely good and endeavour to further their noble struggle at every turn. But, like any bedtime story, this is not the stuff of real social relationships, which are marked by ambiguity and ambivalence. In addition, those in positions of power resist. For instance, managers may subtly sabotage a corporate initiative (Zald and Berger, 1978). And those who resist need to mobilize power in order to do so (Collinson, 1992). Power and resistance are closely knitted together in complex ways.

Because the last two chapters have treated power and resistance as separate entities, it is now time to investigate the relationship between them. The metaphor of 'resistance' relies upon a Newtonian image of natural moving bodies. First there is an action (power) followed by a reaction (resistance). The more closely we look at this relationship, however, the more *dynamic* and codependent it becomes. For example, Max Weber has defined power as 'the probability that one actor within a social relationship will be in a position to carry out his [sic] own will *despite resistance*' (Weber, 1922/1978: 53; emphasis added). Here we notice that power is viewed as an attempt to overcome resistance that is already present. Power is viewed as a response to resistance, or even a response to the response. The nature of this dynamic was debated in some detail in the 1980s, when Barry Hindess (1982), for instance, argued that power should not be seen as the ability of certain agents to overcome a relatively weak party despite some resistance. Rather, power relations ought to be viewed as an ongoing and mutually implicated interplay between subordinates and superordinates. Building on this argument, J. M. Barbalet (1985) claims that resistance might actually shape these power relations. These approaches suggest that, instead of having two diametrically opposed worlds of good and evil, organizations are more like a chiaroscuro of power and resistance, wherein 'light' and 'dark' play off each through a combination of mixture, contrast and blurring.

In this chapter we aim to develop a more robust and nuanced conceptualization of this dynamic in organizations by introducing the term 'struggle'. This concept has been well used in disparate groups of literature. By developing it in the context of critical organization theory, however, we suggest that it may help us better understand the complex and ambiguous interface between power and resistance in workplaces today. This notion will then form the backdrop for the chapters that follow.

The power–resistance dynamic

In recognizing the intertwined nature of power and resistance, we can shift the focus from separate entities to a more complex 'power–resistance' dynamic, in which different forms of power evoke certain types of resistance and vice versa. We can see this dynamic in relation to the dimensions of power/resistance discussed in chapters 1 and 2. Direct refusal by an employee to work on a project is met with more coercive expressions of control, such as an unambiguous command or being escorted from the building by a security guard. An attempt to voice unpalatable political issues is countered by further efforts to manipulate the agenda in order to exclude them before the discussion begins. Acts of organizational escape are met by further internalized forms of domination relating to guilt, family values and sentiments of trust. And the creation of counter-identities is fought by a more carefully orchestrated programme of cultural subjection. Indeed, as Dennis Mumby argues, the study of resistance should not focus on 'the bow (an ostensible act of obeisance to power) nor the fart (a covert act of resistance to power) but rather on the ways in which these intersect in the moment to produce complex and often contradictory dynamics of control and resistance' (Mumby, 2005: 21).

Careful studies of the interplay of power and resistance certainly provide a rich and more nuanced picture of organizational life. Instead of two sharply contrasting images of heavenly resistance and hellish power, the power–resistance couplet is considered in a more earthly light of political purgatory. But, although the notion of 'dynamic' emphasizes the intertwined nature of power and resistance, they are still assumed to be ultimately distinct. Indeed, as a result of holding onto this analytical dividing line, we are tempted to try and decide which actions are resistance and which are power. Recent research has shown that teasing out the two can become a very hard task when faced with current political situations. With the prima facie obliteration of class politics in many Western countries, shareholder attacks on managerial ranks and the emergence of new social movements based around consumerism and non-work issues, the once black and white vista of the controlled and controllers is difficult to retain.

This uncertainty, we suggest, derives from three assumptions that are still present in much of the literature exploring power and resistance in work organizations. First is the assumption that power and resistance are *epistemologically* distinct phenomena. This means that it is possible to know the differences between power and resistance and identify them in empirical settings. But there is difficulty here, as Dorinne Kondo (1990) has most notably argued in her study of a Japanese confectionery manufacturer. She maintains that the power of resistance and resistance of power infused the relation of domination between the factory patriarch and female employees. Indeed, the power to rescript the dominant narratives in the factory in a manner that provided limited freedom actually fuelled the control desired by the manager. Kondo suggests that what we conceptualize as resistance could easy be termed as power and vice versa – the epistemological distinction involves slippage and overlap to such an extent that they fall in on each other.

Deriving from the first, a second assumption underlying much power–resistance research is that the two terms are *ontologically* distinct. While we may acknowledge that our academic concepts are not exactly accurate in identifying the forces underpinning power and resistance, there is still a 'real world' out there that entails these two forces. Otherwise, why would we even choose to research how the powerful control the powerless? Although we also assume that there is a very strong reality in which some enjoy and receive more privileges and control than others, the empirical dynamic of power and resistance relations remains scrambled. As we will argue in later chapters, resistance may involve forms of power that facilitate domination at other points in power/resistance relations. Power wielded by management may involve forms of resistance that are then used to fuel the power of subordinates. Due to the commonality of mechanisms between 'power' and 'resistance', it seems hard to keep them ontologically separate.

Faced with this difficulty of separating power and resistance as epistemological and ontological entities, some have sought to claim that they are *politically* and ethically distinct categories (Fleming, 2006). Here we turn to structures first, and then explore the ensuing dynamics of power–resistance within this frame. By identifying a certain group as powerful and another group as resistors, we are able to make a political intervention that gives legitimacy to an oppressed political group and furthers their struggle for emancipation. Indeed, as Gayatri Chakravorty Spivak (1996) argues, even the most tyrannical technocrat is a victim of sorts, but we would not want to compare his/her victimhood to that of the most impoverished in society. This is certainly a defensible position, which recognizes the broader political context of micro-politics in work organizations. But the danger here is that when we identify the 'powerless' we reinforce a simplistic stereotype that romanticizes subordinate groups. In doing this we may miss the politically regressive aspects of some forms of resistance among the powerless (such as the homophobia discussed in chapter 5), and the progressive elements of the politically dominant. Moreover, by assigning social roles in this way we may further embed the sense of powerlessness and hopelessness associated with resistance. It is no wonder that small communities, for example, should feel disempowered and that radical action is pointless when all they can do is simply 'resist' a significantly more 'powerful' force.

So, given these persistent problems with the concepts of power and resistance, we suggest that the term 'struggle' may provide a supplementary vocabulary that can further our understandings of this complex relationship. In doing so, we do not want to jettison the terms 'power' and 'resistance'. They remain very useful, but at a deeper level (dirtied by the vagaries of empirical situations, perhaps) we think that 'struggle' captures a more nuanced and ambivalent reality.

The concept of struggle

The word 'struggle' evokes a highly antagonistic situation. For example, we talk of two children struggling over a toy that they both long for. We talk about two companies locked in a struggle to dominate a market. There is also the struggle of a colonized group to gain their independence from their colonial masters. Women struggle for equal rights and opportunities. We talk about an individual's struggle for justice. And we might even talk about struggles with ourselves when faced with a moral dilemma or major decision. Each of these expressions of the idea of struggle reveals the intimate, existential and wide-ranging elements of the phenomenon. But, what *exactly* is meant by the term 'struggle'? More specifically, how can the concept of struggle help us understand the dynamic interplay between power and resistance in contemporary workplaces? In order to address these questions and make our argument, we now investigate some theories of struggle that have appeared in social and political thought.

If we return to the power debates, we notice that struggle forms the foundation of modern approaches to power. The work of Niccolò Machiavelli (1515/1997, 1517/1983) is replete with images of struggle between the Prince and his subjects, the Prince and other princes, and the Prince and other members of the nobility. Machiavelli presents a world where actors are 'ungrateful, fickle, false, cowardly, covetous, and as long as you succeed they are yours entirely; they will offer you their blood, property, life and children, as is said above, when the

need is far distant; but when it approaches they turn against you'
(Machiavelli, 1515/1997, chap. 17). Political life involves the constant
attempt by egocentric actors to advance their interests, often at the
expense of others. The result is that politics is a space where mutually
mistrusting actors are consistently locked in a struggle for political
advantage that is not bound by any external reference points, save the
constant calculation of power. We also find images of struggle at the
heart of Thomas Hobbes' (1651/1985) theory of the modern state.
Hobbes argues (chap. 13) that people are largely equal in physical
and mental abilities, but tend to overvalue their own ability vis-à-vis
the ability of others. This gives rise to a situation in which an actor will
seek to use his/her abilities in order to obtain a resource he/she desires
from another person. Because of the limited nature of these resources,
actors begin to fear attack from others, and seek to pre-empt an attack
on their own interests and life by consolidating their power. During this
time there are no human institutions other than mutual struggle; 'a
state of nature' reigns whereby the only important dynamic is perpetual
contestation. Hobbes points out that people desire an escape from this
state of constant war and voluntarily submit their power to a sovereign
who will guarantee them order and life. What interests us is that the
'ground zero' of politics for Hobbes is a situation of mutual, interlocked fierce struggle; law and order come only after the fact to prevent
its negative effects (chapters 14–17). For Machiavelli and Hobbes
alike, struggle forms the very basis of political life.

While Machiavelli and Hobbes demonstrate the foundational nature
of struggle in political life, they are less specific about the interrelation-
ships involved in this struggle. This task fell to Georg Hegel: to demonstrate how struggle occurs *between* two subjects. The subjects involved
are not independent entities who clash. Rather, they are mutually
dependent on their opponent in struggle for their own sense of being.
Perhaps nowhere is this better explicated than in Hegel's (1807/2005:
IVa) famous discussion of the master and slave. Hegel investigates the
process through which we come to be conscious of ourselves. Instead
of this being a process of exploring ourselves and gradually reveal-
ing what is there, Hegel argues that we come to know who we are
through a struggle with another person: 'Self-consciousness exists in
itself and for itself, in that, and by the fact that it exists for another self-
consciousness; that is to say, it *is* only by being acknowledged or
recognized' (Hegel, 1807/2005: 229; emphasis in original). Here, he

argues that our own sense of who we are is to be found only in interaction with another person. For Hegel, the nature of this interaction with another person is struggle. He notes that two individuals enter into a 'life-and-death struggle' to 'bring their certainty of themselves, the certainty of being for themselves, to the level of objective truth'.

This life-and-death struggle is exemplified by the antagonism between the powerful Lord and the dependent Bondsman. The Lord feels that he is independent of the Bondsman because he has control over him/her and can tell him/her what to do. In contrast, the Bondman experiences him-/herself as dependent upon the Master because he/she is often simply an extension of the Master's wishes. Hegel shows us that both these figures, at least initially, are dependent on the other for their sense of who they are. The Master would not be a Master without the Bondsman to recognize him as such and do his bidding. Similarly, the Bondsman would not have an identity without the recognition and fear experienced in the face of his/her Master. Hegel goes even further, by noting that the Bondsman has a relationship independent of his/her relationship with the Master, namely the relationship with the object of his/her work. It is through this struggle with the object of work that the Bondsman develops a sense of recognition and self-consciousness that is independent of the Master. The central point we can take from Hegel's argument about the relationship between the Master and the Bondsman is that both of these figures exist only to the extent that they stand in relation to one another. Hegel shows us how through the political struggle between two actors (whether they are individuals or social collectives) each group gains its sense of identity and existence. This suggests that actors do not just arrive on the scene and then engage in struggle, but develop a sense of themselves as actors through the very process of struggle.

The vital nature of struggle in any social relationship was picked up by Georg Simmel. In much of the early sociological thought, struggle was thought to be a disruption or breakdown of sociality and organization. To put this crudely, the more struggle the less sociality. However, Simmel suggests the opposite: *Kampf* (which is translated as conflict, but also means struggle) 'is a way of achieving some kind of unity, even though it may be through the annihilation of one of the conflicting parties' (Simmel, 1955: 13). For Simmel, struggle is a vital ingredient of social reality, because a completely harmonious social situation is 'not only empirically unreal, it could show no real life process' (13). Like

Machiavelli and Hobbes before him, Simmel argues that 'natural hostility as a form or basis of human relations appear at least side by side
with their other basis, sympathy' (28). Instead of treating struggle as the
opposite of sociality, Simmel argues that struggle plays at least three
vital social roles. First, struggle gives an actor a sense of agency. By
engaging in struggle, an actor is reminded that he/she is not merely a
slave of circumstance. This ultimately builds self-esteem and conviction
that an actor can indeed act upon the world and make a difference.
Second, struggle often promotes social interaction within a group. This
is because 'one *unites* in order to fight, and one fights under the mutually
recognised control of rules and norms' (Simmel, 1955: 35; emphasis
added). For instance, it is often reported that an organization under the
threat of takeover by a corporate raider will have less social disputes
within the organization. Finally, struggle paradoxically promotes social
interaction with the group one struggles with. For instance, if one
department of an organization is in fierce competition with another,
then they are more likely to copy and mimic each other than if they are
completely alien to one another. The central insight we can take from
Simmel is that struggle not only constructs how an actor understands
him-/herself but also deepens social relations between actors. For
Simmel, the very bonds of sociality, and perhaps even our confidence
as social actors, are produced through, by and within struggle.

A common image of struggle is that it is a destructive process that
actors pursue for individual gain, often resulting in mutual destruction.
Indeed, this image of struggle appears throughout Simmel's book on the
subject. However, a tradition of late nineteenth- and early twentieth-
century thought reminds us that struggle, as well as being destructive, is
also a vital force of creativity and development. Probably the foundational insight here can be located in Karl Marx's theory of social class.
According to Marx and Engels, society is driven forward by
the struggle between social classes. They famously declare in the
Communist Manifesto:

The history of all hitherto existing society is the history of class struggles.
Freeman and slave, patrician and plebeian, lord and serf, guild-master and
journeyman, in a word, oppressor and oppressed, stood in constant opposition to one another, carried on an uninterrupted, now hidden, now open
fight, a fight that each time ended, either in a revolutionary reconstitution of
society at large, or in the common ruin of the contending classes. (Marx and
Engels, 1848: 2)

This creative dynamism is a theme that has been developed in countless studies of class struggle. Perhaps most notable for our purposes is E. P. Thompson's (1967) historical study, which maps how various trades were able to constitute themselves as a single identifiable class through the development of a working-class identity and 'class consciousness' during the eighteenth century. What is so interesting about this study is that it demonstrates the creative pressure of social struggle. Thompson shows how, through their struggle with the appearance of early capitalist industries, the working classes were able to create an identity, a way of life and a whole series of institutions, such as clubs, trade unions, political parties and religious movements.

At the heart of the creative dynamics of struggle is *communication*. Indeed, it is the mutual communication of at least two actors that creates new possibilities and potentialities. We find this point made in the philosophy of Karl Jaspers (1932/1970). For Jaspers, our being is always in relation to other people. Our sense of who we are comes into existence only when we confront other people *and* open ourselves to these people through engaging in meaningful communication with them. The fact that we communicate with them opens up the possibility and necessity of difference. That is, the other people will and should call our claims, ideas and even identity consistently into question. Perhaps struggle is central to our very being because 'I cannot be without bringing [struggle] upon myself. There is no way in which I might hold back, since by merely existing I take part in [struggles] constitution' (Jaspers, 1932/1970: 204). Jaspers argues that we engage in three kinds of successive struggles, each of which builds upon the others. First, we struggle for our bodily existence, whereby we attempt to secure our own biological life through expanding our 'living space'. Second, we engage in a struggle for the *agon* of minds, which involves the process of debate, discussion and questioning ideas. This struggle for Jaspers is the 'font of creativity'. The third is what Jaspers calls 'the loving struggle', which involves the continuous process of two people putting 'each other totally in doubt, so as to get at the roots by way of truth resulting from inexorable mutual illumination' (205). The important point for us at this stage is that at the heart of struggle is the process of increasingly frank communication between two individuals.

The relationship between communication and struggle is further developed by Jaspers' erstwhile student and life-long friend, Hannah

Arendt (1958, 1970). As we explored in chapter 1, Arendt suggests that power comes from our ability to act in concert. For her, '[p]ower is never the property of the individual; it belongs to a group and remains in existence only so long as the group keeps together. When we say of somebody that he [sic] is "in power" we actually refer to his being empowered by a certain number of people to act in their name. The moment the group, from which the power originated to begin with (*potestas in populo*, without a people or group there is no power), disappears, "his power" also vanishes' (Arendt, 1970: 137). While Arendt is clearly using the concept of power here rather than struggle, she puts the idea of struggle right at the centre of what power means. For her, power is only the outcome of a group coming together and communicating. Power is the result of a communicative struggle. In *The Human Condition* (1958), politics is action taken to reorganize the relations between people through speech, and, perhaps more precisely, debate. In her study of totalitarianism, Arendt suggests that, when the spaces for actors to engage in communicative struggle are closed down, power begins to drain away and is replaced with hollow brute force. Her investigation of revolution demonstrates how revolt springs up when actors withdraw their communicative struggles from existing institutions. Like Jaspers, Arendt argues that struggle is first and fore-most about communication.

The function of this communicative struggle is a theme picked up by Pierre Bourdieu in a remarkable and dense essay (1983) that showcases some components of his vibrant social theory. Bourdieu argues that what he calls 'symbolic struggles' involves the attempt to change and order our perceptions of the social world. This entails a process of what Bourdieu (drawing on Nelson Goodman [1978]) calls 'world-making'. This occurs when we apply particular schemes of classifica-tion onto the world that distinguish one group from another. This happens through 'objective' and collective representations, such as the official naming of a group, the granting of titles or even official displays of strength and size (for instance, through a protest). It may also occur through more 'subjective' or individualized processes, when actors make creative and ingenious use of classification schemes through insults, innuendo, slander and gossip (Bourdieu, 1983). At the heart of any struggle is not just communication but a communication that classifies people and things into particular social categories and provides an evaluation of these categories. His empirical masterpiece

Distinctions (1984) demonstrates how this process operates in class relations. The book identifies the categories of tastes used by actors to position themselves in broad class structures. For instance, light and dainty food is often used by the upper classes to distinguish their 'fine tastes', whereas hearty, heavier food is used by peasants and the working classes to distinguish their 'earthliness'. Therefore, in the words of the earlier article, 'the struggle over classification is a fundamental dimension of class struggle. The power to impose and inculcate a vision of divisions, that is, the power to make visible and explicit social divisions that are implicit, is political power par excellence. It is the power to make groups, to manipulate the objective structure of society' (1983: 23).

The preceding analysis has identified six definitive features of struggle. First, struggle lies at the heart of *political change*. This directly contrasts with the common assumption that struggle represents stalemate and deadlock. Second, struggle constitutes the *self-consciousness* of the actors involved. This contrasts with the common assumption that actors arrive to the struggle with pre-defined ideas about what they want and who they are. Third, struggle produces the *sociality* of actors, in terms of their ability to relate with themselves (what we might describe as self-esteem), their ability to relate with their own groups and their ability to socialize between groups. This contrasts with the common assumption that struggle leads to the breakdown of sociality. Fourth, struggle is *creative*, in that it produces new identities, institutions and social arrangements. This contrasts with the assumption that struggle is a destructive and inimical force. Fifth, struggle occurs through *communicative* action. This contrasts with the assumption that struggle represents the breakdown of communication. Finally, communicative struggle involves a process of *categorization*. This contrasts with the idea that struggle results in the distortion and/or contradiction of social categories.

Rethinking power and resistance as struggle

Now that we have systematically unpacked the concept of struggle we can return to the issue of power and resistance. We want to suggest that the dynamic that we have identified above between power and resistance can be understood as a single process we call 'struggle'. To put this another way, power and resistance are both manifestations of a more basic and fundamental process of struggle. As we have seen in Arendt's political thought, power is the result of processes of communicative struggles. When these struggles disappear so too does power, and simple tyranny prevails. Similarly, resistance is also a manifestation of deeper processes of struggle. It also springs forth from the collective, communicative struggle that Arendt depicts. Less grandiose forms of 'micro-resistance' also rely on the same kind of collective communicative interaction and classification. Indeed, James Scott's (1985) study of the various forms of 'infrapolitics' (or underground resistance) amongst repressed groups shows that these modes of resistance always flow from collective communication and tactic building on the part of subordinates.

In the context of organizations, we treat struggle as a multidimensional dynamic that animates the *interface* between power and resistance. This is a process of ongoing, multiple and unpredictable calls (power) and responses (resistance) in which power and resistance are often indistinguishable. The interface is one of mutual constitution in which power is never without resistance and vice versa. As a social engagement, struggle entails political change, communication and categorization, constitutive self-consciousness and creativity. We can identify struggle in the various forms of power and resistance relationships discussed in chapters 1 and 2. In these chapters we identified four couplets of power and resistance: coercive power and resistance as refusal, manipulative power and resistance as voice, dominative power and resistance as escape, subjectivity power and resistance as creation. Instead of seeing each couplet of power and resistance as opposing forces, they can be approached as fundamentally interconnected forms of struggle. Let us work through these couplets and identify the type of struggle animating each.

Coercion and refusal

The couplet of coercion and refusal is underpinned by a fundamental struggle around *action*. The focus of this struggle is the 'doing' of the imperative that A communicates to B. It corresponds with Robert Dahl's (1957) investigation of observable actions and decisions regarding 'what is to be done'. An analysis of this kind of struggle would look into the interplay of force and blockage evoked when one is directed to do something that one would otherwise not have done. A simple example of this kind of struggle in the workplace is the fight over carrying out a task in a certain manner (see chapter 8). The activity might either not be undertaken or be done in a different manner from that which was intended by A. Each intervention communicates a political statement and engenders a certain creative tension that constitutes identities and social rituals.

Manipulation and voice

The couplet concerning manipulation and voice is underpinned by the more fundamental struggle around *inactivity*. This is because the focus of this struggle is on what is not to be done, and may involve the imposition of voice as an intervention that disrupts the systematic silencing of issues. This corresponds with Bachrach and Baratz's (1962) emphasis on issues that are rendered non-decisions. An investigation of the struggles around inactivity (as it is played out through manipulation and voice) highlights how certain actions are made impossible and how this 'impossibility' may be reconstituted as an option if voicing politics is successful (see chapter 7). A simple example of this mode of struggle is represented by the various attempts to ensure that employees do not deviate from a standard related to total quality management protocols and the ways employees may speak up about such manipulation in union–management meetings.

Domination and escape

The couplet of domination and escape is underpinned by a fundamental struggle around *interests*. This struggle revolves around the goals of action. This corresponds with Lukes' (1974/2005) focus on the distortion of interests. An analysis of struggle over interests identifies the ways in which groups try and change the goals we aim to achieve when we act (or do not act). In this struggle, parties are constituted as political subjects, just as the self-consciousness of management and workers is created when conflict arises over change initiatives. A simple example of this struggle in the contemporary workplace concerns the promotion of goals such as 'being loyal to the company and customer' through culture management and the escape attempts employees use to avoid subjective identification (see chapter 4).

Subjectification and creation

The couplet of subjectification and creation is underlined by a more fundamental struggle around *identity*. The focus of this struggle is on who controls the means of identity construction in the confines of the workplace (and beyond, as we shall see in chapter 6). This corresponds with Foucault's (1979) investigation of the construction of subjectivity and the types of identity politics that ensue in relation to power. An analysis of struggle around identity examines how managerial discourses of enterprise and empowerment attempt to constitute our selfhood in order to make us more amenable to the post-industrial organization (see chapter 5). An investigation of this sort establishes the contested nature of identity management, and how the process of struggle allows alternative counter-selves to emerge.

We treat all these modes of struggle as flexible conceptual constructs that are not meant to be mutually exclusive. They describe a more complex set of relationships that animate the dynamic between power and resistance. Studies often find various mixtures and connections between these modes, or a situation in which one form of struggle is dominant. For instance, so-called knowledge work may be heavily characterized by struggles around identity (Sveningsson and Alvesson, 2003). In contrast, certain types of repetitive manufacturing work may be more characterized by the struggle around action and non-action (Braverman, 1974), or perhaps even interests (Burawoy, 1979). We describe in the forthcoming chapters how these (and other struggles) may be 'stacked' on top of each other in contradictory and unpredictable ways. There may be cases where one mode of struggle will take centre stage, while other potential struggles remain a latent influence. Moreover, a struggle around one dimension, such as economic interests, may influence other dimensions, such as identity, in unintended and sometimes self-defeating ways. In chapter 5 we show how struggles with sexual identity and economic interests can confound each. The 'progressive' politics of workers striving to address economic inequality involved a rather 'regressive' identity politics of homophobia. There may be attempts to form strategic links between struggles; this is evident in situations where one group has an advantageous position because they are able to connect a number of struggles in a mutually supporting fashion (see chapter 8). For instance, the labour movement at the height of its powers was able to link together struggles around what is done (such as the allocation of jobs in a factory), what is not to be done (shifting the boundaries of what was thinkable in the work relationship), interests (by aligning workers' interests with those of the union) and identities (by constructing a common workers' identity). Actors may also attempt to shift the ground of struggle to gain strategic advantages. For example, a development manager may find that his/her struggle to get employees to identify with the company is failing, so he/she shifts the basis of struggle away from identity towards interests and goals (Fleming, 2005a).

Dynamic cycles of struggle

The most significant aspect of struggle is the fact that it is an ongoing, live, tense and overwhelmingly dynamic social process. Thus it is not sufficient simply to identify what struggle is, what modes of struggle exist and how these modes of struggle relate to one another. To have a proper understanding of workplace struggle it is vital to consider how it unfolds, and what the temporal dynamics of engaging in struggle are. Clearly, any empirical analysis of struggle will reveal a panoply of different tactics. Such tactics might involve attempts, within a given strategically configured relation of struggle, to gain a temporary advantage (de Certeau, 1984). For instance, in the struggle over an action, a group may use a whole range of tactics, from judiciously following the rules of the workplace to temporarily blocking or slowing down the organizational process through which an action will occur. We should note that such tactics are not used solely by dominated or less powerful groups. Rather, tactics are the stuff of all political struggles, and used by both the powerful and the powerless. Indeed, those who are particularly good at engaging in political struggle are also particularly good tacticians.

While this tactical aspect of struggle is vital, what is perhaps even more important for our purposes is the kind of cycle of interaction evident during a struggle. Because any struggle is a two-way process that involves a dynamic of give and take, particular cycles arise. These cycles occur through a process of mutual reinforcement, whereby an initial action on the part of one actor will provoke a certain response on the part of another, which will then be responded to in a particular way, and so on. This is particularly clear in the case of labour disputes where the action (say, management changing working conditions) is responded to by the union (through a threatened strike), which is responded to by management (through the hardening of their position), which then provokes a reaction from the union (calling its members out on strike). In what follows we seek to identify some possible dynamics of struggle.

Destructive struggle

Perhaps the most obvious dynamic of struggle is the destructive one. This involves a situation in which the actors involved in the struggle seek to destroy their opponents through absolute victory. The struggle becomes a kind of zero-sum process whereby one person's gain is another's loss. This is what Karl Jaspers calls struggle by force. It is 'coercive, limiting, oppressive, and conversely space-making: in this struggle I may succumb and lose my existence' (Jaspers, 1932/1970: 206). For Jasper, there are two possible reactions when we are locked in this kind of struggle. The first is simply disgust and absolute rejection of the struggle and all the various gains it brings us. This involves 'non-resistance' and giving up on politics. This would mean we would be swayed by the smallest and most base demands that others make upon us. The result, according to Jaspers, is self-destruction, because we are giving up on the struggle that actually calls us into being, in both an existential sense and a more basic material sense. The second option that Jaspers identifies in the destructive struggle is an utter 'will to power'. This involves the enthusiastic grasping of the instruments of power and engaging in a ceaseless fight for the eventual victory over all. This absolute struggle 'would end with a lone destroyer or conqueror of all the rest. He [sic] would not know what to do with his limitless conquests: he has a task only while he has something to crush. The tendency to rule or ruin everything, to remove all limitations on one's own power, consistently ends in despair at having no one to fight anymore' (Jaspers, 1932/1970: 209). The result of a destructive struggle is, therefore, either utter victory or annihilation. While such a cycle of struggle is most vividly portrayed in the case of war, it occurs frequently within organizations. For instance, particularly bitter battles between unions and management are sometimes based on attempts by one group to destroy the other (such as in de-unionization drives). Similarly, a struggle between two senior managers for the position of chief executive officer may frequently lead to the utter defeat of one candidate. Perhaps the most extreme example of this battle can be found in Gibson Burrell's (1997) argument that organizations function on the principle of basic destruction and always terminate in death.

Resentful struggle

The second cycle of struggle is the dynamic of resentment. In contrast to destructive struggle, those involved in this dynamic do not give up on the possibility of resistance or aim to annihilate their foe utterly. Rather, they seek to show their unhappiness at being dominated, to express their dissatisfaction and drag their feet. In short, they want to show their resentment. Nowhere is this better illustrated than in Scott's (1990) study of forms of underground resistance amongst peasant workers. The forms of resistance that Scott documents in this study rarely pose a large-scale challenge to the system of domination. They are merely attempts to make the conditions of domination more tolerable and give the oppressed a sense of control and perhaps to open small spaces of freedom. However, this ultimately locks these self-same resistors into a kind of sick dependence upon the dominant group. By only going so far, subordinates are able to express themselves only in relation to a system of domination. When trapped in this cycle of resentment, they are patently unable to effect fundamental change to the kinds of politics they are involved in (Brown, 1995). This means that they become fastened to what Friedrich Nietzsche calls the 'slave mentality' – that is, the wish, and even desire, to be dominated by someone. Through being dominated, subordinates are afforded the illicit joys and pleasure of being resentful, the ability to 'bitch and moan' about the sorry state of affairs, while at the same time not actually seeking to change anything. Indeed, why should they? By giving up their resentment, they would abandon the (albeit limited) sense of dignity and agency given to them by the fact they can 'see through the lies' (Sloterdijk, 1987). Furthermore, they would give up their own sense of identity as belonging to 'the oppressed'. This would bring forth an uncertain world, in which they would have to take responsibility for their own struggle and their perpetuation of it. They would be required to make a decision to be absolutely passive (and accept any form of domination) or adopt the attitude of being absolutely against – whereby they would seek to fight ceaselessly and destroy their enemies.

Loving struggle

Are passivity, destruction and resentment the only dynamics associated
with struggle? No, according to Jaspers. He identifies another form,
which he calls 'the loving struggle'. For him (1932/1970: 206),
'[a] loving struggle is non-violent, jeopardizing without a will to win,
solely with a will to manifestation'. At the centre of the loving struggle
is the recognition that the opponent has the right to exist. The loving
struggle involves the attempt to affirm, extend and glorify each
actor's existence through the mutual and consistent process of calling
his/her partner into question. It is through this process of questioning (and being called into question) that we come to know ourselves
and know our partner in struggle. This mutual calling into question
'extends' each actor and the struggle more generally. In this struggle,
'there is no victory or defeat for one side; both win or lose jointly...the
fight is possible only as one simultaneously struggle against both the
other and myself' (Jaspers, 1932/1970: 213). Indeed, this process
involves struggling *with* someone rather than *against* someone. The
example Jaspers intuitively relies on is long-term intellectual friendship, or perhaps even a 'good marriage', in which each partner consistently calls the other into question in an affirmative and expansive
fashion, in a way that is neither destructive nor resentful. Indeed,
examples of this affirmative struggle are replete in organizations too.
For instance, the members of a research and development team may
struggle with each other and their materials during the development
process. In amidst this struggle their own ideas about each other and
themselves are constantly called into question. Similarly, a union and
management may struggle with each other to develop a just and productive employment relationship. The point in each example is that
these relationships are not based on absolute agreement. And the
nature of struggle is not resignation, destruction or resentment but a
process of mutual affirmation in which relations are created and
moulded.

Conclusion

This chapter has aimed to develop a more complex and dynamic
approach to the power/resistance couplet by proposing the notion of
struggle as a supplementary concept. It has not been our intention to

dismiss the current terms of 'power' and 'resistance', for we will continue to use them throughout this book. We do suggest, however, that the notion of struggle points to a different level of complexity, in which a dynamic interplay between cross-cutting forces comes to the fore in the analysis of workplace politics. As such, some forms of resistance might best be termed 'power' and, similarly, some types of power might best be called 'resistance'. We have identified how struggle involves a dynamic process or interplay between superordinates and subordinates that actually defines the parties involved. Moreover, struggle may be for, against or with an opponent – a distinction that gives each struggle a definitive flavour.

In the chapters that follow we provide a number of illustrative examples of struggle at work in organizations. These examples range from the subterranean micro-politics of employee cynicism and humour to the more wide-ranging actions of a new social movement protesting about the commercialization of a public broadcaster. Each chapter will empirically elaborate on the notion of struggle, but also provide additional theoretical background, especially in relation to *justice* – a key concept that we feel is important for understanding everyday expressions of struggle in workplaces today. Finally, what we find striking about Jaspers' notion of struggle is that it is not something we can escape from. Rather, struggle is at the very heart of being human, and is therefore an unceasing aspect of political life. As we will maintain in the concluding chapter, we are undecided on this point. Is struggle something that will always be with us, or should we take a 'utopian risk' and imagine a time when struggle in organizations is no longer required?

PART 2

Forms of resentful struggle

4 | *Dis-identification and resentment: the case of cynicism*

> It can be an unpleasant job, especially when
> you are working for a bank – it happens
> every day on the phone... [*In an angry tone*]
> '*You* have done this, *you* have done that, this
> is *your* fault.' It's like, '*I* haven't done any-
> thing, you motherfucker, go fuck yourself.'
> But you can't say that – you have to always
> be pleasant and say 'Oh, is that right? I can
> appreciate that, that should not have hap-
> pened.' And they're swearing at me and then
> you would rather not be there...
> Management have the rhetoric of 'this is
> what we are doing, we are different'. But
> when you get there and start working you
> find that it is just the same, and this is where
> those corporate strategies fall down because
> they aren't going to convince someone like
> me that this shitty job is 'fun'.
>
> (*Employee interviewed in a 'high-
> commitment' call centre*, Fleming, 2003)

Resentment forms a major dimension of organizational life and is a
particularly interesting way in which subordinates experience relations
of domination and power. This is especially so in contexts where, to
paraphrase de Certeau (1984), people find themselves in power relations that they cannot leave or change. Today it is fashionable, however, to denounce resentment as a perverted, or at least unhelpful,
engagement with power (Brown, 1995). Since Nietzsche's plea for a
praxis of ethical affirmation and the positive transvaluation of the
present, resentment has been derided as an aspect of modernity that
reconciles us even more profoundly to our own domination. As we
noted in chapter 2, resentment at work in the form of ironic humour

and cynicism is often construed as a form of escapism. The passivity of cynical resentment is thought to undermine radicalism rather than further its cause in any efficacious manner. In the next three chapters we aim to examine resentful resistance in more detail and explore it in relation to notions of struggle developed in the last chapter. We suggested that struggle does not necessarily attend to a 'face' of power but is more the formation of an interface between constituted and constitutive power, in the Hardt and Negri (2004) sense. That is to say, political struggle amplifies and accentuates the points at which power becomes its opposite. It was argued that the very term 'resistance' tends to picture the power/ resistance couplet in a very linear and causal way (first there is power, then resistance comes to meet it). While some have reversed this formula (resistance comes first and power then thwarts it), the term 'struggle' is more dynamic and processual in its understanding of how resistance unfolds in the politically contested terrain of the modern workplace.

It is not our intention to redeem unconditionally the resentful elements of resistance. Its problems were outlined in the previous chapter. But neither do we have much truck with the gushing postmodern adoration of 'self-affirmation' as the ethical foundation of struggle. What we do aim to do is to deal with resentment in a circumspect manner. Given the trials and tribulations of a shallow and unfair world of work, resentment, we maintain, is an understandable stance. Although innumerable studies have demonstrated how workers are subjectively co-opted by culture controls, managerial discourse and other ideological regimes, an important stream of research recognizes the ways in which employees dis-identify with management, and in particular are resentfully cynical. Attempts during the late 1980s and 1990s to move away from bureaucratic structures and Taylorist work processes, and instil loyalty, commitment, dedication and fun in organizations, often engendered a credibility gap between reality and heightened expectations. Given the New Right's attack on employment conditions and the right of association that occurred in the 1980s and 1990s, employees found ways to resist without being dismissed or disenfranchised. Ethnographic studies of contemporary work have identified the importance of cynicism. In the work of Gideon Kunda (1992), David Collinson (1992), Catherine Casey (1995) and Paul du Gay (1996), for example, we meet workers who voice statements of disbelief about the official culture, humorously send up attempts to craft 'cultures of WOW' (Peters, 1992) and are rather jaundice-eyed about managerial promises for a more humane environment. Like the employee quoted in the opening excerpt of this chapter, they can 'see through' the hollow promises of human resource departments and do not really 'buy into' the hype of the loyalty pundits. Kunda (1992) finds employees calling the culture 'California bathtub crap'. Collinson (1992) records workers referring to the push to build a culture of excellence as 'Yankee propaganda' and the company newsletter became known as the 'Goebbels Gazette'. Casey (1995) observes workers discerning the gaping contradiction between the 'caring' values of the company philosophy and the ruthless reality of working life in a transnational corporation. Research investigating service organizations shows how employees sometimes 'surface act' the 'culture of the customer' rather than internalize it as their own because they are savvy about its instrumental nature as a form of managerial control (Hochschild, 1983; Sturdy, 1998). In the midst of the frenetic attempts to colonize the subjectivity of workers through corporate culture, self-management teams and enterprise discourse we find not only systems of identification with the company philosophy but also resentful distancing, incredulity and cynical disbelief.

In order to interpret the significance of cynicism, this chapter returns to the third dimension of struggle explored in chapter 2. The reason we revisit the 'resistance as escape' category is because dis-identification has become a major theme in recent research exploring struggle in organizations. Whereas trade unionism, wildcat strikes and class warfare set the tone of struggle during the heyday of industrial capitalism (and still plays a role, as later chapters demonstrate), the political terrain of work has significantly shifted over the last decade or so. Organizations have discovered a 'soul' and have made widespread attempts to empower workers through loyalty campaigns and self-management work systems (Boltanski and Chiapello, 2005). In many ways, these managerial initiatives resonate with a long-standing attempt to 'humanize' work (Barley and Kunda, 1992; Ross, 2004). And employee cynicism is certainly nothing new. But the broad acceptance of the US-orientated commitment-based HRM model means that dis-identification and resentment (such as cynicism, irony and humour) ought to be evaluated in the context in which the very selves of employees are the target of control. In the 'no-collar' (Ross, 2004) world of work, identity and lifestyle are as much fought over as the wage–effort bargain. As we saw in chapters 2 and 3, cynicism has largely been discredited as a form of struggle. For some, it operates as a 'safety valve' or 'ideology' that gives workers a false sense of autonomy and thus encourages them to perpetuate their own exploitation. We want to explore this interpretation of cynical resistance in more detail, and suggest that it has major implications for how we understand power, subjectivity and struggle in organizations. It will be argued that, when we view cynicism as ideological self-deception, we are forced to rethink well-established notions of self and power. In the later part of this chapter we attempt to resurrect the lost radicalism of the cynic, especially that of the original cynic, Diogenes of Sinope. Resentful irony and parody are the weapons of choice for the organizational Diogenes, allowing him or her to master the symbolic underpinnings of domination and reveal the absurdity of the contemporary workplace.

The ideology of cynical escape

There are often times when we intuitively feel that critical negativity towards domination is an inherently disruptive force, which agitates rather than conserves particular relations of power. However, an interesting tradition of research in the sociology of work has identified the ways in which resistance and opposition (usually in connection with working-class counter-culture) can sometimes become an integrative mechanism that reinforces the structures of domination that were the object of resistance in the first place. In North America we can trace this line of analysis back to Paul Piccone's (1976, 1978) oft-cited concept of 'artificial negativity'. Although the term 'artificial' evokes an epistemological minefield, the general idea is that modernity systemically relies upon a degree of internal criticism in order to avert stagnation (also see Boltanski and Chiapello, 2005). Middle-class radicalism, for example, is often absorbed by the state and corporate apparatuses so that an element of vitality is maintained without seriously threatening the foundations of these institutions. In the United Kingdom, Paul Willis' *Learning to Labour* (1977) explores a similar theme by showing how the astute criticisms of capitalism expressed by working-class 'lads' (what he calls 'partial penetrations') created a set of low expectations that were ultimately self-fulfilling, and thus slotted them into an oppressive, class-based social structure.

Willis' findings were confirmed to a large extent by Michael Burawoy's study of shopfloor workers at 'Allied' in *Manufacturing*

Consent (1979). Burawoy depicts the informal 'making out' games workers used to resist the piecework bonus system orchestrated by management. Workers were suspicious and critical towards management and vented their grievances through output restrictions and shirking (goldbricking) – in much the same way that Donald Roy (1952, 1958) had recorded in the same factory some years before. But Burawoy's startling finding was that, because workers gained a sense of freedom and relief from the intolerable boredom by participating in the games, they consented to being exploited by Allied's managerial elite. Their games of subversion actually adjusted them to their lack of privilege at work and thus functioned in an ideological manner. Burawoy draws the conclusion that some forms of resistance have the unintended consequence of maintaining domination because they are articulated in such a way that they undermine more meaningful and effective strategies of opposition.

As we intimated in chapter 2, the idea that some forms of transgression can be a preserving force has informed a number of influential interpretations of employee cynicism. Rather than reading the deep-seated cynicism of employees as a successful strategy of resistance, they point out how it may diminish the efficacy of more transformative workplace politics. Cynicism may accommodate workers to their subordinate position because they are given a specious sense of freedom ('I am not a dupe', 'I am separate from power) that allows them to cope with circumstances perceived to be out of their control. When we dis-identify with our prescribed social roles we often *still perform them* – sometimes better, ironically, than if we did identify with them. From this perspective, cynicism is thought to represent the inadvertent success of corporate power relations rather than their failure. After Slavoj Žižek (1989), cynicism operates as an unplanned *ideological* phenomenon that unobtrusively reproduces relations of power, because cynical employees are given (and give themselves) the impression that they are autonomous agents, but they still practise the corporate rituals nevertheless. The term is not conceived in any vulgar sense, whereby an all-knowing puppet master intentionally dupes the unthinking masses, but in a more post-structuralist vein that points to the way everyday discourses, symbols and signs frame our subjectivity in ways favourable to dominant power relations (Eagleton, 1991). According to Žižek, ideological indoctrination controls not only our ideas but also *what we do* – indeed, the two provinces of human life cannot easily be separated. In an effort to dissolve the perennial mind/body dualism he maintains that 'reality' itself is ideologically structured, imbued with phantasmagorial illusions, and this is what subjects do not see in their everyday lives:

> The illusion is not on the side of knowledge, it is already on the side of reality itself, of what the people are doing. What they do not know is that their social reality itself, their activity, is guided by an illusion... [w]hat they overlook, what they misrecognise is not the reality but the illusion which is structuring their reality, their real social activity. (Žižek, 1989: 32)

Cynicism becomes an ideological force, ironically, because we are under the illusion that we are not victims of ideological obfuscation. Expressions such as 'I'm not a sucker, I have not bought into this phoney rubbish' pervade contemporary social relations of work and seem to sit comfortably alongside obedient practices of arduous labour. But what we often do not realize is that cultural control is not just in our heads but in reality itself, and this is how cynicism can lead to what Žižek paradoxically calls an 'enlightened false consciousness' (also see Sloterdijk, 1987). In being cynical we are enlightened about the ways of the world yet can still enact even the most boorish discourses because we fail to understand that the fantasy is ingrained in our modes of conduct. Such a consciousness is nowhere better explained than by Terry Eagleton in relation to racist ideology: 'Ideology is not just a matter of what I think about a situation; it is somehow inscribed in that situation itself. It is no good my reminding myself that I am opposed to racism as I sit down on a park bench marked "Whites Only"; by the act of sitting on it, I have supported and perpetuated racist ideology. The ideology, so to speak, is in the bench, not in my head' (Eagleton, 1991: 40).

If we go back to our cynical workers in Gideon Kunda's *Engineering Culture* (1992) we can see this process at work. Despite the humour, the mocking of pompous official rituals and the sneering cynicism, the employees performed their roles flawlessly and were highly productive. The ideology of cynicism ensured that Tech operated akin to a well-oiled machine because the corporate culture did not necessarily need to colonize their 'minds' (a concept not easily separated from our behaviour, as we will see below shortly), only their discursive practices. The employees were cynically enlightened about the realities of corporate exploitation, but *they acted as if they were not*. In fact, cynicism in a context such as this may often lead us to feel that we are not fully reducible to the company line but are 'unique individuals': 'I may look like an IBM man, but under this blue suit and corporate lunches is a true, giving human being.' Such ideational distancing gives workers an important sense of 'self-outside-power', allowing the corporate machine to get on with its job and commandeer the 'reality' of the organization's productive system.

As we argued in chapter 2, some interpretations of cynicism in the workplace can also be viewed from this perspective. In his influential article on cultural controls, for example, Hugh Willmott (1993) argues that, although corporate culture does capture the souls of most employees, some inevitably distance themselves from the discourse of commitment. The very capacity to challenge the company culture cynically provokes a counterfeit sense of self-determination that allows the corporate roles to be enacted without the friction that is usually present when people feel they are being hard done by. We argue that this interpretation of employee cynicism implicitly opens up some interesting problems with key concepts in organization studies: those of power, subjectivity and resistance. In explaining cynicism as a possible ideological phenomenon we find that cultural power may work through dis-identification (rather than simply through identification) and subjectivity may be radically 'external' (rather than something 'internal' to us). In the remainder of this chapter we theorize the implications that this interpretation of cynicism has for the concepts of power and subjectivity, then in the final part we turn to the task of resurrecting the spirit of Diogenes in light of the preceding analysis.

Turning the 'resistant subject' on its head

Two of the most striking implications of the ideology of cynicism thesis concern the way we conceptualize subjectivity and power in critical organizational studies. Indeed, we aim to show that common understandings of cultural power and the effects it has on subjectivity in the workplace often rest upon simplistic assumptions and are in need of clarification. Given the popularity of interpreting cynicism as a reproductive mechanism we now build upon that approach to demonstrate how power can work through dis-identification (rather than simply through identification) and subjectivity may be radically 'external' (rather than something 'inside' us). First we discuss each implication in turn.

Power: *from identification to dis-identification*

Narrating cultural power as a process that operates through *identification* is still to a large extent the accepted orthodoxy within organization studies. Interestingly, this assumption is probably spelt out most clearly in the managerialist literature. Working within the parameters of social and behavioural psychology, much of the prescriptive literature maintains that cultural control elicits from workers a positive attachment to the company and its products. When organization members internalize the values and beliefs crafted by management they come to make sense of their self-esteem, confidence and well-being in those terms. Herbert Simon argues in *Administrative Behaviour*, for example, that managerial 'values gradually become "internalized" and are incorporated into the psychology and attitudes of the individual participant. He [sic] acquires an attachment or loyalty to the organization that automatically – i.e. without the necessity for external stimuli – guarantees that his decisions will be consistent with the organization objectives' (Simon, 1945/1961: 198). That is to say, when the goals of the organization (management) and workers are aligned, a positive identification process will ensue whereby subordinates invest their sense of self and personality in the motives and desires of superiors. More recently, this concern with the 'inculcation of motives' (Barnard, 1938) can be found in the rhetoric espoused by corporate culture gurus such as Tom Peters and Robert Waterman (1982), Peter Senge (1990) and Eagar Schein (1997).

The assumption that cultural power works via identification is often shared by much critical research as well. One of the major indictments of corporate culture programmes by critical scholars is that the loyalties and commitments of workers are manipulated in such a way that they lose any desire to resist capitalism. What has been dubbed the 'last frontier of control' (Ray, 1986) penetrates the very desires of workers so that they cannot help but devote and dedicate themselves to the edicts of domination. Carol Ray offers one of the first critical excursions into this more sinister side of corporate culture management. She claims that culture programmes have the result that 'individuals possess direct ties to the values and goals of the dominant elites in order to activate the emotion and sentiment which might lead to devotion, loyalty and commitment to the company' (Ray, 1986: 294). Similarly, Stanley Deetz argues that new management control systems targeting the very selves of workers attempt, and often succeed, in persuading workers to 'want on his or her own what the corporation wants' (Deetz, 1992a: 42). This explicit identification apparently links workers' sense of dignity with accomplishing the goals of the organization, and as a result they say 'yes!' to prevailing regimes of power. Stephen Barley and Gideon Kunda also make the point that, under the ideological control of corporate culture, workers 'make no distinction between their own welfare and the welfare of the firm' (Barley and Kunda, 1992: 382). And, finally, Catherine Casey (1995, 1996, 1999), in her analysis of the corporate fabrication of 'designer selves', has made repeated assertions about the identification mechanisms of team and cultural normalization. She remarks:

Hephaestus Corporation designed its 'new culture program' with the principle objectives to gain employee involvement, to improve production and increase customer satisfaction. . . To achieve this a 'new Haphaestus employee' was required, one who would believe that his or her self-development, source of fulfillment and identity are to be found working for Hephaestus. (Casey, 1999: 160)

The interpretation of cynicism as ideology, however, unsettles the simplicity of the identification thesis. The cynical worker seems to be free from the clutches of cultural incorporation, but this semblance of freedom is the very stuff of insidiously integrative discourses – especially against the background that real domination still evidently prevails. To take an example: instead of a McDonald's worker identifying with the values enshrined in the training programmes (quality, teamwork, cleanliness, efficiency, etc.), she may be extremely cynical towards the company and see through to more base managerial motives (perhaps wearing a 'McShit' T-shirt under her uniform in a clandestine fashion). Crucially, however, she performs as an efficient member of the team all the same. It appears that in cases where employees do not identify with the values and philosophy of the organization a regime of ideology still seems to be at work. This is because, even though our cynical McDonald's employee has transgressive tastes in clothing that dis-identify with her employer, she acts *as if* she believes in the prescribed values of the organization, and it is at this level that cultural power is operating in its most potent form. The importance of understanding how ideological consent can be harnessed through dis-identification rather than simply through identification is underlined by Žižek.

We are dealing here with what one is tempted to call the *ideological practice of dis-identification*. That is to say, one should turn around the standard notion of ideology as providing a firm identification to its subjects, constraining them to their 'social roles': what if, on a different – but no less irrevocable and structurally necessary – level, ideology is effective precisely by constructing a space of *false dis-identification*, of false distance towards the actual co-ordinates of those subjects' social existence. (Žižek, 2000:103)

To return once more to our cynical McDonald's worker, ideological power is present in the strategy of dis-identification because it creates a gap in which the subject feels relieved of the burden of committing to the social role as an active and participating employee. This relief allows the McDonald's worker to claim that, 'even though I slave all day serving high-fat, low-fibre food to children, I am nonetheless free – just look at the 'McShit' T-shirt I wear underneath my uniform!'. Realistically speaking, of course, our imaginary worker would probably not be against the organization absolutely, as there are many shades between the poles of identification and dis-identification (e.g. indifference, ambivalence, anxiety, etc.) and seldom do we maintain one subjective stance over time and contexts. It is simply not the case that some people *are* cynics while others *are* optimists. Subjectivity is without a centre, inconsistent, contradictory, and cannot be pinned down to one set of dispositions or characteristics. However, that does not detract from the argument that, when the dis-identification process is enacted, it can establish an alluring 'breathing space' in which people feel untrammelled by the subjective demands of the organization, but which – ironically – permits them to behave as efficient and meticulous members of the team nevertheless.

Research into the training protocols of customer service workers supports this general idea. Studies conducted by Blake Ashforth and Ronald Humphrey (1993), Robin Leidner (1993) and Andrew Sturdy, Irena Grugulis and Hugh Willmott (2001), for example, note that workers are actually advised not to identify with the routinized identity script too much lest they suffer from 'burnout'. To avert the injuries of conformity they are told by trainers to retain some autonomy, use their own discretion and maintain a degree of subjective distance in order for the script to work properly. These 'indulgency patterns' (Gouldner, 1955; Mars, 1982) have long been recognized by researchers as an important part of maintaining workplace relations of power. In turning a blind eye to minor infringements such as petty pilfering and 'fiddling', for example, more consequential disruptions are avoided. The *desirability* for some sort of dis-identification for corporate power to sustain its machinations is illustrated by Žižek's analysis of the film and subsequent television series *MASH*:

> Contrary to its misleading appearance, Robert Altman's *MASH* is a perfectly conformist film – for all their mockery of authority, practical jokes and sexual escapades, the members of the *MASH* crew *perform their jobs exemplarily*, and thus present no threat to the smooth running of the military machine. In other words, the cliché which regards *MASH* as an anti-militarist film, depicting the horrors and meaningless military slaughter which can only be endured by a healthy measure of cynicism, practical jokes, laughing at pompous official rituals, and so on, misses the point – this very distance *is* ideology. (Žižek, 1997: 20)

Thus, the cynical distance a subject feels towards his/her actions (the 'day job', if you will) often does not present an inherently seditious challenge to domination (as the identification thesis would lead us to believe); rather, it can uphold the continued functioning of this very system because of the sense of freedom it provides.

Subjectivity: from internalization to the objectivity of belief

Another prevalent theoretical approach to subjectivity and control we find in critical organization studies is that which examines how corporate identities are *internalized* by workers. The inside/outside spatial metaphor the term 'internalization' implies harks back to the equally pervasive subjective/objective distinction whereby people are seen to have an internal psychological realm that is somehow divided from external reality (cf. Burrell and Morgan, 1979). Moreover, in much critical research the mind/body dualism is also an important assumption underlying the discourse of internalization, because coercive control is seen to influence our *behaviour* while cultural control manipulates our *minds* (Mitchel, 1990). It seems to us that the term 'subjectivity' is often used erroneously as a synonym for more traditional concepts such as 'personality' or 'world-view', elements that are seen to reside 'within' rather than 'without'. At any rate, cultural indoctrination is construed as if power is poured into the private recesses of the subject, like liquid into a glass.

For example, take Ray's comments comparing bureaucratic and cultural control: 'While bureaucratic control may prompt individuals to act as if the company is their source of meaning and commitment that is an entirely different matter from seriously believing in it. In other words, control remains externalized rather than becoming internalized' (Ray, 1986: 293). Ray makes a clear distinction between the internal and external spheres of human practice in order to analyse the novelty of cultural control. Control in the past governed our visible practices, but with the advent of culture and ideological management we are infected with power to our very soul. Another example of this internalization thesis can be found in Kunda's analysis of culture engineering in the 'Tech' corporation. For Kunda, the strategies of control and power implemented by corporate culture (what he calls 'normative control') were fundamentally different from external controls because the former endeavoured to manage the inner psyche of Tech workers.

Under normative control, members act in the best interests of the company not because they are physically coerced, nor purely from an instrumental concern with economic rewards and sanctions. Rather they are driven by internal commitment, strong identification with company goals, intrinsic satisfaction from work. (Kunda, 1992: 11)

A common theme underlying these approaches and which continues to pervade critical organization studies is the idea that cultural power controls subjects by inducing them to absorb into their private and isolated interiority a set of ready-made beliefs. Although they disavow essentialism, a kind of essentialism continues to predominate insofar as a humanist concept (a private interiority) is maintained as if it was a natural predisposition of humankind. However, studies of the ideological aspects of cynicism draw upon a more (post-)structuralist tradition of thought that is suspicious of the notion of interiority and leads us to challenge the internalization thesis. It has been shown that in the case of cynicism some employees do not internalize the values and norms of the official culture. On the contrary, the cynics keep the norms and values of the organization at a distance and make an effort to ensure they are not internalized. However, the nub of the problem is the fact that they continue to act *as if* they believe in the culture of the organization. The question is why we think belief is seated inside us, because it becomes patently clear that, although we do not believe internally in the values of the culture, we may still *believe externally*. A radically social understanding of subjectivity tells us that belief is not necessarily inside us – a rather psychologistic proposition – but somehow outside us, or, as the Russian linguist Valentin Voloshinov (1973) more accurately puts it, in between us. Indeed, contra Ray (1986), we could make the claim that our (external) actions appear to believe for us. As Žižek explains:

> Contrary to the usual thesis that a belief is something interior and knowledge something exterior (in the sense that it can be verified through an external procedure)...it is belief that is radically exterior, embodied in the practical, effective procedures of people. It is similar to Tibetan prayer wheels: you write a prayer on a paper, put the rolled paper into the wheel, and turn it automatically without thinking... In this way, the wheel itself is praying for me, instead of me – or, more precisely, I myself am praying through the medium of the wheel. The beauty of it all is that in my psychological interiority I can think about whatever I want, I can yield to the most dirty and obscene fantasies, and it does not matter because whatever I am thinking, *objectively*, I am praying. (Žižek, 1989:34)

An external theory of belief does not discount the fact that we often do experience a sense of interiority, a phenomenological space that we feel to be our very own. Indeed, as the above quotation implies, the feeling of interiority plays a vital role in the power network of particular – especially rampant – individualist social configurations. The radical suggestion we find here is that belief in 'the party line', corporate culture, perhaps even late capitalism, does not necessarily have to exist in the realm of interiority. Instead, systems of identification can be externalized, placed onto a series of objects and actions, so that our subjectivity is freed up to fantasize and think about anything we may wish (perhaps bombing our workplace, perhaps a sexual liaison with a co-worker, perhaps what we need from the supermarket). In this sense it is our social practices that believe in our place (one is reminded of Homer Simpson, who points to the fact that he attends church every Sunday as making him a good Christian – even though we know he sleeps through the entire proceedings). A similar line of reasoning can be found in the structuralism of Louis Althusser (1971). In his celebrated essay on ideology he argues that our cultural investments in a system of power do not come from within us but are manifest in our institutionalized rituals and practices. These practices are not to be conceived as different from belief but as a more precise description of what the concept actually entails in a social setting. Althusser gives an example from Blaise Pascal, who advised that, if you do not believe in God, kneel down, begin moving your lips (act as if you are praying, even if you do not believe) and eventually you will believe. To be sure, it is in our habits, our everyday actions, that belief, subjectivity and hence power reside.

If belief can be posited as an uncannily objective phenomenon, we are then directed to a more profound and unsettling deduction: even our most intimate aspects of identity may not be experienced internally either, but are externalized and *experienced for us*. Žižek is fond of emphasizing just how radically exterior our most personally experienced sensations are. For instance, enjoyment and laughter are experienced for us by canned laughter on television sitcoms. When we slip over on a wet footpath, our companion exclaims 'Oops!' instead of us. In some cultures mourners are hired to do the wailing for the bereaved at the funeral of a loved one. Jon Elster (1983) provides yet another example when discussing the out-of-character 'mysticism' expressed by a renowned rationalist: 'Niels Bohr at one time is said to have had a horseshoe over his door. Upon being asked whether he really believed that it would bring him luck, he answered "no, but I am told that they bring luck even to those who do not believe in them"' (Elster, 1983: 5). Examples of this process abound in organizations. Public relations firms are hired by large petroleum companies to believe in the ethical propriety of their destructive oil explorations. Allegiance to corporate culture is enacted by simply letting the rituals experience commitment for us (a bumper sticker of the company on our car, the correct cap whilst playing golf, feigned enthusiasm whilst participating in team-building activities), while we can 'personally' enjoy that space of freedom inside us. But, if believing can be practised 'for us', then is there really any escape from cultural colonization?

Resurrecting Diogenes' cheeky snigger

In the preceding sections we have worked through the implications that the ideology approach to cynicism has for the concepts of power and subjectivity in organization studies. We now focus on what these implications mean for how we understand employee resistance. The reconceptualization of cultural power as a process that can operate through dis-identification and the notion that subjectivity is also external undoubtedly alter some of the more traditional ways of viewing employee resistance. But perhaps a pressing preliminary issue that such a rethinking raises is the question as to whether cynicism in the face of cultural colonization has only conservative and self-defeating effects, as suggested by a strong version of the ideology interpretation. Although this thesis does touch upon an important element of cynical resistance it could be claimed that it offers an overly pessimistic and functional portrayal of power and conflict. Maybe this is because cynicism in the contemporary era has always been frowned upon as negative, unhelpful and symptomatic of a smug capitulation. As Peter Sloterdijk (1987) points out, this kind of modern 'enlightened' cynicism is a far cry from what the ancient Greek and founder of philosophical cynicism, Diogenes of Sinope, had in mind. This ancient brand of cynicism was considered a 'dog philosophy' by Plato (from the word *kynos*, meaning 'dog' in Greek), a radical approach to reflection that enlists the whole body and all its filthy secrets to highlight the pretences and hypocrisies of official power. It is the *identity* of the stray and unkempt dog that draws attention to the dirty reality behind and under the flimsy veneer of 'legitimate' authority.

Perhaps there is something of this meaning in the cynicism that we have been discussing. When a central purpose of cultural control is to target the very selves of workers, then cynicism can be a *disruptive* force (in a limited sense) because employees thwart the managerial demand to become the kind of people the company wants them to be. Such managerial injunctions – to subscribe positively to the corporate philosophy – are an important component of the employment contract in high-commitment organizations, and cynicism may thus disrupt this particular symbolic economy of power at the level of identity. Moreover, cynicism may also be an important way of *facilitating* other forms of opposition rather than undermining them. As Andrew Sturdy and Stephen Fineman write, 'Cynicism is much more than a psychological safety valve; it is a conduit for questioning and resistance which may produce alternative, sceptical rationales and rhetorics. These can provide the basis for challenges to existing orders or, more simply, limit the scope of totalising control' (Sturdy and Fineman, 2001: 146). For example, Suzana Rodriques and David Collinson's (1995) study of Brazilian Telecom demonstrates how the cynical debunking of the engineered culture in the union newsletter helped to bolster traditional modalities of worker dissent. From this angle, the problem is to discern whether cynicism helps or hinders other modalities of resistance, which may be a formidable task due to the ambiguity and contradictory nature of many forms of dissent. As others have also argued, this approach to cynicism identifies the ways in which it can undermine or thwart a key dimension of the employment relationship – what Peter Fleming and Graham Sewell (2002) have called the managerial demand to assume the subject position of the 'happily managed' (also see Thomas and Davies, 2005; Fleming, 2005b).

These points perhaps allow for a more sympathetic view of cynical resistance, and it would be erroneous to reduce the phenomenon to one interpretation, namely the ideology approach. However, by pursuing our reconceptualizations of power and subjectivity derived from the ideology interpretation of cynicism we can also open up some interesting additional possibilities for thinking about employee dissent. It will be noted that the growing literature on 'subjective resistance' is premised on the very concepts of subjectivity and power problematized in the previous section (e.g. Knights and McCabe, 2000). So, what exactly does worker resistance look like if we accept that cultural power may work through dis-identification and that subjectivity also resides in the 'outside' sphere of objects and practice? Let us now look at resistance in terms of these two implications in more detail.

Believing too much

If a possible outcome of cynical dis-identification is the inadvertent shoring up of cultural domination then is the converse proposition also true: that believing 'too much' may have the subversive effect of throwing the reproduction of cultural power into complete disarray? Although at first glance it seems counter-intuitive, it may be worth considering how employees oppose management by (either sincerely or insincerely) *over-identifying* with the culture programme. Take the example of the employee who affixes not one company sticker to his/her car but hundreds, and thereby ridicules the whole ritual by taking it far too seriously. Another worker may stuff hundreds of suggestions (which are not completely useless) in the suggestion box, and burn out both the symbolic and administrative legitimacy of what employees often know to be bogus participation programmes. Indeed, the manoeuvre whereby subordinates can cunningly undermine the authority of the company by inordinately identifying with the orders of superiors is called 'flannelling'. This is a strategy of dissent that quietly subverts the rules of cultural control in such a manner that it is difficult for superiors to confront them directly because employees are, technically, doing what they have been asked to do. Fleming and Sewell explain the logic of flannelling:

Unlike the 'arse-kisser', 'creep', or 'company suck' who displays a conspicuously devotional adherence to the organization's norms in the hope of gaining preferment, the flanneler does not wish to climb the greasy pole. On the contrary, through an elaborate, even exaggerated, display of deference, enthusiasm, or conformity, the flanneler signals the exact opposite, displaying contempt for those very norms. (Fleming and Sewell, 2002: 866)

There are various other strategies of believing 'too much' that can disrupt relations of domination in contemporary organizations. The classic collective bargaining strategy of 'working to rule' can have a devastating impact on the smooth functioning of the work process. When employees disingenuously follow every single rule of the labour process or corporate philosophy, the work regime inevitably breaks down. Employees also often use the rhetoric of empowerment, equality and participation in a subversive way by taking it earnestly and demanding that the organization actually make it a reality (McKinlay and Taylor, 1996). This is, of course, the crucial weakness of corporate culture management: if it actually delivered what it promised it would mount a fundamental challenge to the very foundations of the capitalist and patriarchal corporation. In a similar way, employees who take customer service too seriously resist the organization by putting the interests of customers above those of the organization – selling a cheaper product that is just as good as an expensive one, or not pressuring potential customers into a sale even when the agents know that they could probably close the deal if they did so (Sturdy, 1998).

Externalizing the pathology of work

How does the externality of subjectivity help us understand the way employee resistance to corporate culture may unfold in contemporary workplaces? The ideology approach makes the argument that cynicism may undermine effective resistance to corporate domination because, even though cynical workers disbelieve 'internally', their external actions believe for them. Given our argument that this external feature of subjectivity is very significant, the enactment of a non-functional resistance may mean externalizing that which was previously relegated by the cynical employee as something internal. In other words, resistance to corporate culture and its symbolic web of control calls not only for an internal practice of incredulity but also for an externalization of disbelief.

One way we could examine this externalization of disbelief is through various forms of corporate 'culture jamming' and symbolic sabotage that are enacted almost routinely in organizations. Likewise, we could attempt to delineate an 'external' political economy of objects of disbelief, such as cynically altered company slogans and cultural 'fiddling'. Externalizing disbelief through culture jamming has proved a favourite strategy of activists in the sphere of consumption, who target the brands of large companies and subvert them by adding witty anti-corporate comments (Klein, 2000). The best examples include the 'subvertisments' produced by the Canadian 'anti-media' group Ad-busters. Their campaigns include Calvin Klein subvertisments that feature an emaciated women throwing up into a toilet and a new Marlboro man who is riddled with lung cancer. Similar strategies are deployed in relation to corporate culture when corporate slogans, symbols and other forms of discourse are subverted, usually in the informal sphere of the organization (Collinson, 1992; Fleming and Spicer, 2003).

Perhaps a less obvious connection between the process of externalization and resistance is indicated by the way that workers often attempt to 're-pathologize' the high-commitment workplace by externalizing that which was previously deemed to be internal by management. This is because corporate culture management is based on the principle of situating the success or failure of the organization 'within' the identity and selves of individual workers; otherwise legitimate employee grievances tend to be psychologized by management (and peers) as an individual 'deficiency' or pathology (Hollway, 1991). Resistance in this context is not explained as something related to the inequality of the capitalist labour process but, rather, a matter of personal problems within the worker – a negative attitude, an inability to be a team player or shirking one's duties. In other words, the pathologies of contemporary work are pushed onto employees themselves, and internalized as personal demeanours and characteristics that have to be 'worked through' in team meetings, development assessment seminars and 'self-help' consumption in the private sphere.

If subjectivity has an objective aspect, as was argued in the previous section, then the coordinates of employee resistance to culture management take on an interesting dimension. In this context, where the discourse of individuation is paramount, a degree of subversion may take place when what is constituted as inside workers by the managerial gaze is pushed back as a feature that is beyond individuals and part of the organization of work itself. As Fleming and Sewell (2002) intimate in their research into struggle in high-commitment workplaces, this usually involves a strategic change in the discourse of workers that attempts to re-pathologize the organization by drawing attention to the externality of much that is taken to be a psychological 'defect' within employees. This kind of resistance literally involves talking about organizations in a manner that transforms what is supposed to be perceived as an internal entity into an external one. This is, of course, a common symbolic procedure in traditional collective action and unionism, where the iniquities of the environment are laid bare. But, under the normative rhetoric of unitary interests that pervades culture management, resistance through externalization can have extremely disruptive consequences. In emphasizing the external nature of subjectivity the 'stressed worker' becomes the 'stressful workplace'. The 'tired employee' is now the 'exploitative organization'. Rather than perpetuating the myth of the 'negative employee', attention is instead placed upon the 'negative HRM categories' that stigmatize those who are simply 'realistic' given external circumstances.

Conclusion

This chapter has aimed to illustrate how the 'ideological' interpretation of cynical struggle opens up a number of important insights regarding typical approaches to subjectivity, power and resistance. We have chosen to dedicate a chapter to cynicism because it is both a dominant and significant mode of experience in contemporary organizations. The workplaces of late modernity are peopled with characters who do not believe in the roles they play and actively dis-identify with authority, their organizations and the products/services they produce. But how to interpret and make sense of this cynicism has been a contested issue in the literature. While cynicism may represent a form of escape from power relations that one cannot physically leave, does this escape conserve or reproduce domination? We have pursued the 'ideology' interpretation of cynicism in order to rethink (or even reverse) explanations of how power, subjectivity and struggle intersect in organizations.

As we stated in the previous chapter, the advantage of the notion of 'struggle' over 'resistance' is that we are able to see how it is always the case that the resisting subject is already deeply implicated in the power that he/she is endeavouring to escape. As a dominant mode of struggle in today's work organizations, we do feel that it is important not to write off cynicism and resentment *in toto*, as researchers have tended to do in the past. Although cynicism does not overthrow capitalism, or even glean higher wages, it might have some kind of 'bounded' efficacy in the context of corporate controls that aim to colonize the selves of workers. Indeed, perhaps cynicism is effective in less traditional ways, because it engages with power at the level of subject conformity, which is an important performance criterion in the US commitment-oriented HRM model. And such resentment has ramifications not only for our current theories (which we have endeavoured to discuss above) but also for the abiding politics of social justice in the workplace. We therefore close with a sobering statement by Harry Braverman that is as germane today as it was when published in 1974:

Beneath this apparent habituation, the hostility of workers to degenerated forms of work which are forced upon them continues as a subterranean stream that makes its way to the surface when employment conditions permit. [...] [I]t renews itself in new generations, expresses itself in the unbounded cynicism and revulsion which large numbers of workers feel about their work, and comes to the fore as a social issue demanding solution. (Braverman, 1974: 151)

5 | Desexualizing work and the struggle for desire

> From the discourse of labour to the discourse
> of sex, from the discourse of productive
> forces to that of the drives, one finds the
> same ultimatum, that of *pro-duction* in the
> literal sense of the term.
>
> (Baudrillard, 1990: 34)

As we have noted in previous chapters, a key element that marks contemporary struggles in the workplace is the displacement of traditional forms of conflict. It is not only the labour/capital divide that animates organizational struggle (although that is still an important catalyst) but, rather, a complex admixture of concerns relating to dignity, gender, sexuality and so forth. The modern organization is shot through with a plurality of antagonisms, although some are more prevalent than others. In this chapter, the issue of sexuality is explored in relation to struggles around desire and the labour process, since it provides an excellent example of how the politics of labour and meaning have become so intertwined in organizations.

The struggle over the expression of sexuality in work settings reveals how struggles involve a variety of discourses that are often contradictory, counter-intuitive and even politically regressive. In relation to sex and desire, we find employees struggling to re-eroticize the practice of labour, but often in ways that may undermine other forms of struggle in relation to democratic representation, solidarity and remuneration (Fleming, 2006). In this chapter we hope to demonstrate how the notion of struggle reveals the symbiotic and interdependent nature of power/resistance, as a kind of libidinal dialectic that has rather ambivalent political outcomes. Moreover, the issue of sexuality and its relationship to conflict has received little attention in studies of work. In this chapter we consider claims that sex is now an important part of organizational life, and is even promoted in some workplaces as a method of managerial control. In such a climate, sexuality has important implications for relations of power and resistance between employees and managers, and among employees themselves.

While some workplaces are devoted explicitly to the commodification of sex via prostitution, pornography, adult entertainment and marketing (Brewis and Linstead, 2000), mainstream workplaces too are now recognized to have an important sexual component (Burrell, 1984; Mills and Tancred, 1992; Kakabadse and Kakabadse, 2004). Like gender and power, much of the literature suggests that sexuality widely imbues organizational life, as Rosemary Pringle (1990: 162) vividly argues:

> Far from being marginal to the workplace, sexuality is everywhere. It is alluded to in dress and self-presentation, in jokes and gossip, looks and flirtations, secret affairs and dalliances, in fantasy, and in the range of coercive behaviours that we now call sexual harassment.

The hyperbole here is understandable given the dearth of research on sex and work that has characterized mainstream organization theory (Brewis and Linstead, 2000; Brewis, 2005). Following Gibson Burrell's (1984) landmark analysis of sex and organization, a good deal of the discussion has been couched in terms of power, control and resistance. And it is here that ambivalence persists regarding the political significance of workplace sexuality. On the one hand, organizations are considered formally desexualized spheres in which management have historically attempted to expunge erotic and romantic relations (Weber, 1948; Burrell, 1984, 1992). This is evident with the continuing citation of sexual misconduct in dismissal cases in the United States, United Kingdom and elsewhere (Kakabadse and Kakabadse, 2004). Wal-Mart's recent attempt to impose a legal ban on office romances in Germany is indicative of this trend. In this context, sexuality becomes a refreshingly radical gesture, since it 'forever grants the possibility of breaking a host of rules of organizational life: to not remain in organizational role, to be public in private, to be personal, and so on' (Hearn and Parkin, 1995: 7).

On the other hand, a counter-argument is evident. It suggests that there is little guarantee that re-eroticization will result in new workplace freedoms. Commenting on Burrell's (1992) discussion of the Marquis de Sade, Joanna Brewis and Chris Grey (1994) maintain that the call to emancipate organizational sexuality may actually re-reinforce pre-existing power relations apropos chauvinism, sexual harassment and even sadistic attacks. Supporting this argument is a small but promising line of scholarship that examines how certain expressions of sexuality are sanctioned and utilized by management in nominally non-sexual employment situations (Hall, 1993; Abbott and Tyler, 1998; Brewis and Linstead, 2000). It indicates that organizations are not the ascetic forums they appear to be and certain types of sexuality might facilitate masculine hierarchy, the consumption experience and control.

We suggest that the struggle over organizational sexuality is neither strictly resistance or a form of power, but a complex and multi-levelled admixture of both. In order to illustrate this argument, in the latter part of this chapter we examine an empirical study of a call centre that sanctioned the expression of sexuality among employees. Under the auspices of a 'culture of fun' celebrating lifestyle and 'being yourself', sexuality was part of a general discourse aiming to engender a more industrious climate. While sex was clearly a control mechanism, the concomitant acceptance of gay identities allowed some to challenge the heterosexism found in other workplaces (Cockburn, 1991; Parker, 2002b; Raeburn, 2004). Moreover, a number of employees resisted the sexualized culture via a cynical attitude, part of which involved homophobic views dismissing gay males as distastefully conformist. Given this complex confluence in which sexuality is simultaneously an aspect of control (management), an expression of empowerment (gay males) and an object of derision (homophobic employees), where exactly does power end and resistance begin? To untangle this nexus, we propose a multi-levelled understanding of power and resistance in which struggles around sexuality have manifold consequences. Just as power is capillary and decentred, defiance too has multidimensional effects. Resistance might undermine the regulation of sexuality on one level, but reproduce the capitalist wage–labour relation on another. Alternatively, successful resistance to an imposed sexuality might sustain the subordination of yet another type of sexual identity, and so on. It is argued that Nancy Fraser's (1997) analysis of the politics of recognition and redistribution is particularly helpful for mapping the multi-levelled effects of organizational sexuality and the ambivalent effects that struggle over desire can engender. The chapter concludes by discussing the normative alliances of the critical researcher and the difficulties that arise when sexuality and resistance are de-romanticized.

Sexuality, power and resistance in organizations

According to Jeff Hearn and Wendy Parkin (2001), a major catalyst for the raising of the profile of workplace sexuality in organization studies was the coining of the term 'sexual harassment' in the mid-1970s. This engendered some important research highlighting the latent presence of sex in ostensibly formal organizations (see Korda, 1972; Quinn, 1977; Gutek and Morasch, 1982; Gutek, 1985). Feminist criticism then underlined the dominance of masculinity and the subordination of women's sexualities in paid and unpaid labour (Cockburn, 1983; Waring, 1989). This concern resonated with studies of chauvinist masculinity in working-class counter-cultures (Willis, 1977; Collinson, 1992). In the mid-1980s and the 1990s the growing popularity of Foucault's (1979, 1980) analysis of bio-power and sexuality gave impetus to the topic in organization studies (Burrell, 1984; Brewis and Grey, 1994; Hassard, Holliday and Willmott, 2000). This line of enquiry emphasized the important connections between sex and everyday power relations at work.

Positioning organizational sexuality and eroticism within a political frame redefines them as socially and historically constituted experiences. Broader trends in social theory have been useful for establishing this claim. Gilles Deleuze and Felix Guattari (1977), Foucault (1979) and Judith Butler (1990, 1993), among others, denaturalized sexuality, eschewing both conservative and radical approaches that view it as a fixed biological fact. Just as gender (what makes us 'man' or 'woman') is enacted rather than pre-given (Butler, 1993), sexuality is sensed, expressed and interpreted within very specific socio-political conditions. Gibson Burrell and Jeff Hearn (1990) rightly argue that there is still much to be contested about this reading of sexuality, the body and desire (also see Casey, 2000). For sure, postmodern theory has been criticized for its blasé dismissal of 'strategic' essentialisms (Spivak, 1996; Eagleton, 1996). But, irrespective of the ontology of sexuality, important for us is the contention that sex and gender are closely implicated in the political networks of the employment relationship (Trethewey, 1997). As Hearn and Parkin (1995) have pointed out, sexuality and gender are entwined through the sexualization of bodies in broader cultural flows (also see Tyler, 2004). Thus it is difficult to speak of gender today without reference to sexuality and vice versa.

This political understanding of sexuality implies that it is *inter alia* a site of control and resistance. Our conceptualizations of the control/resistance couplet will determine how we observe it unfolding at the level of sexuality in organizational settings. Burrell (1984) has argued that orthodox Marxism is limiting here because it tends to analytically privilege dramatic and confrontational forms of struggle that coalesce around the labour–capital divide (cf. Edwards, 1979). Some aspects of organizational sexuality can certainly be understood from this perspective; but it relies on a Newtonian metaphor of primary action and reaction that downplays the often contradictory and ambiguous status of power/resistance relations (also see Kondo, 1990; Ackroyd and Thompson, 1999; Thomas and Davies, 2005). With some tentativeness, Burrell draws on Foucault (1979, 1980) to argue that, if power relations are diffuse and corporeal, then resistance too must imply 'fluidity, interpenetration and reversals. It is a processual notion suggesting ambiguity and flux' (Burrell, 1984: 102). Echoing our analysis in chapter 3, resistance is always contaminated by the very power it is contesting and cannot be reduced to a single motivating force. One interesting implication of this stance is that it often makes for tricky empirical observation, because 'when looking at power relationships in organizational contexts it is difficult to recognize who is resisting what control emanating from what direction' (Burrell, 1984: 100; also see Collinson, 1992). Relevant for us here is the conceptual tension evident in this research area regarding how sexuality is managed and the kinds of resistance it may engender.

Organizations as desexualized spheres

A significant avenue of research concludes that organizations have generally suppressed sexuality because it interferes with the axioms of modern work. The proposition here is that capitalist organizations have historically privileged instrumental rationality as a dominant discourse. With the creation of a spatial and symbolic boundary between work and home, labour and leisure, and the public and private in industrialized economies, sex was increasingly marginalized as an inappropriate activity. It still obviously persisted, in the form of flirtation, humour, affairs, harassment and games, but from management's point of view sex is treated as a serious misuse of company time. This argument carries considerable weight given the historical data presented by Max Weber (1948) and E. P. Thompson (1967) regarding rationalization more generally. Weber's classic dissection

of administrative bureaucracy identifies a process of 'eliminating from
official business love, hatred and all purely personal, irrational, and
emotional elements' (Weber, 1948: 216). Thompson (1967) too argues
that pre-industrial concupiscence was antithetical to the sober time
discipline of the capitalist enterprise (also see Pollard, 1965, and
Pena, 1996).

Burrell's excellent article (1984) on sexuality extends this line of
argument in organization studies and raises the problem of resistance.
For Burrell, sexuality is not just genital pleasure or orgasm. It encom-
passes the full gamut of libidinal excitations, including sensuality
and erotic play (Burrell, 1984, 1992). Through a colourful array of
historical examples, including the church, factory and public institutions, Burrell demonstrates how legal-rational authority has attempted
to eradicate sex at work.[1] It is maintained that 'human feelings including sexuality have gradually been repulsed from bureaucratic structures and have been relocated in the non-organizational sphere – the
world of civil society' (Burrell, 1984: 99). A number of historical forces
have driven this purge: the 'civilizing process' (Elias, 1978), the development of religious morality, the spread of calculative rationality and the
increased demand to control time and the body. Each of these interrelated forces led to a steady desexualization of organizations.

Resistance to this punitive sublimation of the sexual impulses,
according to Burrell, consists of a re-eroticized experience of labour:
'It becomes possible to say that *sexual relations at work may be
expressive of a demand not to be controlled*' (1984: 102; emphasis in
original). In an over-rationalized organizational sphere, insignificant
sexual liaisons can be reinterpreted as resistance to managerial control.
Burrell thus explores what Stephen Ackroyd and Paul Thompson
(1999) after him refer to as 'sexual misbehaviour': those practices
that defy bodily rationalization and recast organizations as theatres of
desire. Sodomy in the navy, concentration camp love affairs and prison
dalliances are flagged as some exemplars. The underlying message here
is that such practices are not merely an inevitable consequence of
repressed biological urges but a political engagement of sorts.

Re-eroticization as control

Burrell's (1984, 1992) argument carefully avoids romanticizing sexual
resistance and thus carries an interesting conceptual undecidablilty.

Because resexualization might be used to enact tyranny rather than defy it (e.g. rape, sexual harassment, etc.), we must champion only those sexual relations that evince 'clear expressions of human feelings of love and affection' (Burrell, 1984). However, does this not run the risk of overly sentimentalizing sex? Sigmund Freud (1920/1961), Georges Bataille (1962) and Foucault (1963/1998) all recognize something cruel and morbid in sex that cannot be fully contained by bourgeois notions of love. Brewis and Grey (1994) worry that a truly radical re-eroticization would unleash the full panoply of sexual practices, including some of the more nefarious types that we may not welcome at the next office party (also see Halford and Leonard, 2001). In other words, when translated into practice a re-eroticized organization would, ironically, require *more* policing, because once sexual licence has been granted it is not only the caring kind that might be aroused. These reservations are perhaps confirmed by Burrell's (1992) subsequent arguments about the deconstructive possibilities of a de Sadeian organizational politics (Brewis and Grey, 1994; Brewis and Linstead, 2000).

The emancipatory potential of sex is severely compromised if the libido is simply de-sublimated within pre-existing structures of rule and domination. This is what Herbert Marcuse (1968) suspected when confronted with the iconic promiscuity of the free love hippy movement. In typically sardonic style, he underlines the repressive de-sublimation of sexuality by demonstrating its compatibility with corporate life:

Without ceasing to be an instrument of labour, the body is allowed to exhibit its sexual features in the everyday work world and in work relations... The sexy office and sales girl, the handsome, virile junior executive and floor worker are highly marketable commodities... Sex is integrated into the work and public relations and is thus made susceptible to controlled satisfaction...but no matter how controlled...it is gratifying to the managed individual. (Marcuse, 1968: 70–71; quoted in Pringle, 1990: 163)

Thus our image changes from an Orwellian nightmare of prohibited sex to the equally unwelcoming world of Huxleyian pleasure control. The quote suggests that sexuality is, in some forms at least, functional in contemporary organizations. We can unpack this proposition in two ways. First, a tolerated sexuality at work may actually be useful in terms of morale, as a kind of libidinal 'indulgency pattern' (Gouldner, 1955). Ackroyd and Thompson (1999) and Andrew Ross (2004) maintain that it is an overstatement to claim that managerialism is complete anathema to sexuality. Changing values and cultural trends have meant that pleasure and work are not as incongruous as they might once have been. With more women entering the paid workforce in the post-war period and the boundaries between work and home increasingly blurred of late, management are just as likely to turn a blind eye to the office romance as pounce upon it. As long as it does not interfere with work (Quinn, 1977).

Second, and perhaps closer to Marcuse's position, sexuality may be implicitly encouraged so as to extend instrumental control. Rationality and eroticism in this sense are not mutually exclusive. Feminist investigations conducted by Barbara Gutek (1990), David and Margaret Collinson (1990) and Harriet Bradley (1999) show how masculine sexuality is a basic feature of strategy and formal hierarchy. Often we do not see it because it is so reified (Ferguson, 1984). This institutionalized masculinity reproduces inequality when it induces subordinate expressions of feminine desire, as Pringle (1989) notes in secretarial work. Mike Filby (1992) and Pamela Abbott and Melissa Tyler (1998) have identified how feminized sexualities are organized among customer service workers. Just as Arlie Hochschild's (1983) airline attendants were tacitly obliged to excite male passengers sexually in order to enhance the consumption experience, many other sales and service roles also utilize sex appeal. Waitressing provides another good example (Guerrier and Adib, 2000). These findings are consistent with observations by Silvia Gherardi (1995) and Nanette Fondas (1997) that we are witnessing the advent of a generally feminized service economy that entails a significant sexualized component.

To recap, the indeterminacy of workplace sex engenders some ambivalence about its political significance in relation to power and resistance. This uncertainty is no more evident than in the forthcoming case study. Unlike other research that has concentrated on the promotion of sexuality in the worker/customer relationship, the case study demonstrates how sexuality is encouraged among workers as a lifestyle statement. Guiding the analysis of the case is the question of how we make sense of the contradictory and ambivalent politics of sexuality in organizations. More specifically, is the expression of sexuality at work liberating, controlling or both, and how can we tell? And what does it tell us about the nature of organizational struggle today?

Managing and resisting sex at Sunray

In order to give some empirical nuance to a rather abstract debate, we now analyse the ambiguities and ambivalences of the struggle around sex at work with reference to Sunray Customer Service (a pseudonym). This is an American-owned call centre with around 1,000 employees, based in an Australian city, that was studied by one of the authors. Sunray deals with communication functions outsourced by banks, airlines, insurance firms, mobile phone companies and the like, and thus puts much emphasis on the customer service skills of employees. The company was founded by James Carr (also a pseudonym) in the early 1990s, and he remains the CEO and cultural figurehead. Sunray was selected for this research project because of its broader reputation in the business community as a high-commitment organization staffed by very motivated employees. This is especially interesting given that many call centres tend to employ rather draconian and Tayloristic methods to organize and motivate workers. The initial objective of the research project was to gain an in-depth understanding of how Sunray manipulates the culture in accordance with the customer service demands of the call centre and analyse the different ways employees respond to these initiatives.[2]

The normal shift for Sunray telephone agents requires them to receive calls from customers for eight hours, with one fifteen-minute rest period in the morning and afternoon and a half-hour lunch break. Management consider the company's culture an integral part of the labour process, as market competitiveness is said to depend largely upon the ability of workers to deliver high-quality customer service. Workers' attitudes and demeanour are therefore integral to the firm's success. The culture programme at Sunray focuses on the nature of call centre work and is primarily directed at telephone agents. It is openly accepted by the organization that call centre work is very mundane and monotonous. The culture is not necessarily designed to hide this fact but to help employees better cope with this kind of work. Janis, a human resource manager overseeing the culture programme, explains:

[W]ork in a call centre can be extremely mundane and monotonous, so we have to make it a rewarding experience in order to be successful.

And, again, call centre work

could be one of the most repetitively boring jobs you could ever do if you choose to view it that way, but we don't.

Janis and her team therefore attempt to make working at Sunray a fun and joyous experience that is intrinsically fulfilling. Perhaps the most ubiquitous artefact of Sunray's 'culture of fun' is the slogan 'Remember the "3 Fs": Focus, Fun, Fulfilment'. This phrase encourages telephone agents to perceive call centre work as a playful and good-humoured adventure. Indeed, the belief that call centre work ought to be fun is an integral part of the cultural discourse and is seen to distinguish Sunray from other organizations. In the colourful training booklet call the 'Rainbow Book', new employees are advised:

At Sunray we try to make work fun – in fact we try to make it fun instead of work. How do we deliver our promise? Forget lone rangers – at Sunray we have free-rangers! It's hard to have fun when you're confined to a work-station like a battery hen, so we encourage you to enjoy the freedom and latitude you need in order to fulfil your obligations to Sunray. This includes freedom of movement. You will be encouraged to decorate your workstation with personal mementoes.

According to Janis, employees embody the 3Fs and incorporate the slogan as an important part of their identities. She explains:

Without the culture the place would be drab, and in most workplaces people can't wait to leave. But at Sunray they love to work and really get into it. You know, just the other day I heard someone say 'I can't believe they pay me to have fun!', and that is exactly what happens.

It is interesting to note the prominence of young people working as telephone agents at Sunray. This recruitment rationale aims to support and maintain a fun and energetic environment (also see Alvesson and Billing, 1997). Janis said,

[Y]oung people find our culture very, very attractive because they can be themselves and know how to have fun.

One way Sunray endeavours to inject fun into the call centre labour process is to symbolically blur the boundary between home and work, so that what are perceived to be enjoyable non-work activities are replicated in the organization. In this way, employees can relax and 'be themselves'. For example, recruitment advertisements promote the organization as a party-like space. This theme is also invoked in training and motivation exercises. During one session in the summer, various teams competed in a relay race in a nearby park. At the end of their sprint team members quickly drank a large glass of beer. As a human resource manager said:

It all comes down to our environment – the culture, the freedom to enjoy being themselves and to enjoy being at work.

Another way in which workers can have fun and be themselves is through the relaxed dress code, which centres on fashion labels and slacker cool.[3] Young men and women make an effort to look attractive when they arrive at work. This may involve expensive clothing, in which the ritual of consumption and shopping is implicitly celebrated (also see du Gay, 1996). Or it may involve alternative clothing styles, including grunge or gothic motifs. On a number of occasions during interviews the interviewer felt decidedly unfashionable and drab because of the care that employees had put into their physical appearance. According to one employee,

The idea is to get away from the boring office look and make things fun and happy, like we are going out for the night.

This dress code extends to embrace lifestyle signifiers such as 'punk' orange hair, visible tattoos and facial piercing; the comparison to parties, raves and clubbing is justified in this sense. Difference and diversity are particularly accentuated in the induction process. One exercise asks employees to tick a form entitled '10 Things I Have Learnt Before Lunch', one of which is 'Promote Diversity in the Workplace'.

Sexuality at Sunray

A fascinating aspect of this culture of youth, partying and fun is the sometimes overt, sometimes covert, theme of sexuality. According to some informants (and confirmed by our own observations), the expression of sexuality and flirting among employees is openly condoned at Sunray. For example, a number of informants claimed that the work environment is considered a fruitful space to proposition fellow workers for a date. Relationships on the call centre floor were sexually charged as liaisons were planned and casual affairs ensued. Sexuality at Sunray was spatially sequenced (Giddens, 1992). It was expressed inside the main building in terms of dress and banter, as well as in nominally external spheres, such as the annual away day and the nearby pub (known as the 'Sunray Pub' because of the high proportion of employees that patronized it). Although these latter spaces are probably highly sexualized in most organizations (the obligatory Christmas party fling, for example), Sunray acknowledges them as a positive feature of company life. The managers interviewed never explicitly espoused sexuality as a culture management policy to us. Nor was their evidence that sexuality was considered a *formal* aspect of the customer service function for telephone agents. But its impor- tance to the overall cultural discourse of 'being yourself' is easily identifiable from the observational and interview data (especially as the latter were unprompted). Joanne, a representative for a health insurance firm said,

You can wear what you want – people are allowed to wear low-cut tops and short skirts.

And a team leader said,

We like to think of ourselves as fun, sexy and dedicated.

    The sexual dimension of the Sunray culture is not only heterosexual but also has a strong gay focus, which again resonates with the 'being yourself' theme. The CEO, James Carr, said in the local business press:

We've tried to create a workplace in which people of either sex, gay people and people from other places can come and really enjoy the time they spend with each other and their managers in the environment. . .

This makes Sunray quite different from the heterosexist organizations that Yiannis Gabriel, Stephen Fineman and David Sims (2000) suggest are the current norm. Because of the qualitative nature of this research it was difficult to judge the exact proportion of gay men employed at Sunray. Perhaps what matters more is the prominence of gay themes in the everyday discourse recorded among informants. Rather than con- cealing their homosexual identities at work, as Marny Hall (1990) argues happens with lesbian workers, Sunray is a space in which gay sexuality can be openly disclosed. Joanne said,

There are lots of gay guys here who are *very out* – they don't have to hide the fact that they are gay [emphasis in original].

Notwithstanding the homophobic attitudes of the national government towards gay rights, the Australian city in which the call centre is
located is known for its pro-gay culture. Sunray reflects this progressive
trend by making the work environment gay-friendly. For example, one
project had a 'Fashion Day' in which workers dressed as fashion
models. Leanne, an airline agent, said,

It was amazing the different costumes people wore – they really got into it.
Many of the gay guys dressed in drag, in tiny mini-skirts – and one of them
won.

Here is another interesting reference to the prominence of gay males
in the organization, especially as it pertains to their contribution to the
fun and effervescent atmosphere at Sunray:

INTERVIEWER: What are the Christmas parties like?
JULES: They are really just big booze-ups like any other.
               Although you get lots of gay boys prancing around
               in their Speedos and being very flamboyant.

The gay-friendly atmosphere of the organization works well with the
general cultural message of being yourself, fun, ebullience and out-
goingness. Rob, a telephone operator for a major bank, identifies with
this atmosphere. Without prompting, he raised the topic of gay sexuality in the context of Sunray's celebration of difference and diversity:

Sunray definitely promote it [open homosexuality] – well, not promote it but,
say, you are what you are and you are allowed to be that way, which is a good
thing.

Negotiating sexuality at Sunray

As Filby (1992) points out, although organizations may endorse sexuality with certain ends in mind, its inherent instability renders it somewhat unpredictable. Indeed, employees negotiated Sunray's culture of
sexuality in diverse ways. Some heterosexual males implied that they
enjoyed the sexually charged atmosphere. Daryl, a nineteen-year-old
telephone agent, said, for example:

It's good how we are free to walk around and talk to each other, chat to the
ladies [*laughs knowingly*] – y'know, and have a good time – just as long as we
do a good job for the team.

Little firm data was collected indicating how gay men felt about the homosexual focus of the culture. Observations of the pro-gay environment and the prominence of gay motifs (e.g. the dress-up 'Fashion Days') would seem to imply that gay men received this facet of the organization favourably. Rob's discourse mentioned above appears to support this claim. It is possible, however, that the kind of gay sexuality celebrated at Sunray would not appeal to all gay men.

Some of the women felt uncomfortable with such a strong sexualization of the workplace. For example, a customer service operator said she avoided the Sunray Pub on Friday nights because it was 'too sleazy' and lecherous. In this forum, relationships had to be policed more than usual by female workers. Inside the organization, the derogatory term 'meat market' (a bar or nightclub where people come specifically to pick up dates) was used to describe some aspects of organizational life. This term is interesting because it gives a very different meaning to the 'Sunray party' discourse, one that was perhaps unintended by management. Leanne said,

There are some very sleazy guys at Sunray and you walk past them and they look you up and down and that is very uncomfortable, but it's a boring job and most who work here want to do something else – sex is less boring.

One of the most fascinating reactions to Sunray sexuality was by a cohort that was regularly interviewed. This group consisted of three employees living together in a house of four (the fourth person being the girlfriend of one of the workers). Two of the housemates (a male and female) were telephone agents and the third (male) held an IT position. The girlfriend worked in another call centre but participated in the cynical banter as much as the Sunray employees themselves. Ironically, she would later become a Sunray employee. The group resisted the culture management programme by cynically distancing their sense of self from the organization. They found the message and delivery of the culture patronizing and dishonest because it obscured Sunray's exploitative side. When explaining the '3 Fs', Kim said:

I can't believe a lot of this stuff. I feel like saying 'How dare you stand up there and pretend to be something you are not'. They pretend to be different but they aren't, and in some ways are worse than other companies because they are not real.

This type of cynical engagement is relatively well theorized in the literature we explored in the previous chapter (Gabriel, 1999; Fleming and Sewell, 2002; Fleming and Spicer, 2003). What is significant in the Sunray case is how this resistance entailed pejorative comments about fellow workers. There was frequent mention of 'sluts' and 'sleazy guys'. Gay men in the organization were especially targeted. The cohort frequently referred to the firm as 'Gayray'.[4] Moreover, they colourfully rephrased the '3 Fs' slogan to read 'Fuckwits, Faggots and Freaks'. Kim explained the rationale behind this bawdy slogan:

Well, to 'succeed' at Sunray you are basically gay, have to be really 'alternative' and Sunray likes people who have different-coloured hair and who are into [*in a sarcastic tone*] 'being themselves', or you're just a complete loser. Now, I'm not too sure which one we fitted into, but basically we are plebs. Just plebs.

Kim is expressing a feeling of injustice regarding the patrimonial hierarchy and favouritism at Sunray. One has to be part of the cool crowd in order to be promoted or treated well. In this context, gay men are considered synonymous with the scripted Sunray personality – someone bubbly, extroverted and exaggeratedly supportive of management. Kim told me that Sunray actually wants people to adopt fake and shallow personalities because that is the only way they can perpetuate a culture of fun. The informal dress code is considered especially pretentious. The dialogue below illustrates homosexuality being evoked in the context of anti-management discourse:

MARK:　　People supposedly look at Sunray and see this hip, young, cool crowd.

JACKIE:　They don't, they see a bunch of pretentious fashion victims.

MARK:　　You don't even work there.

JACKIE:　Thank fucking God. [*To me.*] When I go to meet Mark I wait a block down the road because if I wait outside I get looked at by the Sunray people to see what I'm wearing. I hate it; it's like being back at high school. They all must wear stylish clothes to [*sarcastically and impersonating a subscriber*] 'fit in'.

MARK:　　But I don't wear them.

JACKIE:　But you're a guy, it's different.

MARK:　　There are plenty of guys that get fully dressed up.

JACKIE:　But they're all gay, Mark [*laughing uncontrollably*].

MARK:　　That's discrimination! [*Laughs.*] Well, yes there are a number of gay individuals there.

Sexualized resistance or resisting sexuality?

The Sunray case provides a good opportunity to unpack the political effects of the struggle around organizational sexuality. As already stated, ambivalence underlies the literature in this regard. On the one hand, re-eroticization is said to be a radical gesture that creates spaces of freedom given the historical desexualization of work. On the other hand, management may actually use sexuality to control workers, enhance productivity and reinforce masculine norms. Three aspects of the Sunray case are significant here. First, rather than banishing sexuality from the realm of work, we see management condone a particular expression of it. Second, both straight and gay identities are encouraged. And, third, some workers resist the sexualization of work because it involves harassment or is perceived to be part of an increasingly intrusive control system. Underlining some of this resistance is a disturbing homophobia.

So, is the expression of sexuality at Sunray liberating, controlling or both, and how can we tell? An obvious interpretation of re-eroticization at Sunray would emphasize the control side of the tension, highlighting how sexuality enhances the established wage relation. By allowing people to 'be themselves' in ways that facilitate the customer service function (e.g. positive sentiments, flexibility, discretion, creativity, etc.), the 3Fs philosophy enlists the private dimensions of the individual as a corporate resource. This aspect of control utilizes authenticity, difference, diversity and lifestyle rather than the bland conformity recorded in earlier studies of culture management. The themes of fun, partying and sex, usually associated with the private sphere, are discursively integrated into Sunray's team rituals, social events and everyday interactions. Under the rubric of openness and empowerment a form of bio-power (Foucault, 1979; Agamben, 1998) is achieved as the labour process absorbs sex and lifestyle. Perhaps this renders redundant Burrell's insight that workplace sexuality subverts relations of power because it 'would look remarkably like play or joy' (1984: 107).

This line of analysis would lead us to suspect that resistance at Sunray will be enacted against the re-eroticization of work relations. This can be noted among the female workers who felt harassed. For example, some refused to patronize the sexualized Sunray Pub and complained of sleaziness at work. However, Sunray's management of sexuality did more than create new opportunities for masculine domination. It also voiced an otherwise marginalized gay identity. Is this too part of the control system, aiming to make workers more amenable to the production process? It would be difficult to sustain this argument without sounding somewhat condescending. Imagine informing gay employees that Sunray's celebration of their sexuality is merely a power play implicating them more profoundly with their own subordination. Or, worse still, that theirs is not an *authentic* re-eroticization of labour because it plays into the hands of management rather than undermining capitalism. A more nuanced understanding of power and resistance is clearly required.

One way forward is to tease out the multi-levelled effects of Sunray's power/resistance networks by differentiating between the struggle for recognition (redressing marginalized identities) and redistribution (redressing economic inequalities). In a number of influential essays, Fraser (1997) argues that struggles for recognition and redistribution represent interrelated yet different types of political activity. For example, gay struggles are not simply reducible to economic grievances since the former flow from a concern with social recognition. And, while the capitalist labour process is not inherently anti-gay (as the Sunray case illustrates), it does invariably ply an exploitive redistributive politics. The two levels interpenetrate, but they can be conceptually decoupled in order to clarify some of the complexities underpinning resistance and struggle (also see Fraser and Honneth, 2003).[5] At Sunray it is possible to distinguish between management's progressive, if somewhat opportunistic, recognition politics and its more customary redistributive politics. While on the level of sexual identity *some* Sunray employees enjoy an enabling work environment, at another level they (and others) are still part of an exploited workforce. Re-eroticization at Sunray therefore includes both liberation and control, but along different dimensions.

Can we understand the cynical cohort by using the same multi-levelled approach to power and resistance? Kim's description of herself and other telephone agents as plebs is indicative of their redistributive concerns. While the organization apparently champions difference in which agents can 'be themselves', she feels they *all* are ultimately plebs. The culture of fun (with its references to sex, play and good times) is considered disingenuous because it masks the proletarianized nature of the work. The cohort's cynicism influences material redistribution insofar as positive attitudes are considered a competitive resource by management. However, this economically orientated resistance simultaneously enters the politics of recognition in a regressive form when anti-management feeling is expressed in the idiom of homophobia. The cohort was probably homophobic already, but such sentiments were amplified when they became a vehicle for engaging in redistributive politics. Sexuality is thus 'over-determined' by both identity and economics in the struggle for desire.

Conclusion

In addressing the question of whether sexuality is a site of resistance or control in contemporary organizations, we have suggested in this chapter that it is a multi-levelled combination of both. The tension around this issue can be partially resolved if struggles over sexuality and re-eroticization are embedded in a variegated political field. The Sunray case usefully illustrates this approach, because it presents us with a complex scenario in which sexuality is an aspect of managerial control, a site of empowerment and an object of resistance. Using the social theory of Nancy Fraser (1997), it has been possible to note how both recognition and redistribution struggles unfold. This distinction serves as a heuristic for untangling the confusing and contradictory politics of sexuality and work in organizations. Indeed, Fraser's understanding of justice will be expanded in much more depth in chapter 8 in order to demonstrate how it helps us understand the drivers of struggle in contemporary organizations.

Reference to Fraser's framework emphasizes the *political significance* of organizational struggle. Perhaps critical organization studies ought to move beyond simply classifying acts of misbehaviour and study the multiple political outcomes in relation to social justice issues (also see chapter 8). In this respect, the Sunray case demonstrates how the messy realities of organizational politics can put the critical researcher him-herself in an ambivalent position. As critical scholars, we tend to sympathize with those subordinated in uneven power relations and thus side with those who resist (Fournier and Grey, 2000). But empirical research often confounds these normative alliances. The homophobic cohort at Sunray, for example, reminds us that resistance is seldom pure or uncontaminated by its own will to dominate. The analytical approach developed in this chapter disabuses us of the notion that employee resistance is either politically progressive or regressive *in toto*. To put it simply, not all resistance is good. And not all good resistance is only good. Is the solution a withdrawal to a position of objectivity that simply describes what we observe with cold detachment? Perhaps not. We *must* side with the subordinated, but also remain sensitized to the over-determined and contradictory nature of political struggle in contemporary organizations.

6 | *Displacement and struggle: space, life and labour*

> [o]ne is never finished with anything – the
> corporation, the educational system, the
> armed services being metastable states
> coexisting in one and the same modularity,
> like a universal system of deformation.
>
> (Deleuze, 1992: 5)

A common refrain heard among many workers in organizations today is the following: 'I am a different person at work from how I am at home, but with the demands put upon me now I find it difficult to keep the two separated.' For sure, the idea of a 'place of work' in which we give up or repress those aspects of our selves associated with leisure or the home is a very peculiar historical achievement. As the English historian E. P. Thompson (1967) points out, this achievement that we now take for granted emerged from estrangement, conflict and pain. The spatial demarcation of work from 'life' represents a major break from previous economic regimes, in which space, life and labour were all highly integrated.

The spatiality of organizational power and resistance relations has received little attention in employment studies, which perhaps reflects the ease with which sometimes highly unusual configurations of space can become normalized. We argue in this chapter that newly emerging work forms involve struggle around the meaning and utility of space. Organizational space involves relations of force and domination in which *place* comes to signify the desirability of certain behaviours and meanings above others. These meanings are highly contested by various parties. We demonstrate this in an organization in which management attempt a major displacement of traditional spatial configurations in order to enhance control, productivity and cultural subordination (Fleming and Spicer, 2003). Aspects of this struggle were intimated in the previous chapter on sexuality, where it was pointed

out that, typically, non-work emotions and meanings were being intentionally encouraged in the workplace by management – the aim being
to incorporate more of the employee (so to speak) into the post-industrial
labour process. We demonstrate in what follows that managerial
attempts to integrate space, life and labour more fully represent a
major innovation in organizational power relationships – one that is
also a salient fulcrum of struggle and conflict.

It is now almost a commonplace to proclaim the porosity of various
boundaries that have traditionally separated the workplace from more
'private' domains of life. While the notion of the 'boundaryless' organization probably exaggerates the extent of this displacement of the
inside/outside division, transformations in the character of the work/
non-work boundary are nevertheless a fascinating feature of contemporary organizations (Fleming and Spicer, 2003). Permutations
currently redefining the inside and outside spheres of work have a
fundamental geographical aspect – a point that, curiously, has been
missed in some investigations of organizational boundaries (e.g.
Perlow, 1998). Scholarship that has explicitly considered spatiality in
work organizations has done well in focusing on its relationship with
power and domination, aiming to ascertain the often unobtrusive connections between political processes and the physical environment.
Mauro Guillén (1998), for example, argues that the work of modernist
architects such as Le Cobusier and Mies van de Rohe represented a
wilful attempt to build spaces of work (and leisure) that materialized
the power dynamics of scientific management. Inspired by Taylorism,
modernist architects rendered workspace rational, instrumental and,
above all, controllable (also see Sundstrom, 1986, and Sewell and
Wilkinson, 1992). The strong association between managerial control
and workspace has been further developed by Chris Baldry, who argues
'The working environment, as socially-constructed space, must be
reintegrated into analysis as part of both the objective conditions of
the labour process and the subjective mechanisms of control and subordination' (1999: 536). Baldry is careful to point out how these spatial
elements are intentionally manipulated by management in sometimes
subtle ways (also see Palm, 1977, Henley, 1977, and Perin, 1991).

Current research is limited, however, in two important ways. First, it
focuses on the relationships between spatiality and power only as they
unfold *within* organizations. Indeed, the boundary that separates what
happens inside and outside the workplace is simply taken for granted

by Baldry, Guillén and others (e.g. Gagliardi, 1990; Yanow, 1998; Strati, 1999); it is what happens *inside* the firm that is of primary interest. In this chapter we demonstrate how a significant expression of power in contemporary workplaces is not only the control of space inside the organization but also the positioning of the very boundary delineating the inside from the outside. A second limitation is the lack of emphasis on space as a focus of struggle. We argue that resistance, in addition to having a geographical aspect, is now the object of struggle as well. What is the nature of these spatial power relations, and what kinds of struggle do they inspire? This chapter addresses these questions by exploring how the traditional demarcation between work and life, work and leisure, work selves and private selves marked a major victory in the establishment of industrial capitalism and class relations of power. We then show how this boundary is being manipulated and revised in many organizations today with the aim of enhancing control, productivity and more 'creative' employee labour. With the emergence of new forms of corporate management in which employees are exhorted simply to 'be themselves' (a 'warts and all' approach), an attempt is made to erode and reconstitute the spatial division between work and non-work that was, arguably, indicative of industrialism. Managerial discourse challenges the meaning of work both inside and outside the firm. This means that employees no longer create a clear physical distance between employment on the one hand and home life, family or leisure on the other.

   In order to illustrate this process of spatial displacement, we return to the garishly colourful corridors and work-pods of Sunray Customer Service, which we introduced in the last chapter. While other studies of corporate culture have demonstrated how organizations use normative controls to encroach upon the private lives of employees (Kunda, 1992; Barker, 1993; Scase and Goffee, 1989), the specific spatial and social geographic dynamics of this process has had little attention. As we will point out soon, boundaries are usually framed in terms of time or identity rather than in any physical sense. The Sunray case reveals an interesting *two-way* cultural process whereby spatial practices once considered the domain of organizational life are transferred into the homes of employees, and so-called private activities are, conversely, carried back into the organization. Having explored this as an expression of power, we then identify the dynamics of struggle and conflict that emerge. Echoing the findings in chapter 4, we find that cynical resistance to the symbolic integration of work and life appears to be an important modality of contestation.

Spatial boundaries at work

Boundaries that constitute and regulate the inside and outside domains of organizations appear to be an enduring feature of modern employment relations, and a key characteristic that distinguishes them from pre-industrial modes of production. This boundary has obviously been conceived in various ways, including time management, worker identities and gender roles. This section concentrates largely on the spatial nature of the demarcation between work and non-work, a boundary that is also plural, differentiated and a source of contestation. We outline the character of industrial boundaries and the post-industrial transformations that are currently unsettling them, focusing in particular on the deployment and maintenance of culture management programmes. We do not, however, want to overdraw the industrialism/ post-industrialism distinction, or make the mistake of construing each 'epoch' as homogeneous and undifferentiated wholes (cf. Hirschhorn and Gilmore, 1992). We merely sketch certain trends that, although not entirely unproblematic, are generally accepted as useful categories for making sense of the complex vicissitudes of Western economic history (on this point, see Harvey, 1989).

Industrial boundaries

The shift from feudalism to capitalism in Europe during the eighteenth and nineteenth centuries witnessed a major reorganization of both the physical and conceptual spatiality of working life (Braudel, 1961, 1982). Under feudalism peasants and artisans were usually located in close proximity to home, family and leisure (Pollard, 1965). With the emergence of capitalism and factory production, however, the spatial characteristics of the 'putting-out' system in particular were unsuitable due to the lack of worker discipline and control (Thompson, 1967). As Karl Marx's study of the 'dark satanic mills' in *Capital* (1867/ 1976) graphically demonstrated, the physical concentration of wage labourers under a single roof was driven by the capitalist need to discipline and monitor the execution of work (also see Smith, 1777/ 1974).

This spatial reorganization primarily involved the constitution of a boundary that, while by no means impermeable or impervious, formed a line of division between the organization and the outside world. This boundary was first and foremost physical, as commentators of the Industrial Revolution and modernism have closely documented (e.g. Foucault, 1977). Factories were fenced off like prisons and the urbanization of the industrial proletariat created a new geography of work that was markedly different from previous systems. But this division also involved important temporal and subjective elements. As time became the source of wealth under the aegis of capitalist production, the working day was dichotomized between company time and private time (Clegg and Dunkerley, 1980). And, depending on whether one was at home or at work, quite different selves are exhibited (Scott and Storper, 1986). For example, just as Max Weber (1922/1978) highlighted the normative separation of the office-bearer and his/her office in a bureaucratic context, Huw Beynon recounts the Ford philosophy in the factory context: 'When we are at work, we ought to be at work. When we are at play we ought to be at play. There is no use trying to mix the two. When the work is done, then the play can come, but not before' (Beynon, 1980: 40, quoted in Collinson, 2002: 276).

Although the division between work and non-work life was certainly not watertight, with the work ethic (Thompson, 1967) and industrial paternalism (Bendix, 1956), for example, playing a major role outside the factory gates, the spatial division did represent a significant shift from feudalist economic arrangements. The development of such a boundary was not purely accidental but a reflection of the power relations attempting to render labour more amenable to the production process. According to Manuel Castells (1977), the working-class areas of the industrial city are 'centres of habituation', places where labour resides, is replenished and easily monitored. Reproducing the labour power of a society is thus contained in a demarcated area that is controllable (penetrated by police surveillance) and removed from the spaces of governing elites. Moreover, the constitution of workers as 'free sellers' of labour power meant that organizational responsibilities to the workforce ended when they left the company gates. During periods of extreme unemployment or industrial unrest these gates are used not only to keep workers inside the factory *but also to keep them outside*. Similarly, other research has highlighted the instrumental

importance of the inside/outside boundary for firms wishing to exter-
nalize the costs of production to individual workers, the state or the
family (Harvey, 1973; Waring, 1989).

Post-industrial boundaries and culture management

Although many characteristics of industrialism are still prevalent today
it is now commonly accepted that an array of shifts in economic,
cultural and social geography are taking place in Western societies
generally and the workplace specifically (Harvey, 1989; Clegg, 1990;
Castells, 1996). What some have termed postmodern or post-industrial
developments in economic and organizational spatiality have made
social institutions more fluid and fissiparous over time and space,
reshaping people's experiences of their physical environments in fundamental ways (Jameson, 1991). These macro-trends have also had
significant ramifications for the spatial organization of companies
and their workforces as various industries develop employment practices that are deemed more 'flexible', 'empowering' and 'adaptable'.
The popularity of outwork and homework (Felstead, 1996;
Brocklehurst, 2001), so-called 'hot-desking' (Laing, 1997; Duffy,
1997) and the deskless office (Apgar, 1998; van Meel, 2000), for
example, are testimony to the development of a porosity that has
blurred a number of the typical differentiations between work and
non-work spaces.

The stream of research that we want to develop here has focused on
the way some human resource management strategies have attempted
to challenge symbolically and reconfigure industrial boundaries
in order to gain a more committed and dedicated workforce. The
widespread use of culture management practices in particular have
been shown to encroach insidiously into the hitherto untapped areas
of workers' private lives. Gideon Kunda (1992), James R. Barker
(1993) and Catherine Casey (1995, 1996), for example, emphasize the increased demands that so-called high-commitment organizations and managed cultures place on the psychic energies of
employees, compromising their personal lives and the ways they
enact work and non-work roles (also see Scase and Goffee, 1989).
The effects this has is perhaps no more evident in a story related by
the original gurus of culture management Tom Peters and Robert
Waterman, in which the geographical dimension of cultural controls

are implicitly illustrated: 'A Honda worker, on his way home each evening, straightens up windshield blades on all the Hondas he passes. He just can't stand to see a flaw on a Honda!' (Peters and Waterman, 1982: 37).

Kunda's study of a high-tech corporation in the United States revealed that the expectation for long working hours was built into the organizational culture and was very difficult to resist once it had been internalized. The organization he called 'Tech' attempted to appropriate as much time as possible from organizational members, and this could be done only if workers came to actively desire it themselves. The 'Tech culture' was designed to constitute this desire through various mechanisms of role embracement, so that workers would think of themselves as 'Tech employees' *all the time*. As a result of this management approach many employees found their family and home lives suffered, because they gave more and more of themselves to the firm and experienced burnout, role contradiction and other kinds of pathologies (alcoholism, heart attacks, divorce, etc.). Indeed, even though workers endeavoured to maintain some kind of spatial distance, many found that 'work and nonwork aspects of social ties are experienced as hard to separate, requiring constant definition and redefinition and are never fully resolved' (Kunda, 1992: 169).

Casey recorded similar findings in her study of an electronics manufacturer that had built a high-commitment culture. Working very long hours was considered an axiomatic cultural norm at 'Hephaetus' and employees therefore felt obligated to sacrifice their personal lives. As one employee Casey interviewed made clear: 'I try not to but sometimes I come in on Sunday mornings... I also do a lot of work at home after the kids go to bed' (Casey, 1995: 127). Casey's study concludes that it is not only the personal time of employees that is appropriated by the company but also their *identities*, a process she ominously labels 'the corporate colonization of self'. When this occurs workers become 'company people' even at home, and cannot think about anything else other than their job and the well-being of the firm. Many of these employees are classified by Casey as neurotic and obsessive/compulsives because they have allowed the company to erode the identity boundaries that once separated them from the organization. These workers often burn out as psychic anxiety and contradiction become too intense (also see Willmott, 1993, and Barker, 1993).

Although these studies do illustrate how so-called post-industrial management techniques have attempted to challenge the boundaries that have typically demarcated work and non-work activities, they have largely conceptualized them in terms of time and identity. Given that they are predominantly dealing with experiences of immaterial normative controls operating within the firm, this emphasis is perhaps unsurprising. With the changing nature of the division between work and life, more emphasis should be placed on how new management techniques (associated with culture, empowerment, etc.) disrupt and challenge not only time and identity boundaries but also the *spatial dimensions* of what are considered work and non-work places. In order to illustrate these changing dynamics of power relations at work, we want to revisit Sunray Customer Service. This organization provides a salutary example of how innovative management systems are redefining the symbolic meaning of space in order to further the logic of calculative rationality and capitalism. The case also reveals the points and expressions of struggle that such initiatives engender.

Sunray and the politicization of place: a reprise

We recall from chapter 5 that the most distinguishing feature of Sunray is the emphasis placed on a culture of fun, epitomized in the slogan 'Remember the "3 Fs": Focus, Fun, Fulfilment'. Employees in the call centre are encouraged by management to perceive the otherwise banal, alienating and mundane task of the telephone agent as exciting, exhilarating and exuberant. When an employee embodies the '3 Fs' and is seen to be part of the team he or she is said to have the 'right attitude' (also see Callaghan and Thompson, 2002). This seems to consist of a set of display performances of self that communicate a positive personality, a childish playfulness, a bubbly frame of mind and an extroverted and carefree disposition. This kind of personality is deemed to be of utmost importance at Sunray because competitiveness is said to depend largely upon the ability of workers to deliver high-quality customer service. Other call centre studies have also demonstrated the use of techniques such as these (e.g. Hutchinson, Purcell and Kinnie, 2000, and Derry and Kinnie, 2002), but the *spatiality* of these controls remains largely under-theorized and unexamined. As we shall demonstrate, management want not only the minds of employees but also their spaces.

Boundary control at Sunray

As we ascertained in the last chapter, Sunray's culture programme endeavours to manipulate and blur the traditional boundaries that have typically divided work life and private life as a method of extending organizational control. Team development managers feel that it is no longer sufficient to restrict culture management to just the workplace but seek to increase its span in a number of interesting ways. Some of these techniques have also been documented in other studies (e.g. Kunda, 1992, and Barker, 1999). For example, team meetings are often held outside work hours in a downtown café or nearby park, and may take place after or before work, depending on the project. And, as with the organizations investigated by Casey, Kunda and Barker, the culture instigates everyday norms and expectations regarding the time and effort one must devote to the company, often involving unwanted overtime or weekend work.

Other cultural techniques used at Sunray attempted to disrupt and reorganize the traditional inside/outside boundary through a two-way process whereby activities that should have typically taken place outside work were encouraged inside the organization (e.g. wearing pyjamas, alcohol consumption, etc.), and activities seen to be appropriate inside the organization were encouraged to take place at home or in other private spaces (such as memorizing the company slogan). This dynamic of the cultural system not only represented a symbolic challenge to the traditional demarcating boundary but also had material implications in which the social geography of work and non-work were reconfigured in order to further the reach of the culture's influence. Let's look at each part of this process.

From outside to inside

A significant aspect of the Sunray culture initiative involved encouraging employees to evoke traditionally non-work feelings and identities within the sphere of production. It was openly acknowledged that call centre work can be stressful, boring and monotonous, but management argued that employees did not have to perceive it in this way. As Rachel, a telephone agent, told us: 'You have to be able to see the lighter side of things. You have to be able to look at your work and turn it around in a positive way.' Thus, training workshops and everyday cultural messages constantly stress that all those experiences that employees normally wait until after work to have, such as fun, partying, joy, fulfilment, exhilaration and friendship, are appropriate to evoke in the workspace. Many of these evocations are uncontroversial and have been noted in other studies of culture management. For example, the bright colour scheme and 'party atmosphere' is celebrated at Sunray because it attempts to break down the sterile nature of call centre employment. Similarly, workers are encouraged to bring homemade cakes and dishes into work and share with other employees. This cultural protocol is part of the personalization of space that Sunray hopes will make employees feel more 'at home' when working. Telephone agents bring to work personal belongings to decorate their team's work cubicle. Also observed were surfboards, photos of loved ones, sporting trophies and other non-work items displayed in prominent places.

Much of the 'fun culture' at Sunray attempts to emulate what managers believe to be the *esprit de corps* and playfulness displayed by good friends in a school setting. It is interesting to note the conscious recruitment strategy of employing young people. The recruitment rationale here is that 'young people find our culture very, very attractive because they can be themselves and know how to have fun'. With managers and trainers generally over thirty-five, a definite teacher/student thematic is evident. This is typified in many of the cultural rituals as well. For example, away days are held annually and consist of days when everyone travels to a 'party' destination to stage what Janis refers to as a 'kind of school musical'. Other aspects of this school theme verge on the silly by imitating primary school and kindergarten themes. Training games involving mini-golf and quizzes are frequently employed for sales motivation purposes. In one induction session, workers stood and sung the Muppets' *The Rainbow Connection*. Moreover, cubicles display figures of Big Bird and Grover from the children's television programme *Sesame Street*. This gives the call centre what one employee called a 'kindergarten atmosphere' because of the juvenile ambience it creates.

Team-building exercises also attempt to break down the barriers that the organization traditionally constructs between work and private spaces. For example, employees may be asked to bring to the next training workshop a personal item that best represents and sums up their personalities. This may include anything from a teddy bear to a golf club. Or trainees may be asked to think of as many 'square shapes' as they saw while travelling to work in the morning, demonstrating that working as a group can produce many more instances than an individual. In the training workshops the virtues of 'being oneself' and the importance of cultivating a 'Sunray attitude' even outside work are discussed as individual employees engage in a self-assessment process in order to ascertain what type of person they are and how their unique personality contributes to 'the Sunray Way'. For example, one question is 'What are you passionate about?', the answer invariably pointing to some extra-employment activity. Utilizing the private lives of workers is thus a crucial training strategy that aims to have them invest more of themselves in their work and evoke spatial norms commonly reserved for activities outside work (e.g. reflecting on personal passions and existential purpose).

The home lives of workers are also of interest to the company when monitoring and assessing work performance. Teams aim to replicate a clan-like situation in which team leaders assume the role of confidant and counsellor rather than that of supervisor. In this capacity leaders listen to the confessions of workers regarding personal problems at home, give them sound advice and 'work it through with them'. At Sunray, the ritual of confession is activated when a team leader or member notices someone acting abnormally. This is what Sarah, a team leader, said about this part of her role in relation to punctuality:

We have a situation here where an agent can feel comfortable enough to say the reason why they've been coming late is because they have a serious problem at home. I will first recognize a difference in their attitude. It will begin to wane and I will say, 'What's happened? Is it the job or something at home? What can I do to help you with that?'

In this way the company explicitly links home issues to the productive demands of the company. The organization tries to reproduce private spatial practices in a number of more controversial ways, which have received less attention in the literature. For example, team-building exercises involving heavy drinking as well as the consumption of alcohol during the last two hours of work on Friday afternoons are encouraged by management. As we highlighted in chapter 5, the expression of both straight and gay sexuality and 'flirting' are openly encouraged at Sunray. The work environment is considered by a number of employees to be a fruitful place to proposition someone for a romantic liaison. The informal dress code suggests that employees are free to 'be themselves' at work rather than suppress feelings and idiosyncrasies, potentially making work more exciting and fulfilling. A number of the employees interviewed had brightly dyed hair, facial piercing and sported designer clothes in a manner that apparently celebrated the 'whole individual'. To be sure, the cultural norm of wearing designer jeans and footwear suggests that private consumption rituals are an important cultural signifier at Sunray. Displaying one's dedication to the 'culture of cool' thus depends on one's ability to span the boundary between private patterns of consumption and working life.

From inside to outside

Perhaps the most startling finding from our research of Sunray culture is the attempt to transfer workplace activities into the home and the private sphere. Thus employees are encouraged not only to evoke non-work rituals inside the organization but also to reproduce work-related motifs outside the firm. Sometimes this is very explicit. For example, in relation to the evocation of sexuality discussed above, the pub that employees are encouraged to frequent (especially on Friday nights) is deemed to be part of the workplace insofar as sexual harassment regulations are concerned. Moreover, interviews with employees in their homes revealed the extensive reach of the culture, as it is expected to be positively endorsed and talked about both inside and outside the workplace. For example, workers are often asked to attend the away day on a Sunday, which is commonly assumed to be a work-free period. Failing to attend this activity is a sign that they are not fully committed to the firm and lack the required attitude. One employee relayed a story about a fellow worker:

A woman in my team was told that she had to go to the away day but she said she had family commitments: 'I'm a mother.' But she was told, 'No, we are all going. You should go.' She said, 'No I can't.' And again she was told, 'It's expected that you go or you must pay the $65 fee for the end-of-year party.'

Another interesting example of company cultural practices manifesting in 'private space' was discovered when interviewing a group of three Sunray workers who were living together in the same house. On one occasion, the group was being interviewed, and Michael brought home a handbook that included the question 'What are the "3 Fs"?' and had three blank spaces to be filled in with a pen by the reader. These cultural artefacts have been specifically designed to be taken home with employees so that they continue to be processed once the more overt institutional pressures of the organization are not present. If the internalization of the cultural values and norms constitutes a type of 'identity work' (Ezzamel, Willmott and Worthington, 2001) on behalf of the employees, then the various devices that they take home are designed to encourage employees to *continue their work* outside the workplace (so they do not 'lose the habit') and fashion an identity and lifestyle that is conducive to 'the Sunray Way' (also see Sturdy and Fleming, 2003). In labour process theory terms, there is a concerted attempt to render labour power determinate as labour, however momentarily, outside the traditional geographical boundaries of the workplace.

While interviewing Sunray workers at home in the evening, Jonathan was telephoned on two separate occasions by his superior regarding some aspect of his work. His job included various information technology elements and he was thus consulted about certain events while he was at home. Not only were these conversations technical but they also involved an important cultural dimension, because he would still have to present the correct attitude to his boss over the phone, conveying his commitment and dedication to the project in question. Key signifiers were observed being articulated, such as 'fun' and 'commitment', in Jonathan's discourse that suggested he was conducting identity work even in his living room. Indeed, it was surprising how much time (and space) informants used discussing the Sunray culture at home, and in cafés and bars. Even when unprompted by the researcher, it was obvious that Sunray house members had the company in their thoughts a good deal after they had officially left the workplace. Although the discourse that was recorded in this sphere outside work was not always positive it nevertheless occupied a central space in the social geography of employees and the understandings they had of themselves as employees in the company.

Cynical reason and the struggle for place

Sunray provides an interesting example of how management's attempts to revise the boundaries between life and labour involve an important spatial component. In this sense, the management of culture has material effects that are inextricably linked to the social geography of self and identity. It is the 'whole' person that the organization desires, and not just the uniform corporate self of a previous era, since motivation and productivity capabilities such as innovation and creativity are now linked to 'being yourself' (also see Fleming and Sturdy, 2006). But this managerial initiative creates a new area of struggle in which definitions and uses of place are contested. At Sunray, this contestation takes the form of creating a counter-discourse that undermines the symbolic rescripting of the place of labour and life. The management of work and non-work boundaries is experienced by employees as 'problems of self' (integrity, dignity, self-esteem, self-respect, etc.), with cynicism an especially salient manifestation of this discontent. For example, cynical employees find the attempt to make the work process fun by imitating non-work rituals problematic. There is something inexplicably 'unreal' about the silliness, merrymaking and zaniness orchestrated by management in the corporate context. The parties, games and antics do not seem to be as authentic as *actual* parties, or *actual* family get-togethers and so on. Thus the struggle over the redefinition of space is expressed in the meanings and symbolism of place found in the official discourse, especially as it relates to the management of life and labour. Let's look at the main features of this cynical discourse as expressed by a cohort interviewed both at home and in the workplace. We can see that management's manipulation of the work/non-work boundary figures consciously in their struggle.

Condescension

For a number of Sunray employees, being treated like a child was considered condescending. They thought the school and kindergarten environment gave management a rather patronizing and mawkishly paternalistic flavour. Many of the cynical workers rejected the child/teacher roles implicit in the 'culture of fun' because they wanted to be treated as rational, dignified adults. This was especially evident in the cohort of friends who lived and worked together. Indeed, Kim, Sarah, Michael and Mark (pseudonyms) had definite views on the subject. Sarah, an agent for an airline company, says the thing she would love to yell at her team leader the most [*speaking to me as if I was a superior*] is: 'I'm not a child and I won't be spoken to as one!" The idea that the employment setting was analogous to a schoolyard undermined their sense of aplomb and fuelled their cynicism. Kim, a telephone agent for an insurance company, explains:

Working at Sunray is like working for *Playschool* [*a popular and long-running children's television programme in Australia*]. It's so much like a kindergarten – a plastic, fake kindergarten. The murals on the wall, the telling off if I'm late and the patronizing tone in which I'm spoken to all give it a very childish flavour.

The boundary between work and 'school' (especially for the younger workers) appeared to have important esteem and motivation implications. The use of the school and family narrative to instil fun into the work environment at Sunray underestimated the ways in which the traditional 'seriousness' of the employment situation is connected to feelings of integrity and dignity. It is possible to make the surprising inference that the traditional climate of work might not always signify alienation and boredom – an assumption that almost all the literature on 'fun' has. Indeed, it may be the case that employees hold onto the boundary between work and non-work because the traditional employment situation (rational, relatively serious, unpretentious, etc.) is an important source of dignity and self-respect, especially in an environment deemed pretentious and fake. In its most patronizing form, paternalism strips away this rational sense of self and endeavours to instigate a weak, dependent and sometimes ignorant membership role that simultaneously positions management as benevolent caregivers. On one occasion, a group was being interviewed at home when an individual took out a handbook that included the 'fill in the blanks' exercise referred to earlier. Here are some of the exchanges that ensued among the others:

KIM: Yeah, you get a handbook and it says [*in a childish tone*] 'What are the "3 Fs"?' and you think [*in the same sarcastic tone*]. 'Oh, gee, would they be the "3 Fs" I saw on the other page?' It's very much an adult/child relationship they are trying to instigate here.

MARK: [*In a sarcastically immature voice.*] I keep mine with me on my desk all the time. I might just forget the "3 Fs" so I can never be without it.

KIM: [*In a fatherly voice.*] What about your recognition certificate, son – have you got that?

MARK: Of course!

KIM: [*Back to her own voice.*] I don't. I lost mine [*laughs*].

The evocation of family and school fails in this instance because it does not reflect pre-existing notions of what work means for employees in terms of their identities as rounded adults. The negative and unpleasant aspects of the outside institutions that were symbolically recreated in the workplace were not considered. For example, Sarah says she abhorred school, and much of the culture programme at Sunray simply reminds her of this past.

Inauthenticity

Another factor that seems to have contributed to the cynicism among the employees interviewed was a sense of inauthenticity regarding the quest to make work fun by imitating outside experiences and rituals. The failure to reproduce faithfully the complete experiences of 'family' or 'partying' resulted in some employees viewing the culture programme as pretentious and lacking honesty. This perhaps derives from both the rather maudlin depiction of family, school, weekends and parties by the company and also the perception that management are simply 'trying too hard' to recreate these images. In a focus group session with the aforementioned cohort, Kim and Sarah said that much of the culture programme resembled a rather glib charade. Mark and Michael also agreed but were little less abrasive in their evaluations. I asked the group about what they thought the aims of the fun programme were, and Kim said, 'It's all the same thing – its all just an unreal image they're trying to present of the company and I wish they wouldn't say anything at all.' Perhaps for Kim, because the culture fails to mimic successfully the so-called fun experiences of non-work life, management should not even try to make work fun in this manner because it appears disingenuous.

Kim and Sarah tended to use words such as 'plastic', 'fake' and 'cheesy' to describe the most prominent features of the Sunray culture, arguing that it lacked authenticity (or sincerity) and aimed to beguile them into subjectively conforming to the company's rules. Ironically, among these workers at least, the attempt to achieve identification via a culture of fun had the opposite effect: dis-identification and resentment. But it is not only management who are deemed inauthentic. Employees who appear to subscribe enthusiastically to the culture – rancorously labelled 'Sunray people' by the cynics – are similarly spurned. Kim told me, for example, that the company encourages people to adopt shallow personalities because these kinds of people fail to notice the disparity between the Sunray rhetoric of family/school/parties, etc. and the reality of these social roles. The fashion-conscious dress code is especially seen to represent the pretentiousness of subscribers.

Sarah finds the pretentiousness of the culture programme offensive because of the perceived creditability gap between the dominant representation of the organization (fun, egalitarian, empowering, etc.) and the reality of work and non-work experiences. This appears to translate into a poignant distrust of management and supine peers. She puts it in the following manner: 'I can't believe a lot of this stuff. I feel like saying, "How dare you stand up there and pretend to be something you are not?" They pretend to be different but they aren't and in some ways are worse than other companies because they are not real.'

The 'geographical imaginary' of struggle

The Sunray culture programme represents an interesting power strategy since it involved both typical manifestations of spatial blurring, such as the colour scheme, personalization of cubicles and café meetings, and more novel extensions of workspace outwards into the private sphere. The training tasks conducted exclusively at home by workers, the intensive counselling, 'partying' and sexualization of work relations were particularly salient. It is this two-way process, as we have termed it, that perhaps distinguishes this kind of spatial blurring from industrial examples such as paternalism (past and present) and the work ethic. This is especially significant for the literature exploring workers' engagement with call centre employment. Sunray employees did not necessarily escape workplace controls 'at the end of the shift', as Bain and Taylor (2000: 14) argue in relation to their call centre study, but found themselves still embroiled in the managerial discourse outside the workplace.

Today's managerial discourses, associated with culture management and so on, endeavour to change not only how we abstractly perceive the world and ourselves but also our lived experiences of space. As Henri Lefebvre has argued, for any set of power relations to become actualized they must produce an appropriate space: 'Any "social existence" aspiring or claiming to be "real", but failing to produce its own space, would be a strange entity indeed, a very peculiar kind of abstraction unable to escape from the ideological or even the "cultural" realm'

(Lefebvre, 1991: 53). Following this argument, we can see how the production of space at Sunray involved a power dynamic in which place and culture are closely implicated with one another. Indeed, the Sunray case is particularly useful for showing how a 'geographic imaginary' governs our perceptions of space in relation to work and organization. The phenomenologist Gaston Bachelard (1958) echoes the above point nicely when he argues that our sense of a space is as much a product of how we socially imagine it as it is of the physical dimensions of the built environment. In this sense, lived space represents a paradoxically concrete abstraction:

The objective space of a house – its corners, corridors, cellars, rooms – is far less important than what it is poetically endowed with, which is usually a quality with an imaginative or figurative value we can name and feel: thus a house may be haunted or homelike, or prison-like or magical. (Bachelard, 1958: 56)

This re-imagining of work as a space of 'fun, focus, and fulfilment' displaces the imagined boundaries between spaces of consumption, personal and family life, and the workplace. With this displacement or even dissolution between life and labour, the realm of non-work becomes marginalized as more and more of the social landscape is constituted by the post-industrial machine. This occurs at both the individual level and the collective level: individual insofar as more of the person is integrated into the discourse of labour (however it is redefined) and collective in that every non-space of production for one person is invariably the space of production for another. The space of production becomes abstracted from a fixed and isolatable area to cover the entire social body. Indeed, Michael Hardt and Antonio Negri (1994) capture this dynamic succinctly in their application of Gilles Deleuze's (1992) notion of societies of control, in which it is argued that one is never done with anything when it comes to the contemporary logic of production:

Labouring processes have moved outside the factory walls to invest the entire society. In other words, the apparent decline of the factory as site of production does not mean a decline of the regime and discipline of factory production, but means that it is no longer limited to a particular site in society. It has insinuated itself throughout all social forms of production, spreading like a virus. (Hardt and Negri, 1994: 9–10)

The Sunray case illustrates this trend in a particularly striking fashion, since the spread of labouring processes entails a two-way process. Not only has the imaginery of production colonized the non-work sphere, but associated practices such as consumption and leisure – the 'cult of cool', for example – have extended into the realm of production. Sunray employees are simultaneously subjected to the command to be productive workers as well as the requirement to be fashionable, youthful and fun characters who would not look out of place in a Levi's advertisement.

Conclusion

An obvious problem with an overly pessimistic version of the 'societies of control' thesis is that it fails to acknowledge how resistance and conflict are crucial elements of the process. Drawing our inspiration from the Sunray case and the work of Michel de Certeau (1984), the struggle over space for life and labour in contemporary organizations can be thought of in two ways. Firstly, struggle works in the sense of impeding or subverting the powerful geographical imaginary that is being imposed on existing social relations. Political struggle here interconnects the symbolic and the material dimensions of work through the contestation of where and when labour is to occur. Indeed, it is at the symbolic or imaginary level that power transforms culture into a material force, and cynicism into practical intervention with varying outcomes (especially in relation to sexuality, as we saw in chapter 5). Resistance is sparked not necessarily because of the colonization of 'raw' space but because of the discursive meanings that aim to produce certain terrains. For example, in attempting to evoke a 'party' atmosphere within the bounds of the organization, cynical employees found it a poor imitation of the 'authentic' experience. Similarly, when the geographical imaginary of the school is used to motivate workers, they feel it to be condescending and juvenile. The politics of space is therefore cultural and rather ad hoc – there is little in the way of rational and long-term planning. De Certeau argues this in relation to tactics. A tactic is a sort of spatial resistance whereby 'official space' is not used or experience in the way desired by dominant parties:

The space of the tactic is the space of the other... Thus it must play on and with a terrain imposed on it and organised by the law of a foreign power. A tactic does not have the options of planning general strategy and viewing the adversary as a whole within a distinct, visible and objectified space. It operates in isolated actions, blow by blow. (de Certeau, 1984: 93)

This 'blow by blow' vision of struggle over the meaning of space leads to a second and less intuitive perspective. As mentioned in chapter 3, where we posited the concept of struggle as a supplement to current notions of resistance, the very trajectory of power relations is determined partly by resistance, since it is never complete before its application. The configuration of domination that we see emerging on the spatial dimension in contemporary organizations such as Sunray is an incomplete admixture of power and resistance, which worker struggles have determined to some extent. As workers resist the alienation of the uniform corporate cultures prevalent in the 1980s, asserting more of this individuality in the workplace, this very energy was absorbed into the corporate machine (Fleming and Sturdy, 2006). It is now the exhortation simply to 'be yourself' that is being resisted by workers – a form of struggle that involves a very pronounced spatial theme.

PART 3

Overt, organized and collective struggle

7 | Discursive struggle: the case of globalization in the public sector

> Why is it that the word 'globalization' has
> recently entered into our discourse in the
> way it has? Who put it there and why?
> ...words like 'imperialism', 'colonialism'
> and 'neo-colonialism' have increasingly
> taken a back seat to 'globalization' as a way
> to organize thoughts and chart political
> possibilities.
>
> (Harvey, 1995: 1)

In the last two chapters we saw how employees used various tactics to engage an apparently overpowering corporate culture. We found that these close engagements undermined the company culture at the same time as perpetuating the body corporate. Interestingly, most of these struggles against the corporate culture did not appear in public. Like most workplaces, the discontent, anger, concern and hurt experienced by employees took place in the hidden crevasses and folds of organizational life. For some, it is only within these concealed spaces of 'micro-politics' that struggle can be expressed (e.g. Thomas and Davies, 2005; Sennett, 2006). The voices of dissent in organizations are to be found in rebellious subcultures, conspiratorial glances, carefully timed flatulence and the omnipresent 'demotivation poster'. However, we would be sadly mistaken to assume that struggle in today's organizations takes place only through workplace 'infrapolitics' (Scott, 1990). Many aspects of work life are subject to publicly declared political contestation. Struggle sometimes involves 'large-scale, collective changes in the domains of state policy, corporate practice, social structure, cultural norms, and daily lived experience' (Ganesh, Zoller and Cheney, 2004: 177). To draw an accurate image of struggle in organizations, we must recognize the obstinate existence of publicly voiced dissent that haunts the contemporary corporate world and its auxiliary powers.

While much attention has been lavished on the subtle micro-practices of resistance, it must be remembered that the history of the Western workplace is one marked by organized struggle with and against managerial control. Such contestation has come in many different guises, including Luddite protests (Thompson, 1968), guild-based syndicalism (Cole, 1917), worker autonomism (Hardt and Negri, 2000) and, more importantly, the trade union movement. A wide repertoire of formally organized resistance has developed out of the union movement, such as planned strikes, negotiating and bargaining with employers, intervening in national politics, as well as political 'consciousness raising'. Alongside this official repertoire of unionized resistance is a parallel world of unofficial but highly organized strategies for workers' struggles, including wildcat strikes, the go-slow, and working to rule. Despite the decline of union power in the 1980s (Disney, Gosling and Machin, 1995; Wallerstein and Western, 2000), unions continue to play an important role in the workplace (Bradley, Erickson, Stephenson and Williams, 2000). Moreover, new forms of union activism have recently appeared, in the guise of transnational collectivism (Munck, 2000), 'community' or 'social movement' unionism (Clawson and Clawson, 1999) and online unionism (Carter, Kornberger and Clegg, 2003). These innovations remind us that employee unions continue to be an important vehicle of collective struggle in today's organizations.

Trade unions are not the only form of collective resistance in the workplace. Various social movements play an increasingly prevalent part in challenging, transforming and at times destroying corporations, or even whole industries (see, for example, Davis, McAdam, Scott and Zald, 2005, and Zald and Berger, 1978). Social movements seek to do this through cultural innovations such as inventing new symbols, social repertoires and identities (Melucci, 1996). At the centre of these symbolic politics is the struggle for the cultural *recognition* that collective identities are worthy, legitimate and acceptable (Fraser, 1997; Honneth, 1995). It may be recalled that the theme of political recognition was introduced in chapter 5, in relation to sexuality. Apropos social movements, such struggles aim to achieve legitimacy as a rightful and worthy social collective (deserving of the benefits accrued by other dominant parties), and in so doing build a positive sense of identity and community.

Social movements often find their institutional expression in a certain type of organizational structure. These are 'a complex, or formal, organization that identified its goals with the preferences of a social movement or a countermovement and attempt to implement those goals' (Zald and McCarthy, 1989: 20). Social movement organizations are typically formal, semi-hierarchical organizations that have official procedures, practices, systems of offices and a basis in law. The central task of the social movement organization is to articulate the multiple concerns of a grievant collective as a single authoritative voice. A wide range of social movement organizations have played a vital role in struggles around corporate policy. These relate to interventions in connection with pollution and environmental degradation (Lounsbury, 2001), the organization of oligopolistic markets (Hensmans, 2003), the status of gay and lesbian groups (Carroll and Ratner, 2001) and fair trade schemes (Jaffee, Kloppenburg and Monroy, 2004).

In this chapter, we explore the role of unions and social movements in and around the struggle for organization. We do this by considering how a number of unions and social movements have contested restructuring initiatives justified by a discourse of globalization. We focus on one public sector organization – the Australian Broadcasting Corporation (ABC) – and demonstrate how a coalition of senior management and government policy-makers sought to radically reform the broadcaster in the name of globalization. Instead of cynically sneering at this discourse, a coalition of union and social movement organizations opposed it vigorously. This involved an intense and very public struggle. Groups engaged in this struggle by using a surprising range of tactics, which included appropriating dominant discourses, using shared discourses and resurfacing old discourses. Through this struggle with the discourse of globalization, the unions and social movements were able to fundamentally transform what the idea of globalization meant and how it could be used in the ABC. This allowed the resistant movements to undermine the notion that market-driven globalization is inevitable and unquestionable.

Discourses of globalization, discourses of dissent

During the 1990s the discussion about globalization exploded. Managers and consultants scrambled to ensure that their organizations could cope in this new world of planet-wide social relations and international competition. While globalization certainly involves increased transterritorial economic, political and cultural flows (Held, McGrew, Goldblatt and Perraton, 1999), a significant aspect of the phenomenon is the very discourse of globalization (Rosamond, 2003). This discourse had 'the effect of generating institutional structures for the "global", mediated through policies and techniques of *necessary adaptation*' (Cameron and Palan, 1999: 270; emphasis in original). That is, the near-ubiquitous discourses of globalization proffered by economists, politicians and business leaders actually shaped the available options for government policy-making and the management of public sector organizations (du Gay, 2000a). This had a self-fulfilling function, as 'the very discourse and rhetoric of globalization may serve to summon precisely the effects that such a discourse attributes to globalization itself' (Hay and Marsh, 2000: 9).

Despite their apparent power and ubiquity, discourses of globalization have been an object of intense struggle. Perhaps one of the most notable challenges to this discourse during the early part of the twenty-first century has been the so-called 'anti-globalization' movement (e.g. Fischer and Ponniah, 2003; Notes from Nowhere, 2003). This comprises a whole range of social movement and union organizations. Through a range of high-profile campaigns and protests, this loose coalition has engaged in a poignant struggle with the discourses and practices of 'neo-liberal globalization'. Why does globalization inevitably mean economic rationalization, loss of community control and the corporate colonization of the public sphere? This protest movement articulated a loose but collective 'no' to globally oriented market-based initiatives. As well as voicing displeasure about the spreading tendrils of the global commodity market, this disparate movement has offered 'many yesses' by suggesting alternative economies, lifestyles and ideological positions (Kingsnorth, 2003).

In many ways, the 'anti-globalization' movement is a form of 'globalization from below' (Appadurai, 2000). It is made up of a whole series of situated protest groups, ranging from North American ecological activists to southern African AIDS campaigners and South American landless peoples. Through their diverse struggles, each of these groups has sought to modify and shape what globalization is and what it could be. By 'tactically' appropriating the language of globalization, some of these groups have been able to craft alternative discourses of globalization (Banerjee and Linstead, 2001). This involves the language of globalization being 'appropriated and drawn into local spaces by actors who may treat the discourse as a resource' (Fairclough and Thomas, 2004: 392). This opens up the possibility of 'slippage' in the language of globalization. The result is that the apparently all-powerful language of the global marketplace can be actively used and crystallized in radical ways. This gives local people the space to translate what appears to be a standardized discourse of globalization into a language that mirrors their local emancipatory concerns (Salskov-Iversen, Hansen and Bislev, 2000). As this happens, discourses of globalization can be linked to particular local projects in unpredictable and disruptive ways. Through tactical appropriation, the apparently homogeneous language of globalization may be given a significant local flavour that arms communities against the corporate colonization of their worlds.

From nation to market at the ABC

The struggle around the discourse of globalization is well demonstrated in the much-publicised case of the Australian Broadcasting Corporation. The ABC was established in 1933. It was inspired by the BBC (British Broadcasting Corporation) model of public broadcasting, which aimed to create a liberal public sphere to 'educate, inform and entertain' (Reith, 1924; ABC, 1939). It resembles the BBC in that it operates at arm's length under state legislation and is controlled by a government-appointed board. But there are some differences. The ABC has always shared the nation's airwaves with commercial media providers. Also, the public subscription model was replaced by direct government funding in 1948. The ABC has grown from a single national radio network to four radio networks, a national television network with associated production facilities, an international radio service, an internet service, seventeen local radio stations broadcasting in fifty-nine localities and a chain of ABC shops throughout Australia.

The core goal of the ABC until the mid-1970s consisted of *nation building*, particularly through the development of a national public sphere, a unique national culture, the inclusion of far-flung communities and the presentation of a favourable image of Australia abroad. This nationalist framework eroded in the late 1970s as two new goals and accompanying language became central in its day-to-day operations. The first was the call for the ABC to move away from the middle-class ideal of a single Anglo-Irish culture so that Australia's ethnic diversity could be recognized. The second was the rise of a neo-liberal discourse that suggested the ABC should become more business-like and develop an enterprise culture (Inglis, 1983). This discourse was buttressed by funding cuts and a major government inquiry, which resulted in the Australian Broadcasting *Commission* being renamed the Australian Broadcasting *Corporation* (Dix, 1981). Along with opera-tional and legislative changes that made the broadcaster more 'business-like', funding cuts and staff reductions continued throughout the 1980s. These gathered momentum with the election of a liberal government headed by John Howard in 1996 (Williams, 1996; Dempster, 2000).

The new media environment

To justify wide-ranging restructuring, senior management articulated a new discourse arguing that there had been tumultuous changes in the media environment. This discourse appeared between 1990 and 1992, when the belief that the ABC was positioned in a 'national media market' was replaced with the language of the 'new media environ-ment' that was global in scope. While the former discourse situated the ABC's activities in a competitive market made up of other nationally based media companies, the 'new media environment' discourse suggested a groundbreaking change in the nature of this marketplace. New technologies such as pay-TV, satellite broadcasting, digital deli-very mechanisms and the internet would plunge the broadcaster into a competitive international arena. To survive, senior management argued that the ABC now had to adapt or perish. This ushered in a more 'globally' focused operating and management strategy that rein-vigorated pre-existing neo-liberal reforms. In the mid-1990s a series of new media projects explicitly targeting international markets began, many of which were joint ventures with private sector organizations. Another wave of restructuring and downsizing programmes took place, most conspicuously the 1996 'one ABC' (ABC, 1996) project and the 1997 Mansfield Inquiry (Mansfield, 1997), which aimed to build cross-technological relationships to address the challenges of the so-called 'global age'. Government-appointed boards of directors and CEOs sympathetic with the new policy were responsible for pitching this transformed ABC to both the public (or 'consumers') and workers via a new organizational culture.

By articulating a new discourse, senior management sought to create the impression that the world of broadcasting had irrevocably changed with the advent of globalization. Typically this rapid globalization of the media market was framed in terms of globalizing technologies. The 'new media market' was thought to be driven by 'changes in technology, which are revolutionising the delivery and nature of broadcasting services' (ABC, 1991: 13), and necessitated the reorganization of the ABC. The rise of globalizing technologies also led to 'a media environment characterised by new media forms and converging technologies' (ABC, 1997: 11). The advent of these technologies with a global reach was framed as 'momentous' and similar to '1956 with [the introduction of] television, the ABC is today presented with the opportunity to participate in a new medium. The rapid growth of the Internet as a communications system and the emerging popularity of other multimedia products such as CD ROM will have an impact on all media organisations' (ABC, 1996: 48). This new discourse indicated that the shifts were far-reaching and would cause 'revolutionary changes' (ABC, 1993: 13).

Under the auspices of globalization, technological transformations were thought to necessitate organisational restructuring automatically. In order to 'reposition itself to take into account...a media environment characterised by new media forms and converging technologies', the ABC saw 'sound creative reasons for embarking on restructurings' (ABC, 1997: 11). The 'momentous' shift in the broadcasting environment was an opportunity to put forward a 'bold agenda confirming the ABC's role as a comprehensive and creative publicly funded national broadcaster with a vital part to play in the future media-scape' (ABC, 1997: 10). Shifts in strategy emphasized a seamless line connecting different 'content producers' within the ABC:

The ABC is no longer a broadcaster of discrete services – radio, television or online. By breaking down these divisions, the 'One ABC' strategy has responded to the creative challenges of a converging media environment. It has also delivered productivity through rationalisation and collaboration... In a competitive environment marked by inroads of pay TV and accelerated investment in commercial online services, the ABC this year maintained its audience base across radio and television, and saw the continued strong growth of ABC online. (ABC, 1999: 17)

The changes associated with the new media environment discourse were also linked with changing work practices. The discourse 'demand[ed] greater flexibility' and changes to 'existing industrial agreements and work practices' that 'hinder change and flexibility' (ABC, 1999: 56). The rise of new media environment involved the suggestion that new global markets were rapidly appearing. Other markets could emerge from new 'delivery mechanisms' for ABC programming, such as pay-TV and narrowcasting. For instance, Radio Australia (the ABC's international broadcaster) sought to take advantage of 'target markets in Asia':

Radio Australia is discussing initiatives with the tertiary education programming for target markets in Asia. It is hoped this involvement will provide access to programming not otherwise available as well as funding for additional transmission time. (ABC, 1997: 38)

Although many of the restructuring initiatives were merely a continuation of the neo-liberal commercialization project, they now gained a powerful impetus in the 'rhetoric and reality' of globalization. By articulating a new language of the new media environment, senior management deemed globalization to be an external force that was out of the hands of government and bureaucratic officials. By reducing the phenomenon of globalization to a technological issue, senior management was able to legitimate some major institutional changes at the ABC. Perhaps the most notable was an explicit internationalization strategy, which appeared during 1992. The upshot of this was the creation of a satellite television channel broadcast to Asia called Australia Television International (which was later sold to a commercial channel) and an aborted venture with commercial media firms called Australia Information Media, which sought to set up a twenty-four-hour news television channel. The increased emphasis on the global market was also used to legitimate the deepening application of management techniques borrowed from the private sector, which included an increased emphasis on outsourcing functions to private companies, adopting a more 'entrepreneurial' approach by seeking to expand marketing and sponsorship opportunities, and rapidly increasing reliance and spending on management consultancies. Alongside the rise of managerialism there was a notable commercialization of labour relations, through continued and sustained job cuts and contracting out work to independent companies, particularly in the area of producing and programming content. All these changes were legitimated as an objective and consequentially apolitical necessity of changing times.

Contestation at the ABC

The discourse of the 'new media environment' was an important catalyst for institutional changes at the ABC during the 1990s. Corporate advisors and appointed senior management attempted to push through reforms by introducing a new discourse that framed them as inevitable and in the interests of all consumers. This suturing of what globalization means and the range of legitimate interpretations available formed a comprehensive discursive regime but was nevertheless fragile and open to criticism. Given the historically embedded ethos of the public service among ABC workers and an abiding consumer commitment to non-market-based media provision, it is not surprising that the discourse of the new media environment was never totally accepted. Two ABC staff unions (Media, Entertainment and Arts Alliance [MEAA] and the Community and Public Sector Union [CPSU]) and a social movement organization (the consumer pressure group Friends of the ABC [FABC]) promulgated alternative discourses that countered the new policies. In concert, they struggled with the official discourse by way of three tactics.

Appropriating dominant discourses

The first discursive tactic involved resistant groups appropriating and using discourses that were part of management's dominant lexicon and ideology. The first example of this tactic of appropriating dominant discourse was when the language of the *new media environment* was turned back upon policy-makers to criticize the integration of the ABC into a global market. The striking funding cuts of the ABC's international broadcasting arm, Radio Australia, contrasted directly with the operational necessities of a 'global player'. Agreeing with management and the government apropos the importance of globalization, ironically the FABC said that funding cuts could be supported only by a government that was actually ignorant of the new media environment.

Globalization has come to broadcasting in a big way, but word of this does not seem to have filtered down to the present federal government. Or perhaps it has, and for reasons that seemed good a couple of years ago, the government chose to ignore it. (FABC, 1999a: 6)

The new media environment discourse was also tactically utilized by the FABC to question government underfunding of the ABC's attempts to develop a more globally attuned market strategy. They asked, 'Why did the Minister of Communications say his media release budget provides a secure digital future for the ABC and SBS [Special Broadcasting Service] when he gave the ABC only one-third of the money needed to convert to digital?' (FABC, 2000a: 6). If the government was unwilling to fund these extensions into the international media environment then this was noticeably at odds with the dominant rhetoric.

The second case of resistant groups tactically appropriating dominant discourses involved the FABC using *commercial* discourses. They did this by countering charges that the ABC was an inefficient public service and favourably compared the production costs of the organization with other public and commercial broadcasters.

Despite the fact that ABC produces TV and radio with more staff than the commercial networks, relative costs per hour of broadcasting show that the ABC is twice as efficient. For radio services per broadcast hour, the ABC's costs are 40% of those of the commercial sector; the cost of television provision per broadcast hour by the ABC is 36% of the commercial sector's. (FABC, 2000a: 8)

Resistance groups also harnessed senior management's reliance on popularity ratings as the sole criterion for judging the validity of a particular programming strategy. Industry-standard measures of audience *share* typically revealed low ratings for the ABC, which was then used to forward the case for market integration and competition. But the FABC developed an alternative *reach*-based measure, which demonstrated 'that 86% of Australians use an ABC service each week' (FABC, 2000a: 7). By appropriating the managerial criterion of popularity ratings the FABC was able to discredit the 'low ratings' argument. The use of expert knowledge concerning 'best practice' to ridicule ABC management was a comparable attempt to turn the dominant discourse against itself. The MEAA, CPSU and FABC all argued that commercially oriented employment practices almost always 'create a management culture that shies from controversy and offers little reward for taking risks on air' (FABC, 1999a: 3). For an organization that needs to be innovative and dynamic in a global environment this is not a suitable management approach. Indeed, commercial management at the ABC is said to have been akin to 'the goose-step school of leadership... Autocracy doesn't work in creative organizations. That's why the best firms look more like orchestras than like armies' (FABC, 2000a: 10).

Surfacing shared discourses

The second tactic employed by oppositional groups involved surfacing and manipulating relatively uncontested premises shared by management, worker representatives and consumer groups. These assumptions were used to contradict the 'new media environment' policy. The first instance of using a shared discourse involved resistance groups using the assumption that ABC should act as a *civilizing force* in society through supporting debate, arts, culture and sciences. The broadcaster is described as having 'a broad humanizing impact, across many fields of high and popular culture' (FABC, 2000b: 7). In an FABC newsletter the ABC's mission is described as advancing 'the moral and intellectual life of the nation' through excellence in programming aimed at the entire public, which is certainly a sentiment that management forcefully concurred with as well. But, with market concerns and the new media environment dictating the direction of the organization, this public interest agenda was threatened. Instead of programming aspiring towards high cultural standards and debate around diverse issues, it was perceived that marketization would lead to a more populist approach akin to its commercial competitors. Indeed, '[i]f the ABC does not carry the commission to operate in the public interest who else will? The ABC is our only hope' (FABC, 1999a: 3). Here the public interest is understood not only in terms of 'the majority' but also marginalized cultures entirely absent on commercial programming.

This approach led opposition groups to evoke a related shared discourse regarding the ABC's responsibility for nurturing and developing Australian culture. Even though this was still an official organizational objective, it was argued that commercialization and integration into a global media market would see programming inundated with inexpensive American sitcoms and the decline of Australian content. The outcome would be an abdication of the broadcasters role of 'hold[ing] up a mirror to the whole country' and acting as a 'unifying agent, the most important cultural institution in the country' (FABC, 1999b: 5). Further moves towards international content would also 'limit the ability of up and coming Australian musicians to be heard' (CPSU,

1997c). And particular artistic communities were represented as being harmed by cuts associated with new media environment discourse:

'Jazz Tracks' contribution to the Australian jazz community is invaluable. It has given young artists a chance to record original music and have it broadcast nationally. If the ABC doesn't do it no one will', he said. 'Australia's jazz and cultural community will be poorer for the cuts.' (CPSU, 1997b)

The second example of surfacing shared discourses involved resistant groups using *accountability* discourse. The MEAA and CPSU constantly stressed the traditional relationship between public organizations such as the ABC, government policy and the citizenry that elects them. Rather than accountability being constructed as a mechanism of government control through endless inquiries, the unions couched it in more democratic terms whereby the ABC was accountable to a diverse voting public – for example, funding large executive salaries and 'non-core' activities such as satellite broadcasting in contravention of the public accountability of the ABC as well as the principal of quality. 'Money is being diverted away from programme-making to pay for the new executive structure. The ABC is becoming increasingly commercialised. More and more programme-making is being outsourced and quality is being sacrificed' (CPSU, 2001). The ABC's internet joint venture with Australia's largest telecommunications company, Telstra, was also represented as an abdication of norms associated with accountability:

The Parliament and the Australian public have a right to know the precise details of the secret arrangements with Telstra and judge whether the risks associated with this kind of deal should be taken. (CPSU, 2000)

In this example, the theme of accountability is used in at least two senses. It questions the diversion of resources to projects driven by new media environment imperatives. It is also used to challenge the lack of democratic transparency of strategies that positioned the broadcaster in the new media environment.

A third example of resistance groups surfacing shared discourses was when they evoked *independence* discourse. This was used to represent the ABC as an institution autonomous from the state and government that provided value-free information. It was an excellent resource for resistance groups to affirm the broadcaster's non-alignment with state or business. It was used to show how senior management's whole-hearted adoption of media market discourse caused 'the ABC's independence and editorial independence...to be weakened' (CPSU, 2001). Freedom from commercial or government intrusion was represented as particularly important; due to 'the concentration of media ownership in this country, a properly funded and independent ABC is essential' (CPSU, 1997a). The notion of independence also countered commercialization initiatives such as the proposed web-based joint venture between the ABC and Telstra. The CPSU represented the proposed joint venture as a serious threat:

The Australian community expects total independence of their national broadcaster. This independence is threatened by the ABC Board's decision to proceed with plans for the ABC to become a major content provider for Telstra's on-line services. (CPSU, 2000)

Indeed, under the joint venture 'the ABC will be required to specially produce and tailor stories for Telstra. This is a potentially corrupting influence as the ABC places itself on a drip feed for commercial revenue' (CPSU, 2000). Such a prospect indicated the possible danger and corrupting influence of a swift drive towards commercialism. This was highlighted by suggesting that recent scandals in other parts of the Australian media resulted from a lack of independence from market influences. The FABC used the 'cash for comments' scandal involving prominent Sydney radio talkback hosts John Laws and Alan Jones to highlight the susceptibility of commercial media organizations to inappropriate influences. By including paid promotions in editorial slots, Jones and Laws flouted the norms of journalistic independence. The FABC represented this as an implication of commercialization in the industry:

The need for an independent and fearless ABC has never been stronger. It is most obvious in the wake of the talkback/kickback revelations, but there are other trends in the public life of Australia that point to the ABC as our best hope for a healthy democracy. (FABC, 1999a: 3)

Reviving traditional discourses

A third tactic used by resistance groups was the revival of traditional discourses that were once central to the ABC but had since disappeared. A major example of this involved reviving a *non-commercial discourse*. This discourse was prominent in the ABC until the early 1980s but receded with the rise of market-based models of management and resource allocation. The MEAA and FABC selectively returned to this sentiment as a plausible approach to broadcasting.

A non-commercial ethos was articulated through the vilification of business-oriented ventures undertaken by the broadcaster. The perils of commercialism in the ABC are colourfully described as 'ominous' (FABC, 2000a: 1), a 'monster' that 'gobbles up and spits out the standards of public broadcasting' (FABC, 2000a: 7), 'entrepreneurial quicksand' associated with the 'murky waters of sponsorship and advertising' (FABC, 2000a: 5), a 'slippery slide' (FABC, 1999b: 5) and 'the thin end of the wedge' (FABC, 2000a: 2). In each of these instances, commercial forces were represented as being profoundly dangerous, and the ABC was offered as a fragile institution requiring protection from a brutal marketplace.

It was widely argued that the choice of programme content would be compromised by the perpetuation of a market mentality, with the example of the increasing commercial influence on the ABC's website frequently referenced.

How long before an ABC content provider would be told: 'Mate, that science stuff is going down well on-line. Why don't we drop poetry and books and do more about dinosaurs?' That's how you destroy independent broadcasting. That's how the marketing imperative takes over. It's terrifyingly simple. (FABC, 2000a: 3)

Commercialism was also felt to be extending beyond programming decisions and interfering with the daily lives of the Australian people. The ABC would need to abandon its role as 'a truly independent broadcaster' and result in an increasingly centralized media industry bereft of any outlet unburdened by the narrow demands of profit: 'Given the concentration of media ownership in this country, a properly funded and independent ABC is essential' (CPSU, 1997a). An example of why this is the case was seized upon when a former Disney executive was hired as a consultant to identify revenue-raising opportunities in children's programming. Corresponding with the CPSU, the FABC drew on an anti-commercialism discourse to represent the proposed changes as instituting a hyper-commercial 'Disney-style empire from the popularity of ABC for Kids, which would include an ABC site at Fox Studios, ABC characters in theme parks. . .and ABC chairs and videos in the rooms of hairdressers and dentists' (FABC, 2000b: 3). The flagrant disregard for the values of non-commercialism 'horrified ABC employees, and staff board member, Mr Ian Henschke, said the national broadcaster "should not take advantage of children or their parents"' (FABC, 2000b: 3). This anti-commercial stance recovered traditional values that the discourse of globalization had attempted to erase from organizational culture and memory. While management replied by framing this as juvenile nostalgia, the FABC said they were looking forward by viewing non-commercialism as a viable *future* for the ABC.

The spoils of resistance

On the surface, the discourse of the new media environment appeared to be a strong and stable one that legitimated large-scale changes in the ABC's strategy, organizing practices and labour practices. However, it did not prove to be invincible. Through the tactics of appropriating existing discourses, using shared discourses and creating new discourses, three resistance groups were able to seriously call into question the policy-makers' and senior managers' version of the 'new media environment'. There were a number of results of this dramatic unsettling of a discourse that had previously seemed so natural and entrenched. The first was extremely public mass actions, such as street protests and strikes on the part of staff and citizens. These mass actions coalesced under a banner of 'Save our ABC'. While such protests were certainly driven by very material concerns such as job cuts, the way in which protesters voiced their demands and concerns was saturated with the discourses discussed above. These large-scale actions precipitated a less hard-nosed emphasis on market-orientated reforms at the ABC. One example of this included job cuts in Radio Australia being greatly reduced following the protests. A second example was the rolling back of the commercialization of ABC Online (the ABC's website) following popular pressure and a government inquiry (also see Spicer, 2005). Despite these limited victories, market-oriented reforms continued throughout the period studied, and picked up pace following the appointment of a new managing director in 1999.

Notwithstanding the limited successes in challenging institutional changes, the various resistance groups were certainly effective in reaffirming a language of national civil service in connection with the central role of the ABC. This meant that the ABC was forced to legitimate itself and its activities in terms of serving the national interest. Strategic reshuffling led to a move away from internationally focused activities during the latter part of the 1990s. This included selling the international television service to a commercial operator and even seeking to retrench international radio operations. Indeed, the way the ABC legitimates itself continued to be underpinned by a language of nationalism and, occasionally, localism, with some rather anachronistic nation-building goals haunting the way the public broadcaster understands itself. However, it should be said that these nation-building goals are still hotly contested. In the conservative political climate of Australia at the turn of the century, the notion of nation building provided the ABC with a tool for propagating an Anglo-Australian culture across an increasingly heterogeneous population. For others, however, the ABC has served as a space where these nationalistic attitudes may be called into question.

Struggles with globalization

The ongoing tension and struggle at the ABC remind us that collective forms of resistance such as unions and social movements have not been replaced by underground discontent. Rather, unions and social movements play an important role in the struggle for, against and with organizational initiatives. Unions and social movement organizations sought to engage critically with the language of globalization. This discursive struggle had the effect of reshaping the political context in which debate and deliberation about the future of the ABC could occur. In bringing the future of the ABC into the realm of public debate, managers and state officials were forced to justify their restructuring plans rigorously. Much of this involved a dynamic dialogue among the stakeholders that was very public. Not only did the FABC, MEAA and CPSU respond to managerial initiatives in a critical manner, but also those criticisms themselves were subsequently counter-targeted by the government and ABC managers. For instance, the furore over the Disney consultant provoked managerial claims that protest groups were stuck in the past. But such a public outburst prompted normative reflection among all organizational stakeholders and the general public regarding the role of the organization.

This internal and external scrutiny during the reform process has resulted in traditional understandings of the ABC being confirmed as absolutely central to the organization (e.g. providing a civilizing force, being accountable to the public, being independent, etc.). This means that any future globalizing reform on the part of senior management at the ABC would have to incorporate many of these themes. This is evidenced in the fact that even when senior management urged a head-long charge into the new media environment they also acknowledged that the ABC had to remain a public broadcaster. Discourses of public service were also significant in management arguments about how potentially globalizing technologies would be used (Spicer, 2005). This suggests that at least some of the values associated with public sector organizations do not simply disappear with the rise of a globalization discourse. Rather, the public sector may be linked to images of globalization in unexpected ways.

Much of the current debate suggests that the discourse of globalization is relatively singular in that it is equated with the increased spread of borderless markets (Larner, 1998). In contrast, we found that globalization discourses at the ABC were plurivocal and unstable. During the early phases of the reform process, management and government officials had a rather simplistic and formulaic understanding of globalization regarding the ABC – that it simply referred to lower government funding and increased exposure to international market forces. The contestation process, of which discourse played a major role, fragmented the meaning of globalization along certain socio-political fault lines. For example, the FABC, MEAA and CPSU employed the new media environment discourse to lobby for more public funding. Ironically, this dominant 'fixing signifier' (Laclau and Mouffe, 1985) came to represent the opposite meaning to that intended by ABC management. This was also the case with the neo-liberal discourses of economic efficiency and consumer demand. By tactically appropriating the dominant discourse for alternative aims it became possible to reorient and impugn the narrative of 'inevitability' with its own symbolic resources. By tactically occupying the concepts of globalization, managerialism and efficiency, their meanings were significantly changed.

Conclusion

In relation to workplace struggle, the ABC case has implications for how we conceptualize the relationship between the public sector and the forces of globalization. The restructuring conducted under the aegis of globalization has brought about complex changes within the ABC in ways that cannot be explained through a 'zero-sum' equation between the public sector and the global market (Brenner, 1998). Instead, we witness a seemingly antinomian situation in which a public sector organization is used to facilitate an anti-state stance under the auspices of the globalization discourse. Interestingly, this finding seems to run contrary to an emergent stream of thought that suggests the state and public sector institutions are no longer an effective vehicle for resisting global capitalism. In particular, Hardt and Negri's (2000) extremely influential treatise on globalization contends that nation state institutions have all but disappeared as a fruitful locus of resistance because the transnational capitalist 'Empire' has co-opted even the most robust public place into the juggernaut of accumulation. They take the 'Empire' itself as the most propitious terrain upon which to advance a resistant project:

We believe that toward the end of challenging and resisting Empire and its world market, it is necessary to pose any alternative at an equally global level. Any proposition of a particular community in isolation, defined in racial, religious, regional terms, 'delinked' from Empire, shielded from its powers by fixed boundaries, is destined to end up as a kind of ghetto. Empire cannot be resisted by a project aimed at a limited, local autonomy. We cannot move back to any previous social form, nor move forward in isolation. Rather, we must push through Empire to come out the other side. (Hardt and Negri, 2000: 206)

These sentiments express a general tendency in studies suggesting that, to contest processes of globalization successfully, it is necessary for resistance groups to abandon the state and articulate their practices of resistance at a global level (Zeller, 2000; Herod, 2001). Instead, we find that resistant groups were also able to appropriate a political imaginary of the state and public service in order to contest the authority of globalization discourses in a way that permits the reinvention of the public service ethos as a viable project (also see du Gay, 2000b). It is debatable whether this romantic image of the nation state and public service ethos is desirable, especially given its elitist middle-class focus. However, it does appear to be an important discourse for animating struggle. Our findings suggest that resistance groups play an important role in restructuring public sector organizations in a manner that can transform the discourse of globalization. Further, the resistance we observed was not exactly avant-garde radicalism but tinged with cultural conservatism and traditional liberalism. This contrasts with the romanticism informing many studies of resistance to globalization, which often miss the conventional and less exotic activities found in dull middle-class neighbourhoods. In the next chapter, we explore the much-contested notion of 'justice' that often underlies these forms of struggle.

8 | Struggles for justice: wharfies, queers and capitalists

The question is not whether we will be
extremists, but what kind of extremists we
will be. Will we be extremists for hate or for
love? Will we be extremists for the preservation of injustice or the extension of justice?

(Martin Luther King)

Struggle is not exclusively a preoccupation for disgruntled shop-floor
workers. In each chapter of this book we have sought to explore how
struggle lies at the heart of organizational life. We have tried to uncover
some of the ways that people struggle against and with managerial
initiatives. These struggles are sparked by a whole range of situations,
including antagonistic structural positions between workers and
employers, attempts by employees to build dignified identities, the
persistence of subcultures of opposition in the workplace, and so
forth. We propose that almost all these flash points of struggle seem
to point to some elemental concern for a fair distribution of resources,
the recognition of oneself as a dignified and meaningful person, and
the right to make decisions within the organization. In other words,
animating many struggles in organizations is the issue of *justice*.

In this chapter we hope to show how struggles for justice are a central
part of organizational life. In order to do this we use the illustrative
examples of the Melbourne Port dispute (Australia), the gay and lesbian,
transgender and bisexual (GLTB) employee movement and the shareholder rights movement that sought to challenge the managerial control of large corporations in the United States. We will argue that these
struggles are sparked by a sense of violation of basic social justice claims,
however large or small. We revisit the work of the political theorist
Nancy Fraser (1997, 2003, 2005), briefly introduced in chapter 5.
There, her work was used to untangle power and resistance relations
in the context of sexualized control and expression. In this chapter,

we concentrate and expand on three types of justice claims that people make in organizations: the claim for just recognition, the claim for the just distribution of resources and the claim for just political representation.

In unpacking Fraser's analysis of justice in more detail, we position it as a key fulcrum that underlies many forms of struggle in work organizations. In particular, we demonstrate in this chapter how, once a struggle has been initiated around one justice claim, the aggrieved group then often makes broader justice claims. By expanding their claims to other political concerns, resistant groups are able to strengthen the appeal of their claims to potential allies. This usually means that a workplace struggle links its own particular claim for justice to a more general, society-wide justice claim.

Theorizing justice

Many of the struggles that occur in and around organizations involve implicit or explicit claims for justice. At a fundamental level, these calls for justice involve a demand for *parity of participation* in organizational life. Indeed, struggles to overcome injustice involve 'dismantling institutionalized obstacles that prevent some people from participating on a par with others, as full partners in social interaction' (Fraser, 2005: 5–6). According to Fraser this entails a just distribution of resources to all participants, just recognition of all participants and just representation of those who are participants. In what follows, we explain Fraser's conceptualization of justice, focusing on how different struggles seek to achieve recognition, redistribution and participation. We also discuss the criteria we might use to judge a struggle as a successful attempt to achieve justice.

Perhaps the most widely recognized form of justice that Fraser (1997) touches upon is the socio-economic parity of participation. This involves the just distribution of resources and material life chances (e.g. Rawls, 1971; Dworkin, 1981; Sen, 1985). For her, socio-economic injustice involves forms of harm that are rooted in the economy. This includes a range of phenomena, such as 'exploitation (having the fruits of one's labour appropriated for the benefit of others), economic marginalization (being confined to undesirable or poorly paid work or being denied access to income-generating labour altogether), and deprivation (being denied an adequate material standard of living)' (Fraser, 1997: 13). The remedy for these material injustices is the redistribution of economic resources and opportunities, including 'redistributing income and/or wealth, reorganizing the division of labour, changing the structure of property ownership, democratizing the procedures by which investment decisions are made, or transforming other basic structures' (2003: 13). When a collective engages in a struggle for redistribution, they may be defined as 'class or class-like collectives which are defined distinctively by a distinctive relation to the market or the means of production' (2003: 14). Examples of such collectives include the working class, the underclass and perhaps women (insofar as they undertake most unpaid labour in most economies). Attempts to rectify material injustice involve endeavours to banish material differences between groups by ensuring a fair distribution of life chances. Thus, a crucial part of the struggle for justice consists of attempts to create fair patterns of distribution within an organization.

Alongside struggles for socio-economic justice, Fraser identifies a second, more culturally oriented form of justice. This involves cultural or symbolic parity of participation, which requires the proper recognition of individual or group identities. She argues that claims for recognition as a worthy, dignified and valuable individual or group are vital for achieving social justice (also see Honneth, 1995). For her, forms of cultural-symbolic injustices involve patterns of harm that are rooted in how we interpret the world, how we communicate with others and how we identify others and ourselves. Such socio-cultural injustices include

cultural domination (being subjected to patterns of interpretation and communication which are associated with another culture and are alien and/or hostile to one's own); non-recognition (being rendered invisible by means of the authoritative representational, communicational, and interpretive practices of one's culture); and disrespect (being routinely maligned or disparaged in stereotypic public representations and/or in everyday life interaction). (Fraser, 1997: 14)

The remedy for such injustices is the positive recognition of maligned groups through changes in culture and symbolism. Some of these measures include 'upwardly revaluing disrespected identities and the cultural products of maligned groups; recognizing and positively valorizing cultural identity; or transforming wholesale societal patterns of representation, interpretation, and communication in ways that would change everyone's social identity' (2003: 13). When a collective engages in a struggle for recognition, they are usually considered to be a status group marked by 'less respect, esteem and prestige [than] they enjoy relative to other groups in society' (2003: 14). As we saw in chapter 5 in relation to gay identities, the problems that these groups face cannot just be addressed through simple equality. Justice is achieved through the recognition of *difference* and the unique characteristics of a group.

In her most recent work (2005), Fraser has added a third form of justice to her dichotomy of socio-economic and culture justice. This type of justice is political parity of participation, and involves the representation of concerned groups in political decisions. Here, Fraser builds upon recent analysis that questions who is involved in political communities and which groups are afforded the right to participate in political decisions (Waltzer, 1983; Benhabib, 2004). Political injustice involves misrepresentation and is rooted in the configuration of controlling structures such as the state. For Fraser, 'misrepresentation occurs when political boundaries and/or decision rules function to wrongly deny some people the possibility of participating on a par with others in social interaction – including, but not only, in political arenas' (2005: 8). Akin to the second face of power discussed in chapter 1, representational injustices are the result of people being excluded from formal negotiations and decision-making processes and feeling systematically disadvantaged by the rules that govern this process. The remedy for such injustices involves representing the harmed group's concerns so that all who are affected by a certain decision are included in the decision-making process. A pattern of exclusion is typically addressed by shifting the political boundaries that determine who is included or excluded in a decision-making process. It may also be approached by questioning the very notion of traditional political boundaries. In sum, this third form of justice involves groups seeking just representation of their voice in decision-making.

While there are many accounts of justice, what is unique about Fraser's theory is its multidimensionality. For her, justice cannot be reduced to a singular facet, such as the sufficient redistribution of primary goods or opportunities (Dworkin, 1981; Rawls, 1971), the recognition of different identities (Honneth, 1995) or the representation of political voice (Waltzer, 1983). Rather, as we demonstrated in chapter 5's description of Sunray Customer Service, each form of justice (redistribution, recognition, representation) is relatively auto-nomous. This means that one type of justice claim cannot be reduced to other kinds of justice. Some struggles may primarily focus on recogni-tion issues (such as sexuality), other struggles may be addressed to representational issues (such as the governance of corporations) and a third set of struggles may deal with redistribution problems (such as labour rights). Despite the analytic division she affords each struggle for justice, she acknowledges that many real struggles will involve multiple justice claims. She gives the example of gender and race (2003: 19–26; cf. Butler, 1998, and Young, 1997). The injustices suffered around race appear to be caused by patterns of resource maldistribution, the con-sistent presence of harmful patterns of recognition, as well as repre-sentational structures that systematically bar certain groups from decisions that fundamentally affect their lives. This leads Fraser to argue that 'as a practical matter, therefore, overcoming injustice in virtually every case requires redistribution and recognition' (2003: 25), to which she later adds representation (2005).

Fraser's work provides us with a 'moral grammar' to identify and describe the various injustices that people suffer. But, perhaps more importantly, her approach helps us see how struggles result from low participative parity in matters of recognition, redistribution and repre-sentation. Struggles at work can therefore be framed as an attempt to amend and/or redress patterns of misrepresentation, maldistribution and misrecognition. While chapter 5's brief introduction of Fraser's approach allowed us to tease out conceptually the connections between power and resistance, we now want to discuss three illustrative exam-ples that show how the very compulsion to engage in struggle is animated (for the aggrieved, at least) by claims for the kinds of justice discussed above.

Struggles for justice

To explore the role of justice claims in organizational struggles, we look at three social movements that have sought to change some aspect of organizational life. These are a labour movement that aimed to challenge the restructuring of the Melbourne Port industry (involving workers known as 'wharfies'), a sexuality-based movement that sought to challenge the position of gay and lesbian, transgender and bisexual employees, and the shareholder rights movement that set out to challenge the managerial control of large corporations in the United States. These three very different movements exemplify the fundamental kinds of justice claims identified by Fraser. The Melbourne Ports case exemplifies the struggle for distributional justice because it initially appears to address 'material' issues such as wages and life chances. The GLTB case exemplifies the struggle for recognitional justice because it involves attempts to mitigate the negative depictions of their identities. The shareholder rights case exemplifies the struggle for representational justice because it directly addresses issues of who controls decisions within the corporation.

Wharfies

The paradigmatic example of a group engaged in the struggle for redistributional justice is the trade union (also see the previous chapter). Unions are regarded as the typical vehicle for redistributional justice because they enable an employee collective to contest exploitation by advancing claims for higher wages. They also challenge economic marginalization by ensuring equity of access to work. Finally, unions also challenge deprivation by supporting social welfare measures. Although in reality many unions often do not comply with each of these idealized roles, typically they legitimize themselves through a fundamental commitment to ensuring distributional justice for their members. Notwithstanding some conspicuous failures, unions were certainly successful throughout the twentieth century in putting forward justice claims. They have also been instrumental in supporting many of the redistributional measures that are currently enjoyed in Western democracies. To achieve these measures, unions engaged in a range of struggles. One of the most talked about examples of unionized struggle in recent years was the 1997/8 port labour dispute that occurred in Melbourne. In what follows, we sketch out the various claims to justice that underpinned this dispute by drawing on existing research (Spicer, Selsky and Teicher, 2002; Selsky, Spicer and Teicher, 2003, 2005).

Up to 1997 two large stevedoring companies dominated the Australian ports sector – the British company P&O and the Australian company Patrick. Because they were a duopoly in a vital industry, these companies enjoyed consistently good profits. Those working on the docks were all members of the Maritime Union of

Australia (MUA). The unionized workers enjoyed good rates of pay and conditions in return for doing the dangerous and demanding work. This classic 'Keynesian settlement' was disrupted in early 1998 when one of the port companies, Patrick, sought to restructure their labour practices. In secret collusion with the conservative federal government of John Howard, Patrick sought to replace unionized workers with non-unionized workers. The explicit aim of this exercise was to break the union and introduce more flexible working conditions, with an eye to decreasing labour costs. On 28 January 1998 shifts were cancelled for the entire unionized workforce and the docks previously occupied by Patrick were leased to another company, called P&C Stevedores. This company then employed a non-unionized workforce that had been trained, in secret, in Dubai. Members of the MUA established a picket line outside the Patrick port facilities. This set the scene for a clear case of grievance over distributional issues such as the wages and conditions of the unionized labour force. Following Fraser, we would expect that issues of distributional justice would come to the fore during such struggles.

Initially, members of the MUA expressed shock and disbelief. These reactions quickly transformed into clear redistributional justice claims. The claims often involved an appeal to the history of unions, which highlighted the harsh conditions under which people worked, and the significant material gains the union made for its members. The MUA also argued that its members had helped introduce new technology and more flexible working conditions. What is notable in these early claims for redistributional justice is that they were largely framed in terms of benefiting members of the MUA. But these rather limited appeals rapidly changed as the target of the appeals shifted from MUA members to union members more generally. This occurred as the MUA linked their own claims for distributional justice with broader issues shared by other unionized groups. They did this by arguing that the waterfront was the government's first target in a larger campaign against unionized labour in general in the Australian workplace. This was given greater poignancy through images of an 'unholy' coalition of big business and the government. By linking their own specific distributional concerns with the broader distributional concerns of the union movement, the MUA significantly broadened their support base. The unions pushed this strategy even further by making appeals to wider social justice concerns. By defending their own distributional claims in the workplace, it was argued, the MUA were also defending the distributional claims of many other people who were not union-ized. This transformed the ports into a microcosm of the Australian workplace.

While distributional claims clearly stood at the forefront of the MUA's struggle, claims for recognitional justice also played a role. At the beginning of the dispute, there were significant concerns about how the wharfie was represented in the press and popular culture more generally. Initially the MUA sought to tackle directly the images of the wharfie as a slackard or quasi-criminal thug that often circulated in the press. They saw this as a clear instance of misrecognition, whereby a harmful image of the wharfie was propagated by the corporate-led media. At first they sought to challenge this recognitional injustice by portraying the wharfie as an honest figure working in a hard and often dangerous occupation. As the dispute progressed, however, the picture of the wharfie was generalized to being a proud unionist, and then to an ordinary working person whose rights were being threatened by a militaristic government. In generalizing the image of the wharfie, these groups were able to represent threats and assaults on the image of the wharfie as threats and assaults to the image of all unionists, and then all 'working people' more generally. Such generalized claims to recognitional justice seemed to give additional depth to the MUA's campaign against Patrick, by showing that not only were they suffering from maldistributional threats, they were also being threatened by assaults on the way they were recognized by the public.

As the MUA developed increasingly convincing claims around redis-tribution and recognition, a third issue gradually began to come to the fore. This was the question of who was involved in deciding on the rules that govern the working conditions of people in the ports, and Australian industry more generally. Questions about representational justice were initially broached through the image of an 'unholy' coali-tion between business and government, bent on de-unionizing the nation. As a result, the MUA and its allies in the Australian Council of Trade Unions (ACTU) placed much emphasis on the possible illeg-ality of the government aid to Patrick. It became obvious that the government sought to serve the interests of big business and crush the power of the unions in Australia. This was linked with a concern that the interests of multinational business dominated the government agenda, and the voices of citizens more generally were increasingly disappearing from decision-making processes. In other words, through this struggle, the possibility that neo-liberalism was in fact anti-democratic entered the general political debate of the country. The particular struggles of the MUA were expanded to the far wider struggles of various groups across the world against the rising influence of neo-liberal governmentality (Burgmann, 2003).

By making simultaneous appeals to issues of redistribution, recognition and representation, the MUA was able to mobilize significant support for its cause. Indeed, the Webb Dock in Melbourne was the site of some of the biggest labour protests seen in contemporary Australia. People from all sectors of society participated in the protests. This public pressure played an important part in achieving a settlement between the labour hire companies, Patrick and the employers. The settlement meant that MUA members were reinstated, employment moved back from the labour hire companies to Patrick, and an enterprise agreement was eventually reached. The agreement resulted in 626 lay-offs as well as some non-core functions such as cleaning and security being subcontracted (Griffin and Svensen, 1998). But it also meant that the MUA was able to maintain its role as the union of the waterfront and stave off many of the threats to redistributional justice.

Queers

For Fraser, gay groups are an archetypal group who have been denied recognitional justice. This is because their sexuality is 'despised' by some sectors of society. The central injustice faced by this group is being misrecognized, which is rooted in the patterns of symbolic and cultural oppression (Fraser, 2003; cf. Butler, 1997). Attempts to rectify patterns of misrecognition target the cultural and symbolic misrepresentation of homosexual people and restore recognitional justice by ensuring that homosexuals are not barred from participating in society simply because of their sexuality. Indeed, struggles over recognition have been at the heart of the gay rights movement. Their aims have largely been focused on disrupting harmful representations and assumptions about what homosexuality signifies, as well as addressing legal and medical issues that result from patterns of misrecognition (Armstrong, 2005). Various gay rights groups have employed a range of tactics in their struggles, including protests, information campaigns, consciousness-raising activities and cheeky urban interventions. At the centre of these struggles has been an attempt to challenge widespread stereotypes about homosexuality. One example of such attempts in contemporary organizations is the GLTB workers' movement in the United States. This movement consists of a loose set of common initiatives throughout the United States that seeks to displace the stigmatization that GLTB employees regularly face. In what follows, we draw on existing studies of the GLTB movement in the United States to consider how claims for recognitional justice underpin these struggles (Creed and Scully, 2000; Creed, Scully and Austin, 2002; Scully and Segal, 2002).

GLTB employees have typically suffered significant discrimination in the workplace. This has included symbolic discrimination in the form of harmful jokes, a lack of acceptance of certain lifestyles or family configurations and a rejection of sexualized identities at work. These largely symbolic concerns were often linked with more 'material' issues, such as health care for same-sex partners. Early gay rights activism initially targeted the workplace in order to challenge how GLTBs were portrayed in broader society. For instance, gay rights activists in the San Francisco Bay area used a range of protest strategies, including the foundation of gay special interest groups, cultural 'zaps' where gay activists made clever cultural interventions, and 'work-ins' where activists entered government buildings in San Francisco and posed as gay employees (with a large badge to identify them as such) until they were 'fired' (by being ejected by security guards) (Armstrong, 2005). At the centre of all these inventions was an ongoing attempt to challenge the harmful misrecognition of gay identities. However, it is only more recently that sustained campaigns have been mounted to tackle some of the issues faced by GLTB groups in the workplace.

The gay rights movement had an important impact on different sectors of society. Perhaps one of the central sites where this struggle was played out was the 1996 Employment Non-Discrimination Act in the United States. This outlawed employment discrimination on the basis of sexual orientation. The public debate around this bill was an important forum in which the broader struggle for recognitional justice took place. This often involved mobilizing different symbolic frames around the issue of GLTB rights in the workplace (Creed, Scully and Austin, 2002). These included positively framing gay rights as civil rights, appealing to real-life abuses and representing gay-friendly employment policies as a source of competitive advantage. Not everyone accepted such initiatives. The conservative Family Research Council framed gay rights as a perversion of civil rights, a threat to religious businesses and as legitimating homosexuality to children. These negative framings aimed to represent GLTB employees as people who had been the subject of *too much* positive recognition and therefore should not be given any more. At this legislative level, the more positive framings of GLTBs largely won out, as the 1996 Act outlawing discrimination against GLTB employees made its way into law. This change in legislation was supported and perhaps underpinned by the GLTBs' tactical recognition politics, representing gay workers as worthy of dignity, acceptance and legitimacy on their own grounds.

The passage of the Employment Non-Discrimination Act in 1996 certainly led to legal gains for GLTB employees. However, these gains were not as comprehensive as initially hoped. Just because a governmental body adopts a law does not mean that it is automatically implemented in an organization. There are likely to be very different compliance regimes within different firms (Zald, Morrill and Rao, 2005). Because of this, the GLTB movement turned to firm-level tactics. One example of this was a loose regional network that lobbied for the interests of GLTB people in a range of organizations in a Midwestern US city (Creed and Scully, 2000). Workplace-level activists sought to frame GLTB rights in terms of discrimination, as a source of competitive advantage and of importance to the company reputation. Together, these tactics allowed activists to craft a more 'gay-friendly' environment in a number of individual firms. Activism also took place through very small-scale 'micro-mobilizations' (Creed and Scully, 2000). These focused on very specific and everyday situations in the workplace, such as making reference to a member of the same sex when being asked to name a 'dream date' during a team-building exercise. In order to address these specific issues, activists engaged in political 'encounters', at which individuals actively and publicly took hold of their queer identity. They also used educative encounters, where they would put forward personal stories and offer to answer frank questions. Finally, activists engaged in advocacy encounters, when the claims of the GLTB groups were frankly discussed. During these encounters, GLTB employees often made links with other identity groups. For instance, activists acknowledged multiple identities, such as being a gay father or lesbian mother, or being a lesbian from an ethnic minority, etc. Similarly, GLTB activists would often form alliances with other groups through broader drives for diversity (Scully and Segal, 2002). They attempted to form alliances on the basis of ethnicity, sexuality, gender and disability concerns. As a result, claims for the positive recognition of people's sexuality became linked to broader claims for the positive recognition of difference more generally.

Tying these forms of mobilization together, the multiple claims to justice became clearer. Much of the early GLTB activism focused on the cultural exclusion of queer sexualities and the associated harmful stigmatization of gay identity. These negative representations were combated through a whole series of 'cultural' interventions, such as consciousness raising, public 'coming out' events and 'cultural zaps'. Moreover, these interventions probably helped build a more cohesive sense of individual and community identity. But, in order to gain proper workplace parity, a broader struggle for political representation was necessary. This involved GLTB representatives playing an active role in a public inquiry into new laws banning workplace discrimination. Their struggle did not seek to change who had access to political representation. Rather, the central concern was how the laws about sexual discrimination in the workplace were formulated. Alongside this stood a series of claims for redistributional justice, such as allowing same-sex partners to be eligible for domestic partner benefits. What is particularly striking in this case is that mobilization did not take place only through the kind of public protest and judicial action we saw in the Australian ports case. Rather, lobbying also involved subtler and everyday acts of 'micro-mobilization'.

Capitalists

Issues of redistributional justice and, more recently, recognition justice may appear to be more openly acknowledged in many firms. In contrast, representational issues associated with decision-making are not addressed as frequently. This may be due to the fact that our assumptions regarding the 'manager's right to manage' are still deeply embedded. However, as we noted in chapter 1, there is increasing acknowledgement that the decisions of large corporations have a profound effect on people's lives (Crouch, 2004). This has led to an upsurge in debates about who participates in deliberations associated with corporate decision-making and what the rules and procedures for making these decisions are. These questions have given rise to a wide variety of movements that attempt to address the lack of participation in decision-making in large corporations. Examples of these movements include the cooperative movement, the stakeholder movement and the corporate social responsibility movement. But perhaps one of the most notable contemporary struggles around the control of large companies is the 'shareholder rights movement'. In what follows we draw on a cluster of studies of the shareholder rights movement, and work through some of the claims for justice that underpin this movement (Davis and Thompson, 1994; Useem, 1996).

The shareholder rights movement appeared in the United States during the 1980s. This was against the background of the Reagan presidency, which vigorously promoted the idea of the free market. The Securities and Exchange Commission was committed to providing shareholders with more rights. There was also a significant rise in the amount of takeover activity. Spurred on by a lack of exit options and the increasing prevalence of practices that restricted takeovers, such as poison pills, lobbying for anti-takeover legislation, and greenmail,[1] pension funds began to organize collectively. These pension funds hoped to make explicit claims for fuller representation in the control of large corporations. In one of its founding documents ('the shareholder bill of rights'), the shareholder rights movement demanded a say in all 'fundamental decisions which could affect corporate performance and growth' (quoted in Davis and Thompson, 1994: 155). One particular issue that this movement sought to gain control over was executive pay. The controversy around this issue took on many guises, such as public revelations about the gap between the wage of an average factory worker and the corporate executive, and examples of directors being rewarded with large salary increases for operating underperforming companies, as well as claims that 'out of control' executive remuneration represented a serious threat to American democracy. Underlying all these accusations was a perception that undue managerial control of large companies had eroded the influence a shareholder might have in relation to moderating executive extravagance.

Attempts to address representational injustices were closely associated with what shareholder activists perceived to be redistributional injustices. The major claim was that shareholders were not receiving a return that was commensurate with their ownership stake. The central accusation many shareholder rights campaigns made was that, through instituting restrictive measures such as anti-takeover legislation, corporate executives had bolstered their own positions at the expense of shareholder value. Indeed, economic arguments were often mobilized to claim that restrictive ownership measures instituted by managers could result in large declines in shareholder value. These specific claims around redistributional justice for shareholders were subsequently linked to broader claims about the injustices of executive pay. For instance, the huge disparity between CEO pay and the pay of a factory worker was often cited as evidence of greedy management. Broader questions were asked about the huge bonuses given to CEOs of under-performing companies. By targeting 'fat cat pay', the shareholder rights movement was able to successfully link its own rather narrow and quite technical claims for distributional justice with issues of distributional justice in broader society. This made an unlikely couple out of the shareholder rights movement and workers' claims for fair wages.

The studies conducted on shareholder activism do not examine claims around misrecognitional justice. In many ways this is not unexpected, because, after all, share ownership and corporate control are 'political' and 'economic' issues rather than 'cultural' issues. However, symbolic framings associated with recognitional politics do seem to play some role in the debates about ownership and corporate control (Vaara, 2002). In an analysis of press coverage of takeovers, Paul Hirsch identifies a whole range of popular genres used to describe them, including marriage, warfare, the western, chivalry, macho, nautical, games, *Jaws* and sports (Hirsch, 1986). The often highly negative images of hostile corporate takeovers slowly became accepted during the latter part of the twentieth century as the agents of takeovers changed from being pirates to the bearers of 'golden parachutes'. Nonetheless, when the potential bidders in a takeover are hostile, the negative imagery is not difficult to conjure. Building on this work, we would suspect that shareholder activists might use similar tactics to besmirch CEOs and corporate executives. For instance, images of swollen corporate 'fat cats' and irresponsible or unaccountable executives have been used to create a negative reputation for senior executives. By creating these off-putting images, it was possible for shareholder activists to position themselves as the victim of rapacious corporate appetites.

Like the wharfies and GLTB activist, shareholder activists mobilized a range of justice claims. Initial claims around representational issues associated specifically with managerial decision-making and corporate control were linked to wider redistributional claims. Like other activists, the shareholder groups were able to broaden their claims for justice by associating them with those of other groups. In proposing these justice claims, the shareholder rights movement was able to add moral weight to its activities. This enabled the movement to achieve concrete outcomes, such as voting on executive remuneration, forming subcommittees to investigate issues of concern to shareholders and ensuring the public disclosure of executive pay. The ultimate result was some degree of shift in the balance of power in terms of who controlled the corporation.

Conclusion

In all three struggles that we have analysed, justice claims seem to be absolutely central. The illustrations are interesting in that they demonstrate how the three approaches to justice identified by Nancy Fraser were never present in an isolated form. Each claim for justice aimed to gain more power by connecting to wider social justice issues. What we might have expected to have been primarily redistributional justice claims by the wharfies rapidly became linked to broader claims for positive recognition as 'ordinary workers' and more representational say in running firms' affairs. What we might have expected to be a struggle for recognitional justice by the queer activists evolved into claims for representational justice around the laws governing the workplace, as well as redistributional claims associated with same-sex domestic partner benefits. Finally, what we might have expected to be a struggle for corporate control on the part of shareholder activists also involved a broader struggle for redistributional justice as well as struggles for recognitional justice. As each group broadened out its justice claims it also broadened its base of support. This might lead us to suspect that the greater the number of justice claims that a group is able to make convincingly the greater the support that it is likely to gain.

Creating these connections involves crafting what Ernesto Laclau and Chantel Mouffe (1985) call 'chains of equivalence' between previously separate struggles. This has practical effects in terms of maintaining the success of a struggle. Indeed, when a group achieves some success via broader connections, it is able to embed its gains into a settlement that would prove quite difficult for a counter-mobilization to reverse (Zysman, 1994). The wharfies were able to shore up their right to unionize employment relationships through a relatively favourable employment settlement. The queer workers were able to stabilize their rights in the workplace through changing the norms and practices associated with sexuality in the organization, as well as changing the laws around discrimination in the workplace on the basis of sexual orientation. The shareholder activists were able to embed their claims through a series of changes to corporate governance practices and law, especially those relating to the disclosure of information by corporate executives. In each of these cases, the hard-won justice claims of each group were guaranteed and bolstered by an institutional settlement largely based on the *law*. It appears that law continues to prove a vital site for pursuing, and indeed guaranteeing, justice claims.

Finally, in each case of struggle, the *public sphere* proved to be an important stage where each group could pursue its justice claims. The wharfies made significant use of the media and mass public protests to press their demands for justice. The queer workers engaged in the public sphere too, while keeping an eye on the importance of pursuing micro-mobilization in the firm. The shareholder rights movement also made use of public forums such as the press to push forward its own claims. This suggests that struggles for justice generally engage with the public sphere in order to have their somewhat commercialized claims aired and debated. Indeed, we might suggest that it is the very existence of this public space that allows justice claims to be put forward and pursued – and this issue will be discussed further in the next chapter.

9 | *Struggles for common ground in organizations*

> To have a whole life, one must have
> the possibility of publicly shaping and
> expressing private worlds, dreams, thoughts,
> and desires, of constantly having access to
> a dialogue between public and private
> worlds. How else do we know that we have
> existed, felt, desired, hated, feared?
>
> (Nafisi, 2003: 339)

When Apple Computers was challenged recently about the labour conditions in their iPod factories located in China, a public relations representative gave a well-rehearsed defence; the Chinese cultural context is very different from that of the West. While to us the factories appear to be realms of hyper-exploitation, to locals they represent progress and opportunity when compared to the alternatives. Perversely enough, this appeal to cultural relativism resonates with postmodern celebrations of difference, local micro-politics and resistance that eschew grandiose meta-narratives. In this last chapter, we suggest that struggles in contemporary organizations, both in the West and elsewhere (e.g. China), usually involve justice claims that appeal to the broader concerns of others. As we saw from the last chapter, the most successful struggles are those that make clear and multifaceted justice claims, connecting to wider issues relating to work and beyond. It is these claims for justice that transform individual struggles from simple self-serving politics to a common cause (or ground) potentially involving all oppressed parties.

This final chapter pulls together many of the issues and concepts that have been discussed in the book so far. Our argument is this: many analyses of resistance have overemphasized the technical features of micro-struggles (including cynicism, irony and tactical appropriations of culture management practices), with little mention of the quest for justice underlying such actions. When we do study the issue of justice in the context of workplace struggles, we see specific contestations that draw upon wider narratives regarding the society we ought to live in. Given the configuration of contemporary organizations, however, such appeals are usually hampered by an age-old split between public politics and private lives. Indeed, in our culture the realm of politics has traditionally been considered something that takes place in public spaces such as councils, states, regions, parliaments and assemblies. Note that we do not see organizations on this list of public spaces. They are not open to all citizens. They do not welcome public debate or controversy over their policies. Where possible they shun anything as 'radical' as democracy. Indeed, the organization is typically thought to be part of what ancient Greek thought called the *oekios*, or the economy. As we know from Aristotle, the *oekios* is certainly no place for politics. But, if this is still so, then where can the struggle for justice take place? Are such struggles always doomed to go underground and flee into the informal organizational sphere? Or is there some way of crafting a common ground that connects our workplaces to a public space both nationally and internationally, in which global claims for justice can be pursued? If so, where might this common ground be located?

In addressing these questions, we suggest that struggle in organizations today involves an attempt to reconfigure the private world of work into a public space of politics where justice can be pursued more widely. Because the social world has been progressively organized, a 'sublimation' of politics has occurred (Wolin, 2004). As indicated in the cases discussed in this book, this has meant a closure of public spaces (e.g. the ABC), the incessant spread of economic logic (e.g. the Melbourne Port dispute) and the transformation of common political struggles into issue-specific politics (e.g. sexuality at Sunray). It is the task of this final chapter to discuss how we can conceptualize struggle as the creation of a common ground between ostensibly diverse protest groups. Such a 'universal' common ground that binds different factions is important, we suggest, for the realization of organizational justice claims. Echoing the insights from the previous chapter, this often entails an attempt to connect the political and the public by way of universal narratives of justice. It is here that we see specific interests (sexual parity, the wage–effort bargain, environmental concerns, etc.) becoming linked. When this occurs, the isolated and ostensibly apolitical sphere of work is rescripted as a space of justice, a space of hope. There are, however, different ways we can approach this notion of the universal in relation to work organizations; in this chapter we focus on the divergent arguments of Slavoj Žižek (2000), Ernesto Laclau (2000) and Michael Hardt and Antonio Negri (2004) in order to help us navigate the question of a common ground. We conclude by suggesting that Hardt and Negri's (2004) concept of the ever-present multitude may provide a useful perspective on how we understand the idea of universal struggle. First, though, why do we not share a common ground when we are at work?

Arendt, justice and the *polis*

The pursuit of justice cannot take place everywhere. Aristotle argues in his *Politics* that there must be a special space where the pursuit of justice can take place. This he calls the *polis*. For Aristotle, the *polis* is a common space where citizens seek to establish a good life through pubic relationships. This stands in marked contrast to the *oekios*, or the household. The central activity here is the sustenance of basic life through labour. In Aristotle's time, the *oekios* was governed by two elementary relationships: father and family, and master and slave. The *oekios* and the *polis* are governed by very different logics. Because the *oekios* is bound to the sustenance of biological life, it is governed by the logic of efficiency and effectiveness. The *polis* is the realm of political action and is governed by the logic of praxis and politics. It is important that we do not simply equate the *oekios* with the modern suburban home or the *polis* with the modern state. The state, for example, might not be included in the *polis* if it is concerned only with sustaining biological life (Arendt, 1958). Similarly, a home might be part of the *polis* when the focus on common action shifts from simply sustaining life to contesting relations between people (Fraser, 1989). It is the logic displayed in each sphere that is most important.

If a *polis* is the place where political struggles might take place and justice be pursued, we must ask ourselves where we can find such 'common ground' today. Is there a *polis* where a disgruntled employee can speak? Where can citizens contend the actions of large corporations? What spaces do we have today in which people can engage organizations in the struggle for justice? The most obvious location for these struggles is formalized (democratic) politics such as

parliaments and assemblies. According to the dominant liberal democratic ideas of our time, it is here that those engaged in struggles can
find a place to speak. Indeed, many would point to the fact that we have
witnessed a radical expansion of democratic assemblies where justice
might be pursued. This is due to the diffusion of the democratic model
of governance throughout the world in the late twentieth century
(Starr, 1991). It is also due to the rapid multiplication of the 'levels'
of democratic government. The national parliament is not the only
space where democratic politics can be enacted, since a whole range of
sub- and supranational spaces of governance also exist (Scholte, 2004).
Some argue that these spaces open up new possibilities and opportunities for democratic contestation and struggle. Indeed, we would hope
that this dual movement of widening the scope of the democratic model
and deepening democratic governance through more supra- and sub-
state institutions presents an unprecedented opportunity. It should
mean there are far more spaces where people, citizens and employees
can engage in productive political struggle and pursue their claims for
justice in work organizations.

This rosy view that opportunities for democratic struggle have
expanded significantly is not shared by all. Critics might agree that
there has been an increase in the number of spaces that are at least
nominally democratic. However, they would also add that an elected
parliament should not be equated with democracy (Marcuse, 1968;
Hardt and Negri, 2004). They would point out that democracy is not
just about the availability of formal institutions labelled 'democratic'
but, rather, it is about the propagation of a deeper logic of open political
contestation and struggle. For these critics, democracy involves an open,
politicized debate around issues of the day that is accessible to all people.
It involves creating the ability to question, act upon and change the
relations between us. According to the social critic Hannah Arendt
(1958), this has simply not been realized. She argues that we have not
witnessed the kind of radical politicization that is so often celebrated by
conservatives and liberals alike. Rather, we find ourselves in a kind of
democratic regress in which spaces of political life are being progressively closed down, especially in relation to the corporation.

According to Arendt, political space should be characterized by a
logic of action: taking the initiative, beginning, and setting things in
motion (1958). The target of this initiative is not to sustain our own
bare life by nourishing or protecting our body. Nor does political

initiative involve bringing new objects into the world. Rather, it consists of bringing into being new relationships between people that enable the pursuit of justice. The quintessential way this happens is through speech and deeds, and the *polis* provides a vital space for their expression (1958). The danger that Arendt identified in the politics of her own day was that there had been a swift and rather disturbing shift. She argued that the political institutions were no longer characterized by the logic of 'action' but by the economic logic of 'the household'. This meant that, instead of seeking to act on relationships between people, politics involved the search for efficiency and effectiveness. Relationships between people were simply to be treated as a mechanism to be instrumentally manipulated so that they might function in the most efficient manner. The result was that politics became ruled by questions of efficiency and effectiveness. Politics assumed the form of social engineering. For Arendt, the dominance of economic logic was tantamount to the depoliticization of politics itself.

So, why has such a radical depoliticization taken place? According to Sheldon Wolin (2004), it is the dominance of the organizational form that is to blame. He argues that modern political action has fled from traditional spaces of contestation (such as government) and set up shop in typically 'non-political' institutions. The target of politics has become the large-scale organization, and the central means of political action has become building and maintaining organizations. The result is that politics is utterly and completely equated with the organization and its logic of efficiency, effectiveness and cost-benefit analysis. Due to the spread of the organization into politics, social relationships too have become increasingly instrumental. This means that spaces of action have been replaced by spaces of rationalized procedures, methods and rules. Political spaces have largely been rendered into economic spaces (recall the Sunray case and the spread of corporate culture into extra-employment activities). Wolin arrives at the same conclusion as Arendt: the progressive organization of political life has dealt a death blow to the *polis*. But he takes the argument one step further. He claims that this does not necessarily result in a simple anti-policiticism, 'but rather the sublimation of the political into forms of association which earlier thought has believed to be non-political' (2004: 385). For him, the depoliticization of public space means that previously 'private' spaces such as organizations have become the new seats of struggle.

What Wolin foreshadows is the kind of 'micro-politics' that contemporary commentators celebrate. He shows us a world where politics flees from the public realm and seeks to ply its trade in specific struggles (gay identity politics, the wage–effort bargain, individual dignity at work, etc.). This certainly opens up the possibility of multiple and diverse forms of contestation. It provides a space in which many struggles can voice their specific concerns in unique and often idiosyncratic ways. While the positive side of micro-political struggles has been widely celebrated (Alvesson and Willmott, 1992; Fleming and Spicer, 2003; Jermier, Knights and Nord, 1993), there are some important limitations. Perhaps the starkest and most striking is that micro-politics eschews any attempt to make common claims. In postmodern parlance, such claims are considered to be grandiose and merely peddling incredulous grand-narratives. Such a celebration of micro-politics contributes significantly to the erosion of a common ground. As Arendt reminds us, it is precisely this common ground that allows people to engage in political action. Indeed, the very meaning of politics for Arendt is acting on and through the common. If there is no commonality and nothing we share together, to act in common and upon the common becomes a difficult prospect. To act in the name of a specific group merely involves pursuing self-interest at another's expense.

Universalizing organizational concerns

We suggest that workplace struggle often consists of crafting a common ground that connects private work to a public space, so that claims for justice can be pursued. For many, the best way to create a common space is for struggles to put aside their fascination with the uniqueness and specifics of their claims. Instead, they should appeal directly to universal criteria, as was the case with the three illustrative examples discussed in the previous chapter. This involves organizational members transforming a specific claim into one with universal resonance. Instead of focusing on the specificities and details of a particular struggle, those who seek to generalize their claims would appeal to broad principles that they presume to be universal in relation to social justice. This might involve a specific group, such as stevedores, invoking a more general identity, such as 'worker' or 'citizen'. It might involve a struggle appealing to a general, normative end state, such as the just recognition of all social actors on terms they find acceptable (Honneth, 1995). Finally, it might involve appealing to a universal process such as just patterns of debate and deliberation (Benhabib, 1986). What is important here is that the detailed specificities of one group's struggle would be transubstantiated into something of greater universal import. By universalizing its claims, each 'micro-political' struggle would aim to achieve its own specific ends via the defence of universally assumed principles.

Against the postmodern grain

Asserting universal claims for justice, of course, represents a funda- mental and thoroughgoing challenge to other universals quietly taken for granted by both managers and activists in organizations (e.g. 'man- agerialism', 'marketization', 'globalization', etc.). If a group were seek- ing to challenge these new universals seriously, they would certainly need to craft equally universal ideals with regard to different modes of organization (Žižek, 2000). Instead of simply accepting the necessity of market-based measures, a radical political intervention would assert the universal necessity of the living wage or human rights. This would initiate a fundamental break with the existing universals, such as global marketization, which currently structure the horizon of possibilities. It would also show that specific struggles within an organization are often not unique to that organization but have a generally applicability. Indeed, what the powerful find dangerous is that activists may be able to make claims that are far more universal than the technocratic claims of managerial effectiveness, the necessity of marketization or the inevit- ability of global corporatization. By making these universal claims, the concerns of a specific group morph into universal demands. This means that it is more difficult, for example, to dismiss workers' demands as mere greedy self-interest. Rather, they become a group whose concerns are the concerns of everyone.

This is all very unfashionable in the context of postmodern celebra- tions of cultural specificity and micro-political action. But, while radi- cal universalization may sound like a rather grandiose proposition, it does occur. No matter how much we emphasize the importance of localized struggles with specific goals, genuine and gleeful appeals to the universal remain an important part of very many resistant activities in and around organizations. Many of the great political struggles of recent times, such as the labour and feminist movements, sought to make universal claims. As E. P. Thompson's (1967) description of the labour movement in the United Kingdom has demonstrated, workers appealed to the universal proposition that all should benefit from the fruits of the collective labour process. Similarly, the feminist movement appealed to an equally universal proposition of meritocracy and fairness in access and treatment within the workplace. Although these claims were on the face of it grandiose, they were nonetheless an effective part of how the group engaged in struggle. They were fundamental insofar as they demonstrated that struggles were not just struggles for workers or women: they were struggles for a principle that applied to everyone.

The practice of universalizing workplace (in)justice

But *how* exactly does this radical politicization of universal claims occur in organizations? Ironically, perhaps the most elemental way that people seek to make universal claims is through the vehicle of specific acts of informal struggle. This consists of the kind of unorganized and covert moves by employees that momentarily assert their various concerns and justice claims. We have already come across some examples of these fleeting attempts to assert universal rights, such as employees who appeal to their integrity and dignity as competent adults in the context of paternalistic employment relations (see chapter 5). Their jaundice-eyed view of management may be interpreted as a classic instance of micro-politics. However, these same workers made broader and more universal appeals: to their right to be treated as dignified adults and citizens. Although these appeals may involve a reaction to issues that are very specific to that workplace, they are fundamentally structured by a universal claim for dignity. It is an appeal for them to be able to enjoy rights that any other adult should enjoy in normal circumstances.

In contrast to informal resistance, revolt is the open politicization of social relationships (Kristeva, 2000). People engaged in revolt abandon hidden and disguised claims and openly voice their grievances. Revolt involves a direct challenge to powerful groups, and most are underpinned by or at least point to some kind of universalizable claim. These might be for political rights ('votes for all'), economic rights ('bread for all') or cultural rights ('dignity for all'). Indeed, in this book we have already seen examples of this. For instance, the revolt by the workers and consumers of the Australian Broadcasting Corporation was underpinned by a handful of universal claims. These included claims for universal access to public services, the importance of a civilizing national culture and the necessity of an independent broadcaster. By doing this, they were able to link their own rather specific concerns with broader political struggles across the world. They presented their own struggles as if it was not just for the ABC but for far broader aims relating to the ideals of a fair, equal and just society. This was clearly aided by the fact that many of the calls for justice chimed with a longer history of political struggle for universal rights that stretches back to the democratic revolutions of the nineteenth century. Perhaps more surprisingly, we also found that protest groups often sought to universalize the discourses associated with accountability and commercial viability. They did this by arguing for far broader conceptions of each of these discourses. By doing so, they were able to represent their own struggle as actually defending a *proper* conception of accountability and commercialism.

When a momentary revolt develops into a more enduring political change, we have an organizational revolution. Revolutions often involve attempts to institute a particular set of universal claims. The French Revolution sought to establish liberty, equality and fraternity for all. The Russian Revolution utilized the discourse of communism as a universal ideal. The Iranian Revolution aimed to ensure the universal application of Koranic law. These revolutionary demands frame what actors want and how they might seek to achieve their goals. Indeed, these demands continue to live on well after the actual moment of revolution. They colour people's political imagination and nourish them through the daily disappointments that inevitably follow all revolutions. In the previous chapter we also looked at a number of minor revolutions. These included the gay rights revolution in the North American workplace and the shareholder rights revolution in the control of large corporations. We also looked at one counterrevolution, which was the struggle by Maritime Union of Australia members to maintain the rights they enjoyed on the waterfront. What is so striking about each of these very different revolutionary movements is that they all built universalizable narratives within quite specific circumstances. In making these claims, each of these struggles clearly tapped into far deeper universal claims of the past. For instance, the shareholders drew up a bill of rights (reflecting the American Revolution), the wharfies talked about the rights of labour (reflecting the long history of union activism in Australia) and the gay and lesbian groups linked their struggle to the civil rights movement. In doing so, they were able to lay an ideological foundation that could legitimize their own revolutionary aspirations as well as sustain people through the difficulties of the post-revolutionary life that lay ahead of them.

If justice requires a generalized political common to thrive, then radical politicization offers one way of building such a space. It achieves the task by transubstantiating claims of a single political group into a claim that is voiced for all. Wharfies, for instance, are no longer just wharfies; they are representatives of all workers. There are clear political and ideological gains to be made by universalizing a specific claim. However, there are also some significant problems here, which will not be missed by our more postmodern-inclined readers. Perhaps the most pressing of these problems is the fact that the universalization of a single set of rights is a contingent, historically located and situation-specific initiative made by one single group that assumes to express the claims of all other groups. Asserting the absolute universal applicability of a single group's claim often means ignoring the historical uniqueness and contingency of these very same claims (Rorty, 1989). In some cases this may mean that a rather limited series of claims put forward by one group do not match the actual concerns of those engaged in everyday struggle. The result would be an *oppressive* universal that does not speak to its purported audience. In other cases, attempts to universalize might result in the sidelining of the concerns of specific groups that do not fit into a proclaimed universal category. This may happen when actors are stripped of their ability to speak in their own voice and articulate their own *unique* concerns (Spivak, 1988). In losing their voice, do they not begin to lose the power to articulate their own specific and idiosyncratic claims? The final and most acute danger of proclaiming a universal is that it can, in some circumstances, give rise to the active annihilation of voices that do not fit into apparently universal schemes. This might involve groups being forced into an overall framework through debate, rewarding compliance, punishing non-compliance and in some cases using violent coercive force. The classic example of this is 'revolutionary terror', whereby a post-revolutionary movement begins to destroy 'enemies of the people' and eventually turns on itself to destroy 'the enemies within' (also see Butler, 2000).

The empty universal of organizational justice

Recently some political theorists have questioned whether it is in fact desirable to universalize the claims of a particular local political struggle. Most notably, Ernesto Laclau and Chantel Mouffe (1985) have argued that a democratic polity must always provide space for a variety of political voices. These particular struggles can never be fully subsumed under a single universal term such as 'human rights' or 'the rights of labour'. Instead, groups are bound to have different and antagonistic demands. Practically, this means that a polity should not be made up of a group that coalesces around a single revolutionary demand. Rather, a polity is 'radically democratic' when it consists of a whole range of different political demands. Having said this, a radical democracy is not just a set of radically heterogeneous demands either; each particular demand still involves an active appeal to 'the universal'. Indeed, 'the rights of particular groups of agents – ethnic, national or sexual minorities for instance – can be formulated only as *universal* rights' (Laclau, 1996; also see Laclau, 2005). 'The appeal to the universal is unavoidable once, on the one hand, no agent can speak *directly* for the "totality" while, on the other, reference to the latter remains an essential component of the hegemonico-discursive operation' (Laclau, 2000: 58). The crucial point here is that, for a group's particular demands to make any sense, they must be couched in the terms of universality. However, the particular demands of each group can never completely map onto a broad universal demand. This is because the universal, according to Laclau, is not a thing that is waiting to be found. Rather, the universal is an empty space that particular struggles seek to appeal to, but can never completely capture. As he argues,

> The universal is an empty place, a void which can be filled only by the particular, but which, through its very emptiness, produces a series of crucial effects in the structuration/destructuration of social relations. (Laclau, 2000: 58)

We have already argued that what appear to be radically localized and particular struggles, such as the escape from the paternalistic culture at Sunray, often invoke universal principles (dignity and citizenship). And in the previous section we argued that the revolt by the ABC's consumers and employees involved appeals to universal principles ranging from civility to accountability. These 'empty universals' are filled in and organized by the very specific concerns of each resistance group. In the case of the ABC, these specific concerns included the restructuring of Australian television, the state of the public sphere and the history of colonialism in Australia. It was these details that gave light, colour and timbre to the struggle. Nonetheless, this profoundly local struggle was framed in terms of some rather grandiose claims. The worries of staff and the concerns of radio listeners were linked to broader concerns of public access and civility. But it was not just the coalition of audience members and employees that appealed to universal principles. Managers in the ABC also sought to appeal to universal principles. Senior managers sometimes appealed to the global market and, at other times, executives made claims of civility. This reminds us that claims to the universal are multiple and contested. There is not just one true appeal but many. Moreover, it is this antagonistic struggle between different appeals to the universal that enlivens and characterizes revolts. In short, a revolt in and around organizations involves the contingent struggle to lay claim to an empty universal.

Holding particular struggles and universal demands in dynamic tension certainly allows us to skirt around many of the problems posed by simply seeking to universalize a demand. It allows us to hold onto at least some possibility of struggle and contention between different particularities while not losing sight of the fact that these groups make appeals to universal principles. This sets up an ongoing tension between particularities and universals in which radical democracy can flourish (Laclau and Mouffe, 1985). However, some recent commentators have called this approach into question. We might ask just how 'radical' this 'radical democratic' prescription is. In particular, critics point out that, although we are urged to pay attention to the ongoing struggles between different particularities, these particularities are always articulated around a broader political rule. Although this universal might be empty, various particularities try to capture it, which means that the only way political struggles can be said to work is through seeking out and attempting to articulate an aspect of the universal. This struggle for the universal runs the risk of effectively erasing what is unusual, particular and radical in each struggle, that which is in excess of a universal. This may happen when a universal claim is applied in a situation to which it clearly has no relevance. In fact, there are many political struggles that make no claim for the universal relevance of the struggle but instead prefer to focus on particular and local issues. Moreover, there are some struggles that utterly reject the notion of universality altogether, because they see it as irrelevant, dangerous and perhaps colonizing. Some autonomist critics have gone further and argued that, if a movement continues to make universal appeals, it is inadvertently reproducing the assumption that there is a universal political space that can be controlled by the few for the many (Day, 2004). Perhaps Laclau dooms activists to a world in which they struggle to capture the universal, but necessarily fail. By maintaining this split-levelled world of universals and particulars, we consign any struggle to a mere chase after an ongoing absence.

Struggles in common?

By assuming that struggles are singularities that appeal to an empty universal, we approach justice as something we may reach and hope for but can never quite attain. We assume that we inhabit a political universe that is continually lacking. But what if nothing is lacking? What if the possibility of justice is ever-present? What if all the universals we long for, such as liberty, equality and fraternity, are already in existence in our particular practices? This is what some critics have recently suggested. Instead of assuming that struggle consists of particular groups chasing an empty universal, it is possible to conceptualize those who struggle as a variegated *multitude*. A multitude 'is an internally different, multiple social subject whose constitution and action is based not on identity or unity (or, much less, indifference) but on what it has in common' (Hardt and Negri, 2004: 100). In other words, a multitude is a group of singularities that exist and act in common. This ability to act commonly would not be achieved through hegemonic links between groups assumed to be working towards the same goals. Rather, the focus is the common habits shared between different groups – emotions, patterns of communication and 'affinities' that bond resistance groups (Day, 2004). These allow radically singular groups to work in common without being subsumed by just one universal discourse. We have seen this process in action amongst many of the so-called 'anti-globalization' protests (Graber, 2002). Through common habits and felt affinities, these very different groups (churches, non-governmental organizations, anarchists, etc.) have been able to organize a global network of protest, developing media systems, building new software and developing alternative economies. In each of these acts, we see how singular groups can engage in a common struggle without compromising their uniqueness. But we should be clear that '[t]he common does not refer to traditional notions of either the community or the public; it is based on communication among singularities and emerges through the collaborative social process of production' (Hardt and Negri, 2004: 204).

If we listen to the various forms of everyday struggle in the workplace and beyond we come across currently unfashionable words such as 'dignity' and 'respect', and perhaps even 'freedom'. People appeal to universal criteria to negotiate their particular circumstances. However, what is perhaps more interesting is not just the discursive criteria that people appeal to in order to justify or legitimate their acts of refusal, rebellion or rejection. Indeed, in some cases these appeals to overarching criteria are entirely absent. What seems most striking is the fact that very diverse peoples are acting in common when they dissent and experience dissatisfaction. This subterranean sociality often goes unobserved, since we are trained to be individuals from a very young age. What holds our struggles together are the common jokes, reactions to management culture and methods of relating to each other (communication, technology, etc.). In addition to these common practices, forms of resistance are often held together through common patterns of affect. For example, employees at the Sunray call centre were collectivized by common feelings of subordination, condescension and cynicism about the organization's '3 Fs' culture. These common emotional experiences provide a common ground, a point of connection between call centre workers and other potentially rebellious groups dealing with the problem of corporate colonization (e.g. trade unions, anarchists, etc.). Finally, and perhaps most importantly, these groups are held together by common modes of communication. As well as sharing common practices and common emotional experiences, they also shared a common language. The Sunray cynics in particular invented a shared vocabulary to undermine the patently fake culture of fun. It was this common language that allowed them to act in concert and entertain themselves during the boredom or stresses of the workday. By recognizing how commonalities are crafted between people through habit, emotion and communication, we might suggest that resistance does not necessarily need to appeal to the empty universal. Rather, it may be held together anyway by the very act of struggle, since what is common is the very work of protest. Sometimes this protest may involve an appeal to an abstract and empty universal criterion, sometimes it may not.

An analysis of revolt tells a similar story of what we hold in common. The pleas, the marching cries, the manifestos issued during moments of revolt are all certainly vital. But calls for 'liberty', 'equality', and 'fraternity' are not the only thing that is held in common. What holds this experience of antagonism together is the common work of revolt. Indeed, '[a]ny time you enter a region where there is a strong revolt forming you are immediately struck by the common manners of dress, gestures, and modes of relating and communicating' (Hardt and Negri, 2004: 213). Such common style can be found in historical studies of social movements, which show how revolts are often coordinated and underpinned by shared repertoires of contention (Tilly, 1986). These include marching, barricading, petitioning, encampment and, more recently, 'culture jamming'. These shared repertoires are learnt over a long period of time and are deeply rooted in communities of practice. As well as common action, groups share a degree of affective or emotional 'affinity'. This means that, although they may make appeals to quite different discourses, they share a common feeling for an issue. For example, during protests against changes to the ABC, groups that came from very different political persuasions were able to work together on the basis of their shared emotional attachment to the organization and the idea of public broadcasting. These factions also shared common structures and processes of communication, including newsletters, protest placards, speeches and internet sites, which provided a common ground where diverse actors could gather and share their feelings about the ABC restructuring.

What would a common revolution in workplace politics look like? It is obvious that it would not simply involve introducing some kind of absolute rupture where a despised universal was replaced by another more desirable one (cf. Žižek, 2000). Nor would it involve the courageous but ultimately doomed quest by particular struggles to lay claim to an empty universal (cf. Laclau, 2000). Rather, a revolution of the commons would be one that simply embellished current day-to-day practices. Such a revolution would not be about trying to arrive at a utopian future, for it would be realizing the common space *that already exists between us*, which is currently used to fuel the vibrancy of the global capitalist system. Perhaps this is Hardt and Negri's (2004) most radically optimistic claim. The organizational common that can realize justice is not a distant ideal that we are struggling towards but is already present in the multitude of cases where we cooperate, communicate and share on a quotidian basis. It is in the spaces of what Hardt and Negri (2000) call 'elemental communism' that we find evidence of the revolutionary struggles that have already happened and might happen again. It is this spontaneous communism that capitalism and its overarching structures of organizational domination *depend* upon for their own survival, innovativeness and flexibility. Indeed, as a parallel universe, if such communism remains in the informal networks of organizational life, it is actually very useful for perpetuating organizational domination. Hardt and Negri (2004) insist that the building and maintenance of commonality has already happened many times before, and it is occurring right now among all sorts of people, including social activists, professionals, software developers, indigenous peoples, farmers and street traders. It is this latent yet already existing potential that provides a common ground regarding the justice of organizational life.

Conclusion

We began this chapter by pointing out that there is no justice without a space to claim it. In other words, justice cannot take place when there are no grounds on which it can grow. It is this common ground that provides a place where claims to justice can be announced, deliberated upon and pursued. We have argued that this common ground might be in trouble. This is because of the 'sublimation of politics', whereby politics flees from the formal institutions of the state and begins to install itself in previously 'non-political' space, such as family relationships, sexuality, communities and – above all – organizations. This means that any appeal for justice in each particular struggle loses some of its generality and each claim to justice is reduced to isolated groups pursuing their own interests. This, of course, is not too far from the simple self-serving behaviour celebrated by neo-liberal economists.

Three possibilities for crafting a common ground in work organizations have been examined. The first entails creating a direct link between the particularities of a struggle and broad universal principles such as freedom and liberty. A second possibility involves recognizing that people engaged in struggles do indeed make appeals to the universal, but that there will inevitably be many appeals and each will, inevitably, fail to capture or create links with this universal. The final possibility consists of recognizing and celebrating the habits, emotions and patterns of communication (the 'elemental communism') that are already shared. Here, it is through our very interactions, engagements and shared passions that commonality is enabled and sustained. It is by these interactions that we might affirm a space where we can pursue and achieve organizational justice through struggle.

Conclusion

> [I]t is always the bad side that in the end
> triumphs over the good side. It is the bad side
> that produces movement which makes
> history.
>
> (Marx, 1847/1976: 174)

We have all experienced the effects of power in organizations, be it in a corporation, education institution or social club. Most of us too have been agents of resistance, or at least witnessed resistance in organizations. As we have noted in this book, such resistance can take many interesting and often colourful forms. A corporate culture campaign may be lampooned through bawdy and vulgar commentary. A shop-floor union or professional association may organize collective action in the face of an unpopular policy. Gay employees or ethnic minorities may launch anti-discrimination campaigns in their organizations. A software engineer may sabotage a project that has unfairly exploited his/her creative input. A secretary may even piss in the coffee of a sadistic boss. The list could well be endless.

The objective of this book has been to provide a theoretical basis for making sense of such instances of contestation. In particular, we have developed the notion of *struggle*, not only to sharpen our analysis of *power* and *resistance* at work but also to transcend the limitations of these two concepts. The first two chapters placed our concerns within a scholarly tradition that identifies the differing ways in which power and resistance can be conceptualized in relation to work organizations. The four 'faces' of power, as we have outlined them, provide a useful backdrop for this task. We saw that power is a multidimensional entity that can inspire various forms of resistance and opposition. The third chapter introduced the concept of struggle to supplement and extend current approaches. We feel that the idea of struggle gives a more complete and dynamic picture of workplace politics because it moves away from a simplistic Newtonian image of power/resistance relations in which every action results in a reaction. Rather than workplace politics operating in a linear fashion in which an initial expression of power is met by a secondary reaction of resistance, we suggest the image of a dynamic and mutually inclusive process of struggle.

Importantly, we do not necessarily recommend abandoning the ideas of power and resistance. Indeed, we have used them throughout this book. But, if we take the analysis to a deeper level of everyday political action, then the 'knot' of struggle perhaps provides a more nuanced and realistic account of contestation. The concept of struggle, for example, demonstrates how resistance may come first, provoking new types of control that aim either to impede or to exploit various types of escape. In the Sunray case, for example, it is tempting to assert that new managerial innovations in cultural controls evoked the cynical resistance we have already discussed. But, if we watch the development of these controls over time, a more dynamic process is revealed. Workers resisted the traditional call centre control structures by inserting more of 'themselves' in the labour process (i.e. voicing how they really felt). This resistance was seized upon by management as an opportunity to generate a more authentic and fun culture of work ('just be yourself'). This in turn was resisted by various groups in the organization through cynicism and so on. Struggle points to a multidimensional 'dance' of political engagement in which spaces for achieving justice (however that is defined by the parties involved) is forged and occupied.

A key message of this book is this: we ought to approach workplace struggle and political contestation as a *constitutive* feature of work organizations rather than as an aberration that can simply be managed away. The problem with most mainstream management thinking is that it views politics, contestation and resistance as deviations from the default option of a harmonious norm. We are not suggesting that harmony cannot be attained in work organizations. But such a vision of work is merely ideological if it is prescribed within or superimposed upon the current structure of employment relations, domains whereby asymmetrical power relations are taken for granted and the managerial prerogative a natural right. Indeed, work in today's society is fundamentally permeated with differing interests, factions, contradictions and power/resistance relations.

It is hoped that the illustrative examples drawn from our own empirical research demonstrate how struggle is a defining feature of the employment relation. In the Sunray case, for example, we saw this in terms of selfhood and sexuality: management wanted to appropriate aspects of identity that were once the domain of employees' private lives. Workers resisted the culture management initiatives through cynicism, laconic humour and various degrees of ironic disengagement. The ABC case pointed out how the very existence of the public broadcaster represented a fragile political achievement that was increasingly threatened by neo-liberal attempts to commercialize it via the discourse of globalization. The Melbourne Port dispute showed how unionized labour too is the outcome of a long and brutal struggle for workers' rights, of which the action against the Patrick stevedore firm was but the most recent flashpoint. For sure, these (as well as the other) examples of struggle in organizations we have discussed underline the antagonistic and thoroughly political nature of work. If on the surface organizations appear calm and civil social accomplishments, one does not have to peer too deeply to find their dirty 'bad side' as a defining feature, to paraphrase Karl Marx.

Struggle beyond the 'cult of the subject'

Another objective of this book has been to regenerate interest in modalities of resistance that may not exactly be de rigueur in the current academic climate of postmodernist celebrations of micro-political and identity-based subversions. Readers will have noticed from the structure of the book that in unpacking the idea of struggle (from chapter 4 onwards) we move from the inconspicuous and quotidian (e.g. cynicism) to the more 'grandiose' and overt (e.g. the ports dispute). These forms of struggle are by no means mutually exclusive – indeed, various types of categorization in the literature (informal/formal, organized/unorganized) can and do coexist in the very same political event. However, as we have intimated throughout this book, there has been a tendency in recent years to promote the significance of everyday micro-politics (psychological distancing, identity politics, office bitching, hidden transcripts, etc.) as being somehow more in tune with power today. A good deal of the research exploring workplace resistance follows on from the control literature insofar as it conceptually favours struggles that are situated within or around the subjective features of the employment relationship. Now that we have, apparently, entered a new era in which the 'objects for management control are decreasingly labour power and behaviour and increasingly the mind power and subjectivities of employees' (Alvesson and Deetz, 1996: 192), the kinds of resistance we are likely to find are thought to be expressed via selfhood, ethics, identity, self-transformation, re-enchantment and emotions. As Stanley Deetz insists, 'The politics of identity and identity representation may be the deepest and most suppressed struggle in the workplace' (Deetz, 1992b: 59).

Such an emphasis on identity and subjectivity in relation to work-place struggle is an important corrective to the over-totalizing port-rayal of workplace controls that dominated critical organization theory in the 1990s. It also provides a useful antidote to an earlier notion of resistance that relied upon the Fordist cliché of class conflict. But we feel that the current 'cult of the subject' has perhaps outlived its usefulness as a window on workplace politics, resistance and struggle. This is for three reasons. First, there is an assumption that we have now entered a new era in which overt, collective and antagonistic dissent is obsolete. Because 'grandiose' manifestations of resistance were absent in many investigations of identity-based controls (culture management, self-managing teams, etc.), the argument goes, we should turn to more inconspicuous spaces where dissent will invariably flourish. For a start, the timing of this call to privilege ultra-local, subjective emancipations is incredible when we are witnessing the emergence of a 'new world order' that signifies both a deleteriously totalizing system of govern-mentality and the potential for opposition on a scale never before known (Hardt and Negri, 2004). As we have argued in this book, unionism, new social movements and brazen anti-discrimination pro-tests are alive and well, defining the nature of work organizations in important ways. Subjectivity is important here, but more as an out-come of justice claims and material protest rather than as an aim of resistance in and of itself.

A second concern with the postmodern privileging of the subject is the danger of banalizing workplace struggle. Although useful in certain circumstances, the expansion of the concept of resistance to include micro-identity politics (e.g. being 'bothered', mental withdrawal, resig-nation, etc.) can quickly lead to an unhelpful celebration of the most banal social practices. We agree with Meaghan Morris (1996) that the obsession with the prosaic has ushered in a new kind of criticism that envisages anything and everything as 'subversive'. Morris quotes Judith Williamson's criticisms of British cultural studies, which she contends consists of 'left-wing academics ... picking out strands of "subversion" in every piece of pop culture from Street Style to Soap Opera' (Williamson, 1986: 14–15). This is not a necessary consequence of studying the subversive elements of everyday practices but it still stands as a salutary reminder about how and why we interpret things as we do. In relating these concerns to critical organization studies we could ask some provocative questions. For example, might not some of the activities we label as 'transgressive' more plausibly be termed, *inter alia*, 'discretion', 'autonomy' or 'initiative'?

A third danger with the current obsession with 'subjective resistance' is the unfortunate separation of 'new' identity-based modalities of resistance from the more 'outdated' concepts of the wage–effort bargain, economic struggle and so forth. This issue was picked up in chapters 5 and 8 in relation to Nancy Fraser's arguments about justice. Much of the post-structuralist literature in organization studies argues that identity-based struggles occupy a different register compared to those of yesteryear, which emanated from monetary or materialist preoccupations (e.g. unions). The thematic of capitalism is downplayed as irrelevant in these new times of work relations. Some even go so far as actively discouraging an analysis of 'material concerns' (e.g. wages and conditions) because it might enforce the 'dominance of a positivist epistemology' (Alvesson and Willmott, 2002: 621). In this book we hope that the concept of struggle and the multifaceted justice claims discussed highlight the continuing importance of monetary and/or materialist concerns. As we pointed out in chapters 5 and 8, struggles around recognition and redistribution are closely related, and often play off each other in complex ways. We suggest that more needs to be said about capitalism, wealth distribution and class relations since they have been so underplayed in much of the so-called critical management studies literature. Indeed, as Yiannis Gabriel rightly opines, 'What kind of theoretical perspective does it take to view money as something that plays no part in the way individuals construct their identity?' (Gabriel, 1999: 188). Or, to state it differently, is there not something fundamentally symbolic about money and essentially material about identity work? In this sense, and as we argued in chapter 5 and elsewhere, struggles over dignity cannot easily be unravelled from struggles over equity.

Perhaps the distinction between the 'humble' and the 'grandiose' is a false one, given that even large-scale political upheaval usually begins with and is sustained by prosaic agitation. When one surveys the global political scene, it does seem to be infused with some very conspicuous social struggles that invariably filter through the corporation. For example, at the time of writing (June 2006) thousands of workers in the ASDA supermarket chain are threatening to go on strike over wage and conditions claims. Management and union officials are frantically endeavouring to reach an agreement that will avert strike action. In relation to this case, we agree with Harriet Bradley, Mark Erickson, Carol Stephenson and Steve Williams' (2000) argument that the widespread assumption regarding the absence of trade union activity and/or class politics is indeed a 'myth'. Why do critical management scholars favour inconspicuous and subterranean identity-based struggles over these more 'traditionally' based interventions? Academic fads and fashions certainly play a role, and arguably lead to a somewhat conservative research agenda. It is hoped that this book has demonstrated that one can approach such 'grandiose' and traditional struggles while remaining faithful to a nuanced and contemporary social theory of organizational politics.

The place of organizational struggle

The framework of struggle as it has been presented in this book has demonstrated that organizations are not hermetically sealed off from society when it comes to power, politics and resistance. The power of the corporation today extends far beyond the boundaries of work, and deep into the private lives of citizens. This we saw in the Sunray case discussed in chapters 5 and 6, where the culture programme 'haemorrhaged' in a manner that absorbed the lifestyles, consumption patterns and social activities of employees. This quest to build 'cultures of fun' is, in part at least, characterized by the symbolic displacement of work. Employees are strongly encouraged to make their work playful and experience emotions of fun by emulating practices normally reserved for non-work situations. This is different from culture management simply encroaching upon the private lives of employees through overwork or stress (see Scase and Goffee, 1989; Kunda, 1992). Here, the inverse seems to be the case: positive experiences and emotions *presumed* to be associated with the non-work sphere (such as relaxation, recreation, fun, etc.) are actively invoked in organizations rather than suppressed or prohibited.

Andrew Ross (2004) identifies a similar process in the dot.com company he studied in Silicon Alley. This firm wanted to retain the bleeding-edge bohemian ethos of dissent, lifestyle and fun in order to nurture competitive innovation. As a result, the usual distinction between work and self was eroded, so that more significant aspects of the employee (including his/her sexual orientation) became a corporate resource. In addition, with the inexorable spread of commercialism, almost every aspect of society is for someone at least a point of production, a sphere of labour. As Michael Hardt and Antonio Negri write,

The factory can no longer be conceived as the paradigmatic site of the concentration of labour and production; labouring processes have moved outside the factory walls to invest the entire society. (Hardt and Negri, 1994: 9)

When I leave the office tonight, someone else's labour will take me home (a bus driver). When I enjoy my weekend leisure, I also enter someone's place of work. While feminists and Marxists have perhaps always recognized the importance of civil society for subjectively preparing labour and supporting the ostensibly independent organization, for some reason it is still largely absent in many accounts of organizational power relationships in critical management studies.

If the logic of the modern organization is seen in this light, then we must also think well beyond the traditional boundaries of the workplace in order to understand struggle. As we have noted in the chapters above, especially in relation to the ABC protest and the Melbourne Port dispute, broader discourses, the popular media and public sentiment play an enormously important role in shaping the context and outcome of the organizational struggle. For example, new social movements associated with labour rights in both the underdeveloped and overdeveloped worlds have had a major impact on the corporate strategies of Nike, Gap and so forth. But, even in the less obvious case of Sunray, we witnessed the importance of the extra-employment sphere becoming a point of contention and a platform for struggle. The cynical cohort, for example, experienced a strong sense of inauthenticity regarding the quest to make work fun by imitating outside experiences and rituals. The failure to reproduce faithfully the complete experiences of 'family' or 'partying' resulted in some viewing the culture programme as pretentious and insincere. This derived from both the rather maudlin depiction of family, school, weekends and parties by the company and also the perception that management were simply 'trying too hard' to recreate these images.

While exit and absenteeism have been explored as a form of organizational misbehaviour (see Ackroyd and Thompson, 1999), one related issue regarding the logic of struggle in and around the organization has received little attention. This is because these resistors have chosen not to enter the firm due to political and lifestyle concerns. Jana Costas refers to this point in relation to self-alienation when she writes: '[P]erhaps we should therefore not only study resistance within the boundaries of the company, but also recognize those employees who leave or *do not even enter* such "colonizing" zones in the first place. Maybe we need to look more broadly at the resistance process that self-alienation may fuel, in the decisions made outside the company' (Costas, 2006: 46; emphasis in original). This point connects nicely with the argument we made in chapter 9. Struggle is a process of creating spaces where justice can be pursued and achieved – and one way in which this can occur is through an act of abstinence from the very realms that foster injustice (i.e. certain types of work organizations). Indeed, aren't some business schools overflowing with critical management studies students who cannot bear the thought of 'selling their souls' at the market rate offered by consulting companies and investment banks? Innumerable educated middle-class professionals now choose to connect to the anti-globalization movement rather than the corporate world. The struggle for, against and with capitalist employment might just as well take place outside the traditional sphere of organizational life because of self-selection, lifestyle choices and alternative career paths.

An end to struggle in organizations?

If struggle is a process by which power and resistance join together in a search for a place where justice can be achieved in organizations, then is it possible to envisage a time when struggle is no longer required? This is a key question dominating not just critical organization theory but also social theory more generally, since it connects to a number of issues around how we approach progress, freedom and emancipation. This problem is often couched in an artificial dichotomy between 'realistic' and 'utopian' accounts of work. Here, struggle is seen as something that will always need to occur, since politics is endemic to the human condition, and therefore we will always be fighting for something, no matter how we reconfigure relations of employment. To think otherwise is to fall into the trap of 'utopian' thinking, whereby we imagine an end in which total freedom might prevail. Momentary 'settlements' may be possible, but they will always be fragile (Zysman, 1994). The spectre of struggle continues to haunt even the most consolidated institution. Indeed, as the comment by Karl Marx opening this conclusion highlights, struggle may not lead to liberation or emancipation, since 'progress' is never guaranteed. For Marx, the fundamental problem with utopian versions of social critique is that they envisage a better social formation by retroactively inscribing it in history. That is to say, 'the good' is assumed to be a steadfast historical undercurrent that will one day reveal its true hand in the dawn of a new era of freedom.

We are ambivalent on this point. On the one hand, we agree with social critics such as Ernesto Laclau (2000) who feel that antagonism and struggle constitute an end in itself insofar as they represent the possibility of justice and freedom in organizations. Such a possibility may now and then produce results, but as long as it is occurring then we should be happy since some form of democratic spirit is not far away. On the other hand, however, we do see a role for some kind of utopianism (if we must call it that) that harbours a hope for a time without struggle in work organizations. We are very pessimistic about the history of capitalism, but are optimistic about 'what is to be done' and the future of work organizations. This space of hope is undeconstructable, in Jacques Derrida's (1994) sense of the term, because it is always coming, an unpredictable and haunting murmur of a present that has not yet arrived.

Perhaps this will indeed be a future without work. In any event, the aporia between the present and the future is the very stuff of political agency, and it involves challenging the present in a way that is committed to debate about 'how things might be different/better' in relation to work organizations, as well as formulating criteria for making such judgements and organizing thoughtful practice.

Notes

Introduction

1. There are a number of other excellent introductions to the issue of power and politics that the reader might like to consult. Among the best overviews are Pfeffer (1981, 1992), Clegg (1979, 1989) and Clegg, Coupasson and Philips (2006).

Chapter 1

1. Surprisingly, there has never been a strong tradition of normative theories of power in organization. This means that there are often veiled assumptions about what the most desirable means of organizing power are. Only rarely are these veiled assumptions systematically subjected to reasoned analysis. However, a number of contributions have sought to address this shortcoming by applying normative political philosophy to the organization of power. Examples of this work include neo-Marxist theories of emancipation (Alvesson and Willmott, 1992) and liberal theories of bureaucracy (Armbrüster, 2003).

2. The argument that power may be multifaceted and have a number of 'faces' was first suggested by Peter Bachrach and Morton Baratz (1962) in their response to Robert Dahl's theory of power. The concept of faces was subsequently used in Steven Lukes' (1974/2005) classic *Power: A Radical view*, as well as in other subsequent reviews of the field of power such as that by Cynthia Hardy and Sharon Leiba-O'Sullivan (1998). The concept of faces of power has also been called into question recently by Clarissa Rile Hayward (2000).

3. Dahl's theory of power is considerably influenced by Max Weber. This can be seen in Weber's (1924/1947: 152) definition of power as 'the probability that one actor within a social relationship will be in a position to carry out his own will despite resistance'. This definition informed a stream of foundational studies of power, including those by Harold Laswell and Abraham Kaplan (1950), Herbert Simon (1953) and Nelson Polsby (1960). Most mainstream approaches use this understanding of power. Indeed, foundational work on personality factors (Schein, 1977),

skills (Thompson, 1956), resource dependency (Pfeffer and Salancik, 1974) and uncertainty (Hickson et al., 1971) all define power using Dahl's terms.

4. We should note that, when these threats are acted upon in the form of physical aggression, they no longer constitute a form of power. Instead, they become mere violence. Hannah Arendt (1970) points out that we should draw a sharp distinction between power that relies on 'acting in concert' and violence, which is direct physical coercion. She argues that physical violence is not a particularly sustainable way of maintaining control over a population because it requires constant and bloody action. Power, in contrast, can continue to influence the behaviour of a population, even when it remains a veiled threat. Some commentators have noted, however, that power is often bolstered and backed up with the looming threat of physical violence. For instance, Anthony Giddens (1985) points out that the power of the state is maintained through its monopoly over the use of violence.

5. Weber's understanding of power as a feature of formal structural positions is reflected in subsequent work on hierarchy by Henri Fayol (1949), Alvin Gouldner (1954), Peter Blau (1965) and Derek Pugh, David Hickson, C. Robert Hinings and C. Turner (1968).

Chapter 2

1. For some reviews of resistance in organizations, see Mayer Zald and Michael Berger (1978), Paul Edwards, David Collinson and Giuseppe Della Rocca (1995), Stephen Ackroyd and Paul Thompson (1999), Calvin Morrill, Mayer Zald and Hayagreeva Rao (2003) and Peter Fleming (2005a).

2. This paragraph draws on joint work with Steffen Böhm.

Chapter 5

1. Burrell (1984) uses the term 'repression' in order to explain this eradication process. But he accepts Foucault's (1979) critique of the repression hypothesis. The eradication of sexuality from the workplace is not a denial of human nature but a political manoeuvre that seeks to close down the ever-present potential for sex. This potential does not stem from a universal libido but from the explosion of discourse about sex in the West.

2. In accordance with other studies of this type (Kunda, 1992; Barker, 1993; Casey, 1995; etc.), qualitative data collection methods were chosen in

order to gain an intensive situational understanding of the meaning systems in play (van Maanen, 1998). These included one-on-one interviews, focus group interviews, shadowing, observation and document analysis. A sample of three human resource managers and thirty employees was selected and interviewed at various intervals over eight months. The size of the sample was limited to thirty employees because of the in-depth nature of the interviews. The sample consisted of eighteen females and fifteen males. The average age of telephone agents interviewed was twenty-three (which had significance for the research findings, as will be discussed shortly). The human resource managers were in their mid- to late thirties. The initial selection process was randomly taken from a sampling frame of ten projects and forty teams provided by the organization. However, one interviewee introduced me to his 'cohort', consisting of three other informants, which then became a focus in the project. This non-probability sample was not representative in a quantitative sense, but nor did it intend to be, given the qualitative nature of the project (Silverman, 2001).

Document analysis focused on discourse pertaining to the culture programme found in a training handbook for new recruits (called the 'Rainbow Book'), specific project manuals, recruitment advertisements, extensive newspaper and magazine reports from the business press and booklets from training sessions. Observation and shadowing were used at the beginning of the project to give the researcher a more grounded feel for the job task and environment before the interviews began. Human resource managers were interviewed on-site for periods ranging from forty-five minutes to one and a half hours. Telephone agents were interviewed about the culture programme both on-site (at their desks and in a conference room provided by the company) and outside the firm (homes, cafés, etc.), the latter yielding opinions that would not have been as evident had the interviews been conducted only on-site. Data from the aforementioned cohort of four employees were gathered from semi-structured focus group interviews outside working hours, which were conducted in an informal and conversational manner.

3. The term 'slacker cool' has positive connotations within youth culture, meaning someone who is capable, yet wry and underground.

4. I have phrased this rewording using the pseudonym, which does not quite capture the creative wordplay intended by informants.

5. Fraser's ideas were developed via a critical dialogue with Judith Butler. Fraser (1995) argued that struggles for recognition and redistribution could be conceptually positioned at different ends of the political continuum. Butler (1997) responded by arguing that marginalized gay identities, for example, are not 'merely cultural' but have material effects that

are both economic and non-economic; they cannot be separated. Fraser (1998) rejoined by agreeing that marginalized identities often do suffer redistribution inequalities but claimed that this is more an effect of the cultural discrimination guiding material distribution. Indeed, as the Sunray case illustrates, capitalism is not inherently anti-gay. In her latest work, Fraser (2005) adds the third dimension of political representation in order to map claims for social justice in a globalized world. These notions of justice are unpacked in more detail in chapter 8.

Chapter 8

1. A poison pill is an arrangement whereby a firm can buy back its shares at a discounted rate if a corporate raider threatens to take over ownership of the firm. Anti-takeover legislation has been adopted by over a half of the American states in order to stop local companies being bought by corporate raiders. Greenmail is a situation in which a firm buys shares off a corporate raider who threatens to take over the company at a higher price than the shares would trade for on the open market. Each of these practices makes it more difficult to take over the company, making it harder for shareholders to influence the company and thus reducing the value of the shares in the company.

References

Abbott, P., and M. Tyler (1998). 'Chocs away: weight watching in the contemporary airline industry', *Sociology*, 32 (3): 433–50.

ABC (1939). *ABC Annual*. Canberra: Government Publishing Office.

(1991). *ABC Annual Report*. Sydney: Australian Broadcasting Corporation.

(1993). *ABC Annual Report*. Sydney: Australian Broadcasting Corporation.

(1996). *ABC Annual Report*. Sydney: Australian Broadcasting Corporation.

(1997). *ABC Annual Report*. Sydney: Australian Broadcasting Corporation.

(1999). *ABC Annual Report*. Sydney: Australian Broadcasting Corporation.

Ackroyd, S., and P. Thompson (1999). *Organizational Misbehaviour*. London: Sage.

Agamben, G. (1998). *Homo Sacer: Sovereign Power and Bare Life*. Stanford, CA: Stanford University Press.

Alexander, E. R. (1979). 'The design of alternatives in organizational contexts: a pilot study', *Administrative Science Quarterly*, 24 (3): 382–404.

Althusser, L. (1971). 'Ideology and ideological state apparatuses (notes towards an investigation)', in *Lenin and Philosophy and Other Essays* (trans. B. Brewster). London: New Left.

Alvesson, M., and Y. D. Billing (1997). *Understanding Gender and Organizations*. London: Sage.

Alvesson, M. (1987). *Organization Theory and Technocratic Consciousness: Rationality, Ideology and Quality of Work*. New York: de Gruyter.

Alvesson, M., and S. Deetz (1996). 'Critical theory and postmodernism approaches to organizational studies', in S. R. Clegg, C. Hardy and W. Nord (eds.), *Handbook of Organization Studies*. London: Sage.

Alvesson, M., and H. Willmott (1992). 'On the idea of emancipation in management and organization studies', *Academy of Management Review*, 17 (3): 432–64.

(2002). 'Identity regulation as organizational control: producing the appropriate individual', *Journal of Management Studies*, 39 (5): 619–43.

Apgar, M. (1998). 'The alternative workplace: changing where and how people work', *Harvard Business Review*, 76 (3): 121–38.

Appadurai, A. (2000). *Globalization*. Durham, NC: Duke University Press.

Arendt, H. (1958). *The Human Condition*. Chicago: University of Chicago Press.

196

(1970). *On Violence*. London: Allen Lane.

Armbrüster, T. (2003). *Political Liberalism, Management, and Organization Theory*. Paper presented at the 19th European Group for Organizational Studies Colloquium, Copenhagen, 3–5 July.

Armstrong, E. (2005). 'From struggle to settlement: the crystallization of a field of lesbian/gay organizations in San Francisco, 1969–1973', in G. F. Davis, D. McAdam, W. R. Scott and M. N. Zald (eds.), *Social Movements and Organization Theory*. Cambridge: Cambridge University Press.

Aronowitz, S., and H. Gautley (eds.) (2003). *Implicating Empire: Globalization and Resistance in the 21st Century*. New York: Basic.

Ashford, S. J., N. P. Rothbard, S. K. Piderit and J. E. Dutton (1998). 'Out on a limb: the role of contest and impression management in selling gender-equity issues', *Administrative Science Quarterly*, 43 (1): 23–57.

Ashforth, B., and R. Humphrey (1993). 'Emotional labour in service roles: the influence of identity', *Academy of Management Review*, 18 (1): 88–115.

Bachelard, G. (1958). *The Poetics of Space* (trans. M. Jolas). Boston: Beacon Press.

Bachrach, P., and M. Baratz (1962). 'Two faces of power', *American Political Science Review*, 56 (4): 947–52.

(1963). 'Decisions and nondecisions: an analytical framework', *American Political Science Review*, 57 (3): 641–51.

Bain, P., and P. Taylor (2000). 'Entrapped by the electronic panopticon? Worker resistance in the call centre', *New Technology, Work and Employment*, 15 (1): 2–18.

Baldry, C (1999). 'Space – the final frontier', *Sociology*, 33 (3): 535–53.

Banerjee, B., and S. Linstead (2001). 'Globalization, multiculturalism and other fictions: colonialism for the new millennium?', *Organization*, 8 (4): 683–722.

Barbalet, J. M. (1985). 'Power and resistance', *British Journal of Sociology*, 36 (4): 531–48.

Barker, J. R. (1993). 'Tightening the iron cage: concertive control in self-managing teams', *Administrative Science Quarterly*, 38 (4): 408–37.

(1999). *The Discipline of Teamwork: Participation and Concertive Control*. London: Sage.

Barley, S. R., and G. Kunda (1992). 'Design and devotion: surges of rational and normative ideologies of control in managerial discourse', *Administrative Science Quarterly*, 37 (3): 363–99.

Barnard, C. (1938). *The Functions of the Executive*. Cambridge, MA: Harvard University Press.

Bataille, G. (1962). *Eroticism: Death and Sensuality* (trans. M. Dalwood). San Francisco: City Lights.

Baudrillard, J. (1990). *Seduction*. London: Palgrave Macmillan.

Bauman, Z. (1991). *Modernity and the Holocaust*. Cambridge: Polity Press.

Bendix, R. (1956). *Work and Authority in Industry: Ideologies of Management in the Course of Industrialization*. Berkeley: University of California Press.

Benhabib, S. (1986). *Critique, Norm and Utopia: A Study of the Foundations of Critical Theory*. New York: Columbia University Press.

   (2004). *The Rights of the Other: Aliens, Residents and Citizens*. Cambridge: Cambridge University Press.

Bennett, T. (1998). *Culture: A Reformer's Science*. Sydney: Allen and Unwin.

Bensman, J., and I. Gerver (1963). 'Crime and punishment in the factory: the function of deviancy in maintaining the social system', *American Sociological Review*, 28 (4): 588–98.

Berger, P., and T. Luckmann (1966). *The Social Construction of Reality*. Harmondsworth: Penguin.

Beynon, H. (1980). *Working for Ford*. Harmondsworth: Penguin.

Blau, P. M. (1965). *Exchange and Power in Social Life*. New York: Wiley.

Boltanski, L., and E. Chiapello (2005). *The New Spirit of Capitalism* (trans. G. Elliot). London: Verso.

Bourdieu, P. (1983). 'Social space and symbolic power', *Sociological Theory*, 1: 14–25.

   (1984). *Distinctions: A Social Critique of the Judgement of Tastes*. Cambridge, MA: Harvard University Press.

Bradley, H. (1999). *Gender and Power in the Workplace*. London: Macmillan.

Bradley, H., M. Erickson, C. Stephenson and S. Williams (2000). *Myths at Work*. Cambridge: Polity Press.

Braudel, F. (1961). *Chapters in Western Civilisation*. New York: Columbia University Press.

   (1982). *Civilization and Capitalism, 15th–18th Century* (trans. S. Reynolds). New York: Harper and Row.

Braverman, H. (1974). *Labor and Monopoly Capital*. New York: Monthly Review Press.

Brenner, N. (1998). 'Global cities, global states: global city formation and state territorial restructuring in contemporary Europe', *Review of International Political Economy*, 5 (1): 1–37.

Brewis, J. (2005). 'Signing my life away? Researching sex and organization', *Organization*, 12 (4): 493–510.

Brewis, J., and C. Grey (1994). 'Re-eroticizing the organization: an exegesis and critique', *Gender, Work and Organization*, 1 (2): 67–82.

Brewis, J., and S. Linstead (2000). *Sex, Work and Sex Work*. London: Routledge.

Brocklehurst, M. (2001). 'Power, identity and new technology homework: implications for "new forms" of organizing', *Organization Studies*, 22 (3): 445–66.

Brown, G. (1977). *Sabotage*. Nottingham: Spokesman.

Brown, R. H. (1978). 'Bureaucracy as praxis: toward a political phenomenology of formal organization', *Administrative Science Quarterly*, 23 (3): 365–82.

Brown, R. H. (1987). *Society as Text: Essays in Rhetoric, Reason and Reality*. Chicago: University of Chicago Press.

Brown, W. (1995). *States of Injury*. Princeton, NJ: Princeton University Press.

Burawoy, M. (1979). *Manufacturing Consent: Changes in the Labor Process Under Monopoly Capitalism*. Chicago: University of Chicago Press.

Burchell, G., C. Gordon and P. Miller (1991). *The Foucault Effect: Studies in Governmentality*. London: Harvester Wheatsheaf.

Burgmann, V. (2003). *Power, Profit and Protest: Australian Social Movements and Globalisation*. Sydney: Allen and Unwin.

Burrell, G. (1984). 'Sex and organizational analysis', *Organization Studies*, 5 (9): 97–118.

(1992). 'The organization of pleasure', in M. Alvesson and H. Willmott (eds.), *Critical Management Studies*. London: Sage.

(1997). *Pandemonium: Towards a Retro-Organization Theory*. London: Sage.

Burrell, G., and J. Hearn (1990). 'The sexuality of organization', in J. Hearn, D. Sheppard, P. Tancred-Sheriff and G. Burrell (eds.), *The Sexuality of Organization*. London: Sage.

Burrell, G., and G. Morgan (1979). *Sociological Paradigms and Organisational Analysis*. London: Heinemann Educational.

Butler, J. (1990). *Gender Trouble: Feminism and the Subversion of Identity*. New York: Routledge.

(1993). *Bodies That Matter: On the Discursive Limits of 'Sex'*. New York: Routledge.

(1997). 'Merely cultural', *Social Text*, 52–3: 265–77.

(1998). 'Merely cultural: non-material leftist movements', *New Left Review*, 227: 33–44.

(2000). 'Restaging the universal: hegemony and the limits of formalism', in J. Butler, E. Laclau and S. Žižek (eds.), *Contingency, Hegemony, Universality: Contemporary Dialogues on the Left*. London: Verso.

Callaghan, G., and P. Thompson (2002). 'We recruit attitude: the selection and shaping of routine call centre labour', *Journal of Management Studies*, 39 (2): 233–54.

Cameron, A., and R. Palan (1999). 'The imagined economy: mapping transformations in the contemporary state'. *Millennium*, 28 (2): 267–88.

Cannetti, E. (1962). *Crowds and Power*. London: Phoenix.

Carroll, W. K., and R. S. Ratner (2001). 'Sustaining oppositional cultures in "post-socialist" times: a comparative study of three social movement organizations', *Sociology*, 35 (3): 605–29.

Carter, C., M. Kornberger and S. R. Clegg (2003). 'The polyphonic spree: the case of the Liverpool dockers', *Industrial Relations Journal*, 34 (4): 290–304.

Casey, C. (1995). *Work, Self and Society: After Industrialism*. London: Sage.

(1996). 'Corporate transformations: designer culture, designer employees and "post-occupational" solidarity', *Organization*, 3 (3): 317–39.

(1999). '"Come, join our family": discipline and integration in corporate organizational culture', *Human Relations*, 52 (2): 155–78.

(2000). 'Sociology sensing the body', in J. Hassard, R. Holliday and H. Willmott (eds.), *Body and Organization*. London: Sage.

Castells, M. (1977). *The Urban Question: A Marxist Approach*. London: Edward Arnold.

(1996). *The Rise of the Network Society*. Oxford: Blackwell.

Clawson, D., and M. A. Clawson (1999). 'What has happened to the US labor movement? Union decline and renewal', *Annual Review of Sociology*, 25: 95–119.

Clegg, S. R. (1975). *Power, Rule and Domination*. London: Routledge.

(1979). *The Theory of Power and Organization*. London: Routledge and Kegan Paul.

(1981). 'Organization and control', *Administrative Science Quarterly*, 26 (4): 545–62.

(1989). *Frameworks of Power*. London: Sage.

(1990). *Modern Organizations: Organization Studies in the Postmodern World*. London: Sage.

Clegg, S. R., D. Courpasson and N. Philips (2006). *Power and Organizations*. London: Sage.

Clegg, S. R., and D. Dunkerley (1980). *Organization, Class and Control*. London: Routledge and Kegan Paul.

Cockburn, C. (1983). *Brothers: Male Dominance and Technological Change*. London: Pluto.

(1991). *In the Way of Women*. London: Macmillan.

Cohen, S., and L. Taylor (1992). *Escape Attempts: The Theory and Practice of Resistance to Everyday Life*, 2nd edn. London: Routledge.

Cole, G. D. H. (1917). *Self-Government in Industry*. London: Hutchison Education.

Collinson, D. (1992). *Managing the Shopfloor: Subjectivity, Masculinity and Workplace Culture*. London: Sage.

(1994). 'Strategies of resistance', in J. Jermier, D. Knights and W. Nord (eds.), *Resistance and Power in Organizations*. London: Sage.

(2002). 'Managing humour', *Journal of Management Studies*, 39 (3): 269–88.

Collinson, D., and M. Collinson (1990). 'Sexuality in the workplace: the domination of men's sexuality', in J. Hearn, D. Sheppard, P. Tancred-Sheriff and G. Burrell (eds.), *The Sexuality of Organization*. London: Sage.

Connel, J., and P. Waring (2002). 'The BOHICA syndrome: a symptom of cynicism towards change initatives?', *Strategic Change*, 11 (7): 347–56.

Costas, J. (2006). *'From Who We Are' to 'Who We are Not': Revisiting the Concept of Self-Alienation in Organization Studies*. Masters dissertation: Judge Business School, University of Cambridge.

CPSU (1997a). *Mansfield Report Delivers the Government's ABC Cuts Agenda*. Media release, 24 January. Sydney: Community and Public Sector Union.

(1997b). *Howard Refuses Petition to Save ABC*. Media release, 24 September. Sydney: Community and Public Sector Union.

(1997c). *ABC Cuts Music Recording in Australian Music Week*. Media release, 19 November. Sydney: Community and Public Sector Union.

(2000). *CPSU Calls for Full Public Inquiry into ABC Plans to Sell On-line Content to Telstra*. Media release, 7 Febuary. Sydney: Community and Public Sector Union.

(2001). *Save the ABC Rally: Huge Turnout Expected*. Media release, 20 April. Sydney: Community and Public Sector Union.

Creed, W. E. D., and M. A. Scully (2000). 'Songs of ourselves: employees' deployment of social identity in workplace encounters', *Journal of Management Inquiry*, 9: 391–412.

Creed, W. E. D., M. A. Scully and J. R. Austin (2002). 'Clothes make the person: the tailoring of legitimating accounts and the social construction of identity', *Organization Science*, 13: 475–96.

Crouch, C. (2004). *Post-Democracy*. Cambridge: Polity Press.

Crozier, M. (1964). *The Bureaucratic Phenomenon*. Chicago: University of Chicago Press.

(1972). 'The problem of power', *Social Research*, 40: 211–28.

Dahl, R. (1957). 'The concept of power', *Behavioural Science*, 2: 201–15.

Davis, G., and T. A. Thompson (1994). 'A social movement perspective on corporate control', *Administrative Science Quarterly*, 39 (1): 141–73.

Davis, G., D. McAdam, W. R. Scott and M. N. Zald (eds.) (2005). *Social Movements and Organization Theory*. Cambridge: Cambridge University Press.

Day, R. J. F. (2004). 'From hegemony to affinity: the political logic of the newest social movements', *Cultural Studies*, 18 (5): 716–48.

de Certeau, M. (1984). *The Practice of Everyday Life*. Berkeley: University of California Press.

Dean, M. (1999). *Governmentality*. London: Sage.

Deetz, S. (1992a). 'Disciplinary power in the modern corporation', in M. Alvesson and H. Willmott (eds.), *Critical Management Studies*. London: Sage.

 (1992b). *Democracy in the Age of Corporate Colonization: Developments in the Communication and the Politics of Everyday Life*. Albany, NY: SUNY Press.

Deleuze, G. (1992). 'Postscript on the societies of control', *October*, 59 (Winter): 3–7.

Deleuze, G., and F. Guattari (1977). *Anti Oedipus: Capitalism and Schizophrenia* (trans. R. Hurley, M. Seem and H. R. Lane). Minneapolis: University of Minnesota Press.

Dempster, Q. (2000). *Death Struggle*. St Leonards, New South Wales: Allen and Unwin.

Derrida, J. (1994). *Spectres of Marx: The State of the Debt, the Work of Mourning, and the New International* (trans. P. Kamuf). New York: Routledge.

Derry, S., and N. Kinnie (2002). 'Call centres and beyond: a thematic evaluation' *Human Resource Management*, 12 (4): 3–13.

Dick, P., and C. Cassell (2001). 'Barriers to managing diversity in a UK constabulary: the role of discourse', *Journal of Management Studies*, 39 (7): 953–76.

Digeser, P. (1992). 'The fourth face of power', *Journal of Politics*, 54 (4): 977–1007.

DiMaggio, P. J., and W. Powell (1983). 'The iron cage revisited: institutional isomorphism and collective rationality in organization fields', *American Sociological Review*, 48: 147–60.

Disney, R., A. Gosling and S. Machin (1995). 'British unions in decline: determinants of the 1980s fall in union recognition', *Industrial and Labour Relations Review*, 48 (3): 403–19.

Dix, A. (1981). *The ABC in Review: National Broadcasting in the 1980s*. Canberra: Australian Government Publishing Service.

Douglass, F. (1857/1985). 'The significance of emancipation in the West Indies', in *The Frederick Douglass Papers, Series 1: Speeches, Debates, and Interviews*, Vol. III, *1855–63* (ed. J. W. Blassingame). New Haven, CT: Yale University Press.

Dubois, P. (1979). *Sabotage in Industry*. Harmondsworth: Penguin.

du Gay, P. (1996). *Consumption and Identity at Work*. London: Sage.

(2000a). 'Representing globalization: notes on the discursive ordering of economic life', in P. Gilroy, L. Grossberg and A. McRobbie (eds.), *Without Guarantees: In Honour of Stuart Hall*. London: Verso.

(2000b). *In Praise of Bureaucracy: Weber, Organization, Ethics*. London: Sage.

Du Gay, P., and G. Salaman (1992). 'The cult[ure] of the customer', *Journal of Management Studies*, 29 (5): 615–33.

Duffy, F. (1997). *The New Office*. London: Conrad Octopus.

Dworkin, R. (1981). 'What is equality? Part 2: Equality of resources', *Philosophy and Public Affairs*, 10 (4): 283–345.

Eagleton, T. (1991). *Ideology: An Introduction*. London: Verso.

(1996). *The Illusions of Postmodernism*. Oxford: Blackwell.

Edwards, P., D. Collinson and G. Della Rocca (1995). 'Workplace resistance in Western Europe', *European Journal of Industrial Relations*, 1 (3): 283–316.

Edwards, R. (1979). *Contested Terrain: The Transformation of the Workplace in the Twentieth Century*. New York: Basic.

Elias, N. (1978). *The Civilizing Process*. Oxford: Blackwell.

Elster, J. (1983). *Sour Grapes: The Subversion of Rationality*. Cambridge: Cambridge University Press.

Ezzamel, M., H. Willmott and F. Worthington (2001). 'Power, control and resistance in the factory that time forgot', *Journal of Management Studies*, 38 (8): 1053–79.

FABC (1999a). *Background Briefing*, 1 (3). Sydney: Friends of the ABC.

(1999b). *Background Briefing*, 1 (4). Sydney: Friends of the ABC.

(2000a). *Background Briefing*, 2 (3). Sydney: Friends of the ABC.

(2000b). *Background Briefing*, 2 (4). Sydney: Friends of the ABC.

Fairclough, N., and P. Thomas (2004). 'The discourse of globalization and the globalization of discourse', in D. Grant, C. Hardy, C. Oswick and L. Putnam (eds.), *The Handbook of Organizational Discourse*. London: Sage.

Fayol, H. (1949). *General and Industrial Management*. London: Pitman.

Felstead, A. (1996). 'Waged work at home: the social organization of industrial outwork in Hong Kong', *Work, Employment and Society*, 10 (3): 588–9.

Ferguson, K. (1984). *The Feminist Case Against Bureaucracy*. Philadelphia: Temple University Press.

Filby, M. P. (1992). 'The figures, the personalities and the bums: service work and sexuality', *Work Employment and Society*, 6 (1): 23–42.

Fischer, W. F., and T. Ponniah (2003). *Another World is Possible: Popular Alternatives to Globalization at the World Social Forum*. London: Zed.

Fleming, P. (2003). *Diogenes Goes to Work: Cynicism, Resistance and Culture in the Workplace*. Unpublished doctoral thesis: Department of Management, University of Melbourne.

(2005a). 'Metaphors of resistance', *Management Communication Quarterly*, 19 (1): 45–66.

(2005b). 'Workers' playtime? Boundaries and cynicism in a "culture of fun" program', *Journal of Applied Behavioural Science*, 41 (3): 285–303.

(2006). 'Sexuality, power and resistance in the workplace', *Organization Studies*, forthcoming.

Fleming, P., and G. Sewell (2002). 'Looking for the good soldier, Švejk: alternative modalities of resistance in the contemporary workplace', *Sociology* 36 (4): 857–73.

Fleming, P., and A. Spicer (2003). 'Working at a cynical distance: implications for subjectivity, power and resistance', *Organization*, 10 (1): 157–79.

Fleming, P., and A. J. Sturdy (2006). *Just be Yourself, or Else: Towards Neo-Normative Control in Organizations?* Working paper: Judge Business School, University of Cambridge.

Fligstein, N. (1987). 'The intraorganizational power struggle: rise of finance personnel to top leadership in large corporations, 1919–1979', *American Sociological Review*, 52 (1): 44–58.

Fondas, N. (1997). 'Feminization unveiled: management qualities in contemporary writings', *Academy of Management Review*, 22 (1): 257–82.

Foucault, M. (1963/1998). 'A preface to transgression' (trans. D. Bouchard and S. Simon), in D. Bouchard (ed.), *Language, Counter-Memory, Practice*. Ithaca, NY: Cornell University Press.

(1977). *Discipline and Punish: The Birth of the Prison* (trans. A. Sheridan). London: Penguin.

(1979). *The History of Sexuality*, Vol. I. London: Penguin.

(1980). *Power/Knowledge: Selected Interviews and Other Writings 1972–1977* (trans. C. Gordon). Brighton: Harvester Press.

(1982). 'Afterword: the subject and power', in H. Dreyfus and P. Rabinow (eds.), *Foucault: Beyond Structuralism and Hermeneutics*. Brighton: Harvester.

Fournier, V., and C. Grey (2000). 'At the critical moment: conditions and prospects for critical management studies', *Human Relations*, 53 (1): 7–32.

Fraser, N. (1989). *Unruly Practices: Power, Discourse and Gender in Contemporary Social Theory*. Minneapolis: University of Minnesota Press.

(1995). 'From redistribution to recognition: dilemmas of justice in a postsocialist age', *New Left Review*, 212: 68–95.

(1997). *Justice Interruptus: Critical Reflections on the 'Postsocialist' Condition*. London: Routledge.

(1998). 'Heterosexism, misrecognition, and capitalism: a response to Judith Butler', *New Left Review*, 228: 140–9.

(2003). 'Social justice in the age of identity politics: redistribution, recognition and participation', in N. Fraser and A. Honneth (eds.), *Redistribution or Recognition? A Political–Philosophical Exchange*. London: Verso.

(2005). 'Reframing justice in a globalizing world', *New Left Review*, 36: 69–88.

Fraser, N., and A. Honneth (2003). *Redistribution or Recognition? A Political-Philosophical Exchange*. London: Verso.

French, J. R. P., and B. Raven (1968). 'The bases of social power', in D. Cartwright and A. Zander (eds.), *Group Dynamics*, 3rd edn. New York: Harper and Row.

Freud, S. (1920/1961). *Beyond the Pleasure Principle* (trans. J. Strachey). London: Hogarth Press.

Friedman, A. L. (1977). *Industry and Labour: Class Struggle at Work and Monopoly Capitalism*. London: Macmillan.

Gabriel, Y. (1999). 'Beyond happy families: a critical reevaluation of the control–resistance–identity triangle', *Human Relations*, 52 (2): 179–203.

Gabriel, Y., S. Fineman and D. Sims (2000). *Organizing and Organizations*. London: Sage.

Gagliardi, P. (ed.) (1990). *Symbols and Artefacts of the Corporate Landscape*. Berlin: de Gruyter.

Ganesh, S., H. Zoller and G. Cheney (2004). 'Transforming resistance, broadening our boundaries: critical communication meets globalization from below', *Communication Monographs*, 72 (2): 163–91.

Garnsey, E., and B. Rees (1996). 'Discourse and enactment: gender inequity in text and context', *Human Relations*, 49 (8): 1041–64.

Gherardi, S. (1995). *Gender, Symbolism and Organizational Cultures*. London: Sage.

Giddens, A. (1985). *The Nation-State and Violence*. Cambridge: Polity Press.

(1992). *The Transformation of Intimacy: Sexuality, Love and Eroticism in Modern Societies*. Cambridge: Polity Press.

Goodman, N. (1978). *Ways of Worldmaking*. Indianapolis: Hackett.

Gordon, C. (1991). 'Governmental rationality: an introduction', in G. Burchell, C. Gordon and O. Miller (eds.), *The Foucault Effect: Studies of Governmentality*. London: Harvester Wheatsheaf.

Gouldner, A. (1954). *Patterns of Industrial Bureaucracy*. Glencoe, IL: Free Press.

(1955). *Wildcat Strike*. London: Routledge and Kegan Paul.

(1970). *The Coming Crisis of Western Sociology*. New York: Basic.

Graber, D. (2002). 'The new anarchists', *New Left Review*, 13: 61–73.

Gramsci, A. (1929–35/1971). *Selections from the Prison Notebooks* (trans. Q. Hoare and G. N. Smith). New York: International.

Grant, D., C. Hardy, C. Oswick and L. L. Putnam (2004). 'Introduction: organizational discourse: exploring the field', in D. Grant, C. Hardy,

C. Oswick and L.L. Putnam (eds.), *The Sage Handbook of Organizational Discourse*. London: Sage.

Griffin, G., and S. Svensen (1998). 'Industrial relations implications of the Australian waterside dispute', *Australian Bulletin of Labour*, 24 (3): 194–202.

Guerrier, Y., and A.S. Adib (2000). "No, we don't provide that service": the harassment of hotel employees by customers', *Work, Employment and Society*, 14 (4): 689–705.

Guillén, M. (1998). 'Scientific management's lost aesthetic: architecture, organization, and the Taylorized beauty of the mechanical', *Administrative Science Quarterly*, 42 (4): 682–715.

Gutek, B. (1985). *Sex and the Workplace: The Impact of Sexual Behaviour and Harassment on Women, Men and Organizations*. San Francisco: Jossey-Bass.

(1990). 'Sexuality in the workplace: key issues in social research and organizational practice', in J. Hearn, D. Sheppard, P. Tancred-Sheriff and G. Burrell (eds.), *The Sexuality of Organization*. London: Sage.

Gutek, B., and B. Morasch (1982). 'Sex ratios, sex role spill-over and sexual harassment of women at work', *Journal of Social Issues*, 22: 30–48.

Habermas, J. (1971). *Towards a Rational Society*. London: Heinemann.

(1991). *The Structural Transformation of the Public Sphere*. Cambridge: Polity Press.

Hage, J. and R. Dewar (1973). 'Elite values versus organizational structure in predicting innovation', *Administrative Science Quarterly*, 18 (3): 279–90.

Halford, S., and P. Leonard (2001). *Gender, Power and Organizations*. Basingstoke: Palgrave.

Hall, E. (1993). 'Smiling, deferring and flirting: doing gender by giving good service', *Work and Occupations*, 20 (4): 452–71.

Hall, M. (1990). 'Private experiences in the public domain: lesbians in organizations', in J. Hearn, D. Sheppard, P. Tancred-Sheriff and G. Burrell (eds.), *The Sexuality of Organization*. London: Sage.

Hardt, M., and A. Negri (1994). *The Labor of Dionysus: A Critique of the State Form*. Minneapolis: University of Minnesota Press.

(2000). *Empire*. Cambridge, MA: Harvard University Press.

(2004). *Multitude: War and Democracy in the Age of Empire*. New York: Penguin.

Hardy, C., and S. Leiba-O'Sullivan (1998). 'The power behind empowerment: implications for research and practice', *Human Relations*, 51 (4): 451–83.

Hardy, C., and N. Phillips (1998). 'Strategies of engagement: lessons from the critical examination of collaboration and conflict in an interorganizational domain', *Organization Science*, 9 (2): 217–30.

Harvey, D. (1973). *Social Justice and the City*. London: Edward Arnold.

(1989). *The Condition of Postmodernity: An Inquiry into the Origins of Social Change*. Oxford: Blackwell.

(1995). 'Globalization in question', *Rethinking MARXISM*, 8 (4): 1–17.

Hassard, J., R. Holliday and H. Willmott (eds.) (2000). *Body and Organization*. London: Sage.

Hay, C., and D. Marsh (2000). *Demystifying Globalization*. Basingstoke: Macmillan.

Hayward, C. R. (2000). *De-Facing Power*. Cambridge: Cambridge University Press.

Hearn, J. and W. Parkin (1995). *Sex at Work: The Power and Paradox of Organizational Sexuality*. Hemel Hempstead: Prentice Hall/Harvester Wheatsheaf.

(2001). *Gender, Sexuality and Violence in Organizations: The Unspoken Forces of Organization Violations*, 2nd edn. London: Sage.

Hegel, G. W. F. (1807/2005). *The Phenomenology of Mind*. Oxford: Oxford University Press.

Held, D., A. McGrew, D. Goldblatt and J. Perraton (1999). *Global Transformations: Economics, Politics, Culture*. Oxford: Polity Press.

Henley, N. (1977). *Body Politics: Power, Sex and Non-Verbal Communication*. Englewood Cliffs, NJ: Prentice Hall.

Hensmans, M. (2003). 'Social movement organizations: a metaphor for strategic actors in institutional fields', *Organization Studies*, 24 (3): 355–81.

Herod, A. (2001). *Labor Geographies: Workers and the Landscape of Capitalism*. New York: Guilford Press.

Hickson, D. J., C. R. Hinings, C. A. Less, R. E. Schneck and J. M. Pennings (1971). 'A strategic contingencies theory of intraorganizational power', *Administrative Science Quarterly*, 16 (2): 216–29.

Hindess, B. (1982). 'Power, interests and the outcomes of struggles', *Sociology*, 16 (4): 498–511.

Hirsch, P. (1986). 'From ambushes to golden parachutes: corporate take-overs as an instance of cultural framing and institutional integration', *American Journal of Sociology*, 26: 800–37.

Hirschhorn, L., and T Gilmore (1992). 'The new boundaries of the boundaryless firm', *Harvard Business Review*, 70 (3): 104–55.

Hjorth, D. (2005). 'Organizational entrepreneurship: with de Certeau on creating heterotopias (or spaces for play)', *Journal of Management Inquiry*, 14 (4): 386–98.

Hobbes, T. (1651/1985). *Leviathan*. London: Penguin.

Hochschild, A. (1983). *The Managed Heart: Commercialisation of Human Feeling*. Berkeley: University of California Press.

Hodson, R. (1995). 'Worker resistance: an underdeveloped concept in the sociology of work', *Economic and Industrial Democracy*, 16 (1): 79–110.

Hollway, W. (1991). *Work Psychology and Organizational Behaviour: Managing the Individual at Work*. London: Sage.

Honneth, A. (1995). *The Struggle for Recognition*. Cambridge: Polity Press.

Hoskin, K., and R. Macve (1986). 'Accounting and the examination: a genealogy of disciplinary power', *Accounting, Organization and Society*, 11 (2): 105–36.

 (1988). 'The genesis of accountability – the West Point connections', *Accounting Organizations and Society*, 13 (1): 37–73.

House, R. J., W. D. Spangler and J. Woycke (1991). 'Personality and charisma in the US presidency: a psychological theory of leader effectiveness', *Administrative Science Quarterly*, 36 (3): 364–96.

Hutchinson, S., J. Purcell and N. Kinnie (2000). 'Evolving high commitment management and the case of the RAC call centre', *Human Resource Management Journal*, 10 (1): 63–78.

Hyman, R. (1972). *Strikes*. Glasgow: Fontana.

Inglis, K. (1983). *This is the ABC*. Melbourne: Melbourne University Press.

Jackall, R. (1988). *Moral Mazes: The World of Corporate Managers*. Oxford: Oxford University Press.

Jacques, R. (1996). *Manufacturing the Employee: Management Knowledge from the 19th to 21st Centuries*. London: Sage.

Jaffee, D., J. Kloppenburg and M. Monroy (2004). 'Bringing the moral change home: fair trade within the North and within the South', *Rural Sociology*, 69 (2): 169–96.

Jameson, F. (1991). *Postmodernism, or the Cultural Logic of Late Capitalism*. London: Verso.

Jaspers, K. (1932/1970). *Philosophy*, Vol. II. Chicago: University of Chicago Press.

Jermier, J., D. Knights and W. Nord (eds.) (1994). *Resistance and Power in Organizations*. London: Sage.

Kakabadse, A., and N. Kakabadse (2004). *Intimacy: An International Survey of the Sex Lives of People at Work*. London: Palgrave.

Kane, P. (2004). *The Play Ethic: A Manifesto for a Different way of Living*. London: Macmillan.

Kanter, R. (1977). *Men and Women of the Corporation*. New York: Basic.

Kelley, G. (1976). 'Seducing the elites: the politics of decision making and innovation in organizational networks', *Academy of Management Review*, 1 (3): 66–74.

Kingsnorth, P. (2003). *One No, Many Yeses: A Journey to the Heart of the Global Resistance Movement*. New York: Free Press.

Klein, N. (2000). *No Logo*. London: Flamingo.

Knights, D., and D. McCabe (2000). '"Ain't misbehavin"? Opportunities for resistance under new forms of "quality" management', *Sociology*, 4 (3): 421–36.

Knights, D., and G. Morgan (1991). 'Strategic discourse and subjectivity: towards a critical analysis of corporate strategy in organizations', *Organization Studies*, 12 (3): 251–73.

Knights, D., and H. Willmott (1989). 'Power and subjectivity at work: from degradation to subjugation in social relations', *Sociology*, 23: 534–58.

Kondo, D. (1990). *Crafting Selves: Power, Gender and Discourse of Identity in a Japanese Workplace*. Chicago: University of Chicago Press.

Korda, M. (1972). *Male Chauvinism! How it Works*. New York: Random House.

Kristeva, J. (2000). *The Sense and Non-sense of Revolt: The Powers and Limits of Psychoanalysis*. New York: Columbia University Press.

Kunda, G. (1992). *Engineering Culture: Control and Commitment in a High-Tech Corporation*. Philadelphia: Temple University Press.

Laclau, E. (1996). *Emancipation(s)*. London: Verso.

(2000). 'Identity and hegemony: the role of universality in the constitution of political logics', in J. Butler, E. Laclau and S. Žižek (eds.), *Contingency, Hegemony, Universality: Contemporary Dialogues on the Left*. London: Verso.

(2005). *On Populist Reason*. London: Verso.

Laclau, E., and C. Mouffe (1985). *Hegemony and Socialist Strategy*. London: Verso.

Laing, A. (1997). 'New patterns of work: the design of the office', in J. Worthington (ed.), *Reinventing the Workplace*. York: Architectural Press.

Larner, W. (1998). 'Hitching a ride on the tiger's back: globalization and spatial imaginaries in New Zealand', *Environment and Planning D – Society and Space*, 16 (5): 599–614.

Laswell, H. D., and A. Kaplan (1950). *Power and Society*. New Haven, CT: Yale University Press.

Lefebvre, H. (1991). *The Production of Space* (trans. D. Nicholson-Smith). Oxford: Blackwell.

Leidner, R. (1993). *Fast Food, Fast Talk: Service Work and the Routinization of Everyday Life*. London: UCLA Press.

Lounsbury, M. (2001). 'Institutional sources of practice variation: staffing college and university recycling program', *Administrative Science Quarterly*, 46 (1): 29–56.

Lukes, S. (1974/2005). *Power: A Radical View*, 2nd edn. London: Palgrave.

Machiavelli, N. (1515/1997). *The Prince*. London: Penguin.

(1517/1983). *Discourses on Livy*. London: Penguin.

210   *References*

Mansfield, B. (1997). *The Challenge of a Better ABC*. Canberra: Australian Government Publishing Service.

Marcuse, H. (1968). *One Dimensional Man: Studies in the Ideology of Advanced Industrial Society*. New York: Beacon Press.

Mars, G. (1982). *Cheats at Work: An Anthropology of Workplace Crime*. London: Allen and Unwin.

Marx, K. (1847/1976). 'The poverty of philosophy', in K. Marx and F. Engels, *Collected Works*, Vol. VI. London: Lawrence and Wishart.

(1867/1976). *Capital* (Vol. I, Pelican Marx Library). London: Pelican.

Marx, K., and F. Engels (1848). *The Manifesto of the Communist Party*. London: Penguin.

McGivern, G. (2005). *The Introduction of Consultant Appraisal: Playing the Tick Box Game*. PhD thesis: Imperial College, University of London.

McKinlay, A., and P. Taylor (1996). 'Power, surveillance and resistance: inside the "factory of the future", in P. Ackers, C. Smith and P. Smith (eds.), *The New Workplace and Trade Unionism*. London: Routledge.

Mechanic, D. (1962). 'Sources of power of lower participants in complex organizations', *Administrative Science Quarterly*, 7 (3): 349–64.

Melucci, A. (1996). *Challenging Codes: Collective Action in the Information Age*. Cambridge: Cambridge University Press.

Merelman, R. (1968). 'On the Neo-Elitist critique of community power', *American Political Science Review*, 62 (2): 451–60.

Merry, S. E. (1995). 'Resistance and the cultural power of law', *Law and Society Review*, 29 (1): 11–26.

Meyer, J. W., and B. Rowan (1977). 'Institutional organizations: formal structure as myth and ceremony', *American Journal of Sociology*, 83: 340–63.

Mills, A. J., and P. Tancred (eds.) (1992). *Gendering Organizational Analysis*. London: Sage.

Mills, C. W. (1956). *The Power Elite*. Oxford: Oxford University Press.

Mitchel, T. (1990). 'Everyday metaphors of power', *Theory and Society*, 19 (5): 545–78.

Morrill, C., M. N. Zald and H. Rao (2003). 'Covert political conflict in organizations: the view from below', *Annual Review of Sociology*, 29: 391–415.

Morris, M. (1996). 'Banality in cultural studies', in J. Storey (ed.), *What is Cultural Studies? A Reader*. London: Arnold.

Mumby, D. K. (1987). 'The political function of narratives in organizations', *Communication Monographs*, 54: 113–27.

(2005). 'Theorizing resistance in organization studies: a dialectical approach', *Management Communication Quarterly*, 19 (1): 19–44.

Munck, R. (2000). *Globalisation and Labour: The New Great Transformation*. London: Zed.

Nafisi, A. (2003). *Reading Lolita in Tehran*. New York: Random House.

Newton, T. (1998). 'Theorising subjectivity in organizations: the failure of Foucauldian studies?', *Organization Studies*, 19 (3): 415–47.

——— (1999). 'Power, subjectivity and British industrial and organizational sociology: the relevance of the work of Norbert Elias', *Sociology*, 33 (2): 411–40.

Notes from Nowhere (2003). *We are Everywhere: The Irresistible Rise of Global Anti-Capitalism*. London: Verso.

Ong, A. (1987). *Spirits of Resistance and Capitalist Discipline: Factory Women in Malaysia*. Albany, NY: SUNY Press.

Palm, G. (1977). *The Flight from Work*. Cambridge: Cambridge University Press.

Parker, M. (2002a). *Against Management: Organization in the Age of Managerialism*. Cambridge: Polity Press.

——— (2002b). 'Queering management and organisation', *Gender, Work and Organisation*, 9 (2): 146–66.

Pena, D. (1996). *The Terror of the Machine: Technology, Work, Gender and Ecology on the US–Mexico Border*. Austin, TX: CMAS Books.

Perin, C. (1991). 'The moral fabric of the office: panopticon discourse and schedule flexibilities', in P. Tolbert and S. R. Barley (eds.), *Research in the Sociology of Organizations*. Greenwich, CT: JAI Press.

Perlow, L. (1998). 'Boundary control: the social ordering of work and family time in a high-tech corporation', *Administrative Science Quarterly*, 43 (2): 328–57.

Perrow, C. (1972). *Complex Organizations: A Critical Essay*. Chicago: Scott Forsman.

Peters, T. (1992). *Liberation Management: Necessary Disorganization for the Nanosecond Nineties*. London: Pan.

Peters, T., and R. H. Waterman (1982). *In Search of Excellence*. New York: Harper and Row.

Pfeffer, J. (1981). *Power in Organizations*. Mashfield, MA: Pitman.

——— (1992). *Managing with Power: Politics and Influence in Organization*. Boston: Harvard Business School Press.

Pfeffer, J., and W. L. Moore (1980). 'Power in university budgeting: a replication and extension', *Administrative Science Quarterly*, 25 (4): 637–53.

Pfeffer, J. and G. R. Salancik (1974). 'Organizational decision making as a political process: the case of a university budget', *Administrative Science Quarterly*, 19 (2): 135–51.

Piccone, P. (1976). 'Beyond identity theory', in J. O'Neil (ed.), *On Critical Theory*. New York: Seabury.

——— (1978). 'The crisis of one-dimensionality', *Telos*, 35: 43–54.

Pollard, S. (1965). *The Genesis of Modern Management*. London: Edward Arnold.

Polsby, N. (1960). 'How to study community power', *Journal of Politics*, 22: 474–84.

Pringle, R. (1989). *Secretaries Talk: Sexuality, Power and Work*. London: Verso.

(1990). 'Bureaucracy, rationality and sexuality: the case of secretaries', in J. Hearn, D. Sheppard, P. Tancred-Sheriff and G. Burrell (eds.), *The Sexuality of Organization*. London: Sage.

Pugh, D. S., D. J. Hickson, C. R. Hinings and C. Turner (1968). 'Dimensions of organizational structure', *Administrative Science Quarterly*, 13 (1): 65–105.

Quinn, R. E. (1977). 'Coping with Cupid: the management of romantic relationships in organizations', *Administrative Science Quarterly*, 22 (1): 30–45.

Raeburn, N. C. (2004). *Changing Corporate America from Inside Out: Lesbian and Gay Workplace Rights*. Minneapolis: University of Minnesota Press.

Ranson, S., C. R. Hinings and R. Greenwood (1980). 'The structuring of organizational structures', *Administrative Science Quarterly*, 25 (1): 1–17.

Rawls, J. (1971). *A Theory of Justice*. Harvard, MA: Harvard University Press.

Ray, C. (1986). 'Corporate culture: the last frontier of control?', *Journal of Management Studies*, 23 (3): 287–97.

Reed, M. (1998). 'Organizational analysis as discourse analysis: a critique', in D. Grant, T. Keenoy and C. Oswick (eds.), *Discourse and Organization*. London: Sage.

(2004). 'Getting real about organizational discourse', in D. Grant, C. Hardy, C. Oswick and L. L. Putnam (eds.), *The Sage Handbook of Organizational Discourse*. London: Sage.

Reith, J. C. W. (1924). *Broadcast Over Britain*. London: Hodder and Stoughton.

Rodrigues, S., and D. Collinson (1995). 'Having fun? Humour as resistance in Brazil', *Organization Studies*, 16 (5), 739–68.

Rorty, R. (1989). *Contingency, Irony and Solidarity*. Cambridge: Cambridge University Press.

Rosamond, B. (2003). 'Babylon and on: globalization and international political economy', *Review of International Political Economy*, 10 (4): 661–7.

Rose, N. (1990). *Governing the Soul: The Shaping of the Private Self*. London: Routledge.

Ross, A. (2004). *No-Collar: The Humane Workplace and its Hidden Costs.* Philadelphia: Temple University Press.

Roy, D. (1952). 'Quota restriction and goldbricking in a machine shop', *American Journal of Sociology*, 57 (5): 427–42.

— (1958). 'Banana time: job satisfaction and informal interaction', *Human Organization*, 18: 158–68.

Salancik, G. R., and J. Pfeffer (1974). 'The bases and uses of power in organizational decision making: the case of a university', *Administrative Science Quarterly*, 19 (4): 435–73.

Salskov-Iversen, D., H. K. Hansen and S. Bislev (2000). 'Governmentality, globalization, and local practice: transformations of a hegemonic discourse', *Alternatives*, 25 (2): 183–222.

Scase, R., and R. Goffee (1989). *Reluctant Managers: Their Work and Lifestyles.* London: Unwin Hyman.

Schein, E. (1997). *Organizational Culture and Leadership*, 2nd edn. San Francisco: Jossey-Bass.

Schein, V. (1977). 'Individual power and political behaviours in organizations: an inadequately explored reality', *Academy of Management Review*, 2 (1): 64–72.

Schlosser, E. (2002). *Fast Food Nation.* New York: Harper Perennial.

Scholte, J. A. (2004). *Globalization: A Critical Introduction*, 2nd edn. Basingstoke: Palgrave.

Scott, A., and M. Storper (1986). *Production, Work, Territory: The Geographical Anatomy of Industrial Capitalism.* London: Allen and Unwin.

Scott, J. C. (1985). *Weapons of the Weak: Everyday Forms of Peasant Resistance.* New Haven, CT: Yale University Press.

— (1990). *Domination and the Art of Resistance: Hidden Transcripts.* New Haven, CT: Yale University Press.

Scully, M. A., and A. Segal (2002). 'Passion with an umbrella: grassroots activism in the workplace', in M. Lounsbury and M. J. Ventresca (eds.), *Social Structure and Organizations Revisited.* Oxford: JAI Press.

Selsky, J., A. Spicer and J. Teicher (2003). "Totally un-Australian!" Discursive and institutional interplay in the Melbourne Port dispute of 1997–98', *Journal of Management Studies*, 40 (7): 1729–60.

— (2005). *War on the Waterfront: The Failure of Institutional Change in Two Labour Disputes.* Paper presented at Industrial Relations Research Unit, University of Warwick, May.

Selznick, P. (1949). *TVA and the Grass Roots.* Berkeley: University of California Press.

Sen, A. K. (1985). *Commodities and Capabilities.* Amsterdam: North Holland.

Senge, P. (1990). *The Fifth Discipline: The Art and Practice of the Learning Organization.* New York: Doubleday.

Sennett, R. (1998). *The Corrosion of Character.* New York: W. W. Norton. (2006). *The Culture of the New Capitalism.* New Haven, CT: Yale University Press.

Sennett, R., and J. Cobb (1977). *The Hidden Injuries of Class.* New York: W. W. Norton.

Sewell, G., and B. Wilkinson (1992). 'Someone to watch over me: surveillance, discipline and the just-in-time labour process', *Sociology*, 26 (2): 271–89.

Silverman, D. (2001). *Interpreting Qualitative Data: Methods for Analysing Talk, Text and Interaction*, 2nd edn. London: Sage.

Simmel, G. (1955). *Conflict.* Glencoe, IL: Free Press.

Simon, H. (1945/1961). *Administrative Behaviour: A Study of Decision Making Processes in Administrative Organization.* London: Macmillan. (1953). 'Notes on the observation and measurement of political power', *Journal of Politics*, 15: 500–16.

Sloterdijk, P. (1987). *Critique of Cynical Reason.* Minneapolis: University of Minnesota Press.

Smith, A. (1777/1974). *The Wealth of Nations.* New York: Penguin.

Spicer, A. (2005). 'The political process of inscribing a new technology', *Human Relations*, 58 (7): 867–90.

Spicer, A., J. Selsky and J. Teicher (2002). 'Paradoxes in symbols and subjects: the politics of constructing the wharfie', in S. R. Clegg (ed.), *Management and Organization Paradoxes.* Amsterdam: Benjamins.

Spivak, G. C. (1988). 'Can the subaltern speak?', in C. Nelson and L. Grossberg (eds.), *Marxism and the Interpretation of Culture.* Urbana: University of Illinois Press. (1996). *The Spivak Reader: Selected Works of Gayatri Chakravorty Spivak* (ed. D. Landry and G. MacLean). New York: Routledge.

Starr, H. (1991). 'Democratic dominoes: diffusion approaches to the spread of democracy in the international system', *Journal of Conflict Resolution*, 35 (2): 356–81.

Strati, A. (1999). *Organization and Aesthetics.* London: Sage.

Sturdy, A. J. (1998). 'Customer care in a customer society: smiling and sometimes meaning it?', *Organization*, 5 (1): 27–53.

Sturdy, A. J., and S. Fineman (2001). 'Struggles for the control of affect: resistance as politics *and* emotion', in A. J. Sturdy, I. Grugulis and H. Willmott (eds.), *Customer Service: Empowerment and Entrapment.* London: Palgrave.

Sturdy, A. J., I. Grugulis and H. Willmott (2001). *Customer Service: Empowerment and Entrapment.* London: Palgrave.

Sturdy, A. J., and P. Fleming (2003). 'Talk as technique: a critique of the words and deeds distinction in the diffusion of customer service cultures in call centres', *Journal of Management Studies*, 40 (4): 753–74.

Sundstrom, E. (1986). *Workplaces*. New York: Cambridge University Press.

Sveningsson, S., and M. Alvesson (2003). 'Managing managerial identity: organizational fragmentation, discourse and identity struggle', *Human Relations*, 56 (10): 1163–93.

Thomas, R., and A. Davies (2005). 'Theorising the micro-politics of resistance: new public management and managerial identities in the public service', *Organization Studies*, 26 (5): 683–705.

Thompson, E. P. (1967). 'Time, work discipline and industrial capitalism', *Past and Present*, 38: 56–103.

——— (1968). *The Making of the English Working Class*. London: Penguin.

Thompson, J. D. (1956). 'Authority and power in "identical" organizations', *American Journal of Sociology*, 62 (3): 290–301.

Tilly, C. (1986). *The Contentious French*. Cambridge: Cambridge University Press.

Townley, B. (1993a). 'Foucault, power/knowledge, and its relevance for human resource management', *Academy of Management Review*, 18 (3): 518–45.

——— (1993b). 'Performance appraisal and the emergence of management', *Journal of Management Studies*, 30 (2): 221–38.

Trethewey, A. (1997). 'Resistance, identity, and empowerment: a postmodern feminist analysis of clients in a human service organization', *Communication Monographs*, 64: 281–301.

Tyler, M. (2004). 'Managing between the sheets: lifestyle magazines and the management of sexuality in everyday life', *Sexualities*, 7 (1): 81–106.

Useem, B. (1996). *Investor Capitalism*. New York: Basic.

Vaara, E. (2002). 'On the discursive construction of success/failure in narratives of post-merger integration', *Organization Studies*, 23 (2): 211–48.

van Maanen, J. (ed.) (1998). *Qualitative Studies of Organization*. Thousand Oaks, CA: Sage.

van Meel, J. (2000). *The European Office: Office Design and National Context*. Rotterdam: 010 Publishers.

Voloshinov, V. N. (1973). *Marxism and the Philosophy of Language*. London and New York: Seminar Press.

Wallerstein, M., and B. Western (2000). 'Unions in decline? What has changed and why', *Annual Review of Political Science*, 3: 355–77.

Waltzer, M. (1983). *Spheres of Justice*. New York: Basic.

Waring, M. (1989). *If Women Counted: A New Feminist Economics*. London: Macmillan.

Weber, M. (1922/1978). *Economy and Society*. Berkeley: University of California Press.

(1924/1947). *The Theory of Social and Economic Organization* (eds. and trans. A. H. Herderson and T. Parsons). Glencoe, IL: Free Press.

(1948). *From Max Weber: Essays in Sociology* (eds. and trans. H. Gerth and C. W. Mills). New York: Oxford University Press.

Williams, R. (1996). *Normal Service Won't be Resumed: The Future of Public Broadcasting.* St Leonards, New South Wales: Allen and Unwin.

Williamson, J. (1986). 'The problems of being popular', *New Socialist*, 41: 14–15.

Willis, P. (1977). *Learning to Labour: How Working Class Kids Get Working Class Jobs.* Westmead: Saxon House.

Willmott, H. (1993). 'Strength is ignorance; slavery is freedom: managing cultures in modern organizations', *Journal of Management Studies*, 30 (4): 515–52.

Wolfinger, R. (1971). 'Nondecisions and the study of local politics', *American Political Science Review*, 65 (4): 1063–80.

Wolin, S. (2004). *Politics and Vision*, 2nd edn. Princeton, NJ: Princeton University Press.

Wray-Bliss, E. (2002). 'Abstract ethics, embodied ethics: the strange marriage of Foucault and Positivism in LPT', *Organization*, 9 (1): 5–39.

Wrong, D. H. (1968). 'Some problems in defining social power', *American Journal of Sociology*, 73: 673–81.

Yanow, D. (1998). 'Space stories: studying museum buildings as organizational spaces while reflecting on interpretive methods and their narration', *Journal of Management Inquiry*, 7 (3): 215–39.

Young, I. M. (1997). 'Unruly categories: a critique of Nancy Fraser's dual systems theory', *New Left Review*, 222: 147–60.

Zald, M. N., and M. A. Berger (1978). 'Social movements in organizations: coup d'état, insurgency, and mass movements', *American Journal of Sociology*, 83: 823–61.

Zald, M. N., and J. D. McCarthy (1989). *Social Movements in an Organizational Society: Collected Essays.* New Brunswick, NJ: Transaction.

Zald, M. N., C. Morrill and H. Rao (2005). 'The impact of social movements on organizations: environment and responses', in G. F. Davis, D. McAdam, W. R. Scott and M. N. Zald (eds.), *Social Movements and Organization Theory.* Cambridge: Cambridge University Press.

Zeller, C. (2000). 'Rescaling power relations between trade unions and corporate management in a globalizing pharmaceutical industry: the case of the acquisition of Boehringer Mannheim by Hoffman–La Roche', *Environment and Planning A*, 32 (9): 1545–67.

Žižek, S. (1989). *Sublime Object of Ideology.* London: Verso.

(1997). *Plague of Fantasies.* London: Verso.

(2000). 'Class struggle or postmodernism? Yes, please!', in J. Butler, E. Laclau and S. Žižek (eds.), *Contingency, Hegemony, Universality*. London: Verso.

(2004). *Revolution at the Gates: Žižek on Lenin, the 1917 Writings*. London: Verso.

Zysman, J. (1994). 'How institutions create historically rooted trajectories of growth', *Industrial and Corporate Change*, 3: 243–83.

Index